The new structure of school improvement

D0144681

The new structure of school improvement

Inquiring schools and achieving students

Bruce Joyce, Emily Calhoun, and
David Hopkins

Open University Press
Buckingham · Philadelphia

Open University Press
Celtic Court
22 Ballmoor
Buckingham
MK18 1XW

email: enquiries@openup.co.uk
world wide web: http://www.openup.co.uk

and
325 Chestnut Street
Philadelphia, PA 19106, USA

First Published 1999

ISBN 0 335 20294 2

A catalogue record of this book is available from the British Library

Library of Congress Cataloging-in-Publication Data
Joyce, Bruce R.
    The new structure of school improvement: inquiring schools and achieving students/Bruce Joyce, Emily Calhoun, and David Hopkins.
        p. cm.
    Includes bibliographical references (p.) and index.
    ISBN 0-335-20294-2 (pbk.)
    1. School improvement programs–Great Britain. 2. School improvement programs–United States. 3. School-based management–Great Britain.
4. School-based management–United States. I. Calhoun, Emily. II. Hopkins, David, 1949– . III. Title.
    LB2822.84.G7J69 1999
    371.2–dc21   98-55535
                                                                                          CIP

Copy-edited and typeset by The Running Head Limited, London and Cambridge
Printed in Great Britain by Redwood Books, Trowbridge

To Love. When you write about school improvement, you come to realize that no matter how good we get technically, it is love that makes the school improvement world go round. Love of children, primarily. But love of colleagues as well. Love is *why* we inquire into the inquiry that can create a luminescent education for all our children.

Contents

PART I CREATING THE SCHOOL AS A CENTER OF INQUIRY: SEARCHING FOR A NEW STRUCTURE

The quest is for a structure that can guide school improvement with a high probability that both staff and students will be in a rich state of growth.

PART II ELABORATING THE HYPOTHESES: THE DETAILED WORK OF SCHOOL IMPROVEMENT

We turn to the nuts and bolts. The structure is described in detail, with attendant support from research and practice.

PART III REFINING, RENOVATING, AND REDESIGNING: TAKING STEPS LARGE AND SMALL

School improvement is sometimes accomplished by many small improvements in the learning environment (refinements), sometimes by reconstructing entire curriculum areas (renovations), and sometimes by redesigning the whole place.

PART IV POLICYMAKING FOR SCHOOL RENEWAL: MAKING THE CONTEXT THROUGH NATIONAL, STATE, AND LOCAL EDUCATION AUTHORITY POLICY

National, state, and district policies create the context for school
renewal and deserve careful scrutiny. Both external initiatives
and efforts to support site-based efforts have foundered badly in
the past. We review the policies and suggest serious inquiry into
ways of improving them.

Foreword

Everyone wants schools to improve. The difficulties are that not everyone shares the same meaning of *improvement* and so there is little agreement over who ought to be undertaking the improvement.

I welcome this new book on school improvement because the authors are in no doubt where they stand on these issues. Improvement is about creating what the authors term *evolutionary schools* – able to sustain the continuous efforts needed to meet the challenging needs of our societies without losing sight of their prime purpose as centers of individual learning. The people who should be doing the improving are what the authors call the *Responsible Parties* – coalitions of teachers working with parents, community members, institutions, and businesses.

The New Structure of School Improvement extends the scope of Joyce and his US colleagues' 1983 publication, *The Structure of School Improvement*, in two important ways. First, the authors endeavor to take account of the many educational developments of the last 16 years. Second, through the involvement of a British co-author, they address their subject in terms designed to make sense to readers on both sides of the Atlantic. As they note, "very few books cross the Atlantic," despite the common heritage and language and many of the same problems. Thus, educationalists in both countries are denied the opportunity to learn from experiences of the other. The Anglo-American alliance represented by this book is further strengthened because it has been formed from detailed knowledge of how schools, in some 20 or so other countries, actually improve.

The concerns of business and industry – that future workers will need greater skills than was common in the past and that lasting employment will demand the capacity to keep learning new skills – have been accepted by educationalists and are repeated endlessly in publications about schooling. Moving beyond this recognition, however, is more of a problem. How can the skills of our students be increased significantly? How should schools seek to engage their students with the learning enterprise so that the desire to learn is fostered rather than – as so often in the past – extinguished? And how can we create schools that meet these objectives while retaining those qualities remembered and valued by so many of the generation who now make up the Responsible Parties? Joyce, Calhoun, and Hopkins grapple with these questions in a book that is full of illustrations from a wealth of case studies, surveys, and clinical experiences yet is written in a style that also draws on the power of metaphor and simile.

The authors define a series of issues (the need for collective inquiry, the democratic involvement of the community, the creation of an information-rich environment, the involvement of the Responsible Parties in the teaching and learning knowledge base, the importance of staff development both as an input and as a process, and the use of small work groups) from which they construct the seven hypotheses that form the framework of their structure for school improvement. In compiling these hypotheses they reveal their belief that lasting improvements can only be achieved by the creation of what they call an inquiring school. In this they acknowledge their debt to Lawrence Stenhouse, the British educationalist who sought so passionately to define teaching as an inquiry-based activity.

The New Structure of School Improvement is an optimistic book that rejects the over-gloomy judgments of schools made by so many political commentators. Yet it is far from complacent. It recognizes that many attempts to improve have failed and it analyzes why. It spurns the over-eager attempts of governments (national and local) to take control of improvement. It focusses – rightly, in my judgment – the responsibility for improvement on the individual school but, having done so, lays down a tight timetable for success within the first year of any initiative.

At a time when, in many countries, teaching is seen as a fairly lowly profession, this book serves to remind everyone concerned with education that teachers are the key to the improvement of schools. Teachers cannot do it all by themselves and, from time to time, they need expert help. Nevertheless, they are the principal actors. In the twenty-first century "age of intelligence" their role will be even more crucial than it is today: expecting more of their students; stimulating and facilitating the learning process; and monitoring and evaluating the quality of the learning that takes place, both among the students and within themselves.

I commend the authors for their work over many years with many schools, for their careful scholarship, and for the clear way in which they have set out their ideas. Most of all, I commend them for their faith in the power of education to transform individuals and institutions. The book deserves to be read widely by teachers, academics, and others interested in improvement. It also needs to be read by policymakers as a salutary reminder that school improvement is an inquiry and not a formula. They need to trust the teachers in order to empower them to create the self-critical, ever-evolutionary school for the sake of the students, the teaching profession and our future societies.

Peter Mortimore
The Institute of Education, University of London

Mission and style

This book on school improvement is written by two people who work primarily in the United States and one who works primarily in the United Kingdom. The three try to address school improvement in terms that they hope will speak to educators and policymakers in both countries and in the nations of the Commonwealth. Complicating things further, they have among them participated in school improvement initiatives in 20 other countries and have, in their discussions, come to the conclusion that the need for, and structures for, school improvement are very similar in those nations as well as the United States and the United Kingdom.

To prepare the book, they have drawn on their experiences with intensive school improvement programs in their countries and the others with which they are affiliated. They have tried to combine their experiences with research on school improvement, curriculum, and teaching, and to generate an inquiry-oriented structure that suggests there is important knowledge that schools, school districts or local education authorities, and governmental policymakers, can use to increase the likelihood that student learning will become richer and better – *much* richer and better. *Increased student learning is their objective.*

In the past, very few books have crossed the Atlantic Ocean to speak to both American and English educators. Frequently the reason has been that slight differences in terminology have led educators to the conclusion that the social contexts are so different that knowledge about education developed in one is unlikely to be useful to the other. We don't think so and believe that each country has lost knowledge and perspectives as a result. The differences should be enriching rather than impoverishing, just as literature, science, and technology float comfortably across the ocean.

To help bridge the gap the following differences in terminology that often separate English and American educationese are identified. The authors use them somewhat interchangeably, sometimes using an English term and sometimes an American one, and sometimes using both in the same paragraph, which is how we talk to each other.

administrator = senior management team
chief education officer = superintendent
enquiry = inquiry
faculty = staff
head = principal
local education authority = school district
school governors = school board
state = public
term = semester

Part I Creating the school as a center of inquiry: searching for a new structure

Our topic is the school's capacity to improve, simultaneously, the learning capability of the students and the faculty (all staff), parents, and community – the people who are responsible for the education of the students. We call these the Responsible Parties. We speak of this school as *evolving* and the process as *evolutionary*. It is a culture secure in the knowledge that seeking to improve is what learning is all about. The people who work in it know that they have permission to spend their lives learning, inquiring into their work and seeking for ways to do it better. The students are not *clients*. They are members of the society of the school and fortunate enough to be members of one that embodies life-long learning.

The focus is on school improvement that

- is school-based;
- involves the whole faculty/staff;
- builds a learning community that includes faculties, parents, community agencies and business partners, and local school district support personnel;
- is information-guided – characterized both by data about the school and student progress and by knowledge from the professional research literature;
- energizes through continuous collegial study ("staff development");
- is in service of student ability to inquire (learn), and thus
- centers around the study of teaching and curriculum and the development of initiatives to improve them.

All this sounds familiar enough, doesn't it – a reprise of the trends of the times? But although the words are familiar, the tune is somewhat different from the norm and is partly, though not entirely, a matter of emphasis.

Our approach comes from our inquiry into the literature on schooling and school change, and from our clinical experience and the formal research we have conducted. We are in the midst of our personal/professional searches for a reliable structure of school improvement. Our recommendations for how to build an evolutionary school – an ever-inquiring community – take the form of hypotheses. We present them strongly, but they *are* hypotheses and together they make up a *theory* to be tested and revised. We are convinced that a major dimension of school improvement will be disciplined inquiry; that the successful structure for school improvement will have the nature of a clinical science, where communities of educators treat their best ideas as stepping stones to better ones. We offer here our best current ways across the river and hope that some of them will not turn out to be lilypads masquerading as solid ground. Others following our path will find that their inquiry leads them to pick up some of the rocks, turn them over and reseat them, or find better ones to replace them with.

We have said in other places that school improvement is an inquiry, not a formula (Joyce and Calhoun 1996). We like Huberman's (1992) concept that models of social process are "rolling," rather than fixed. Each phase tumbles into the next and we frequently have to go back in order to go forward. We have grown to like the ambiguous processes of trying to learn more by learning to inquire.

We have come to believe that living within an inquiring school, living with people engaged in the active study of their profession, living with the changes necessary to the constant pursuit of excellence, may have a greater effect on children's lives than the specifics of the curriculum or the most luminescent teaching. The medium of inquiry may turn out to be the message of education where the school is truly evolutionary.

In our work we scrape together information from a variety of types of research – on schools, teaching, curriculum, staff development, school renewal strategies, student achievement – and lay their products next to one another to see what's consistent, what one field says that can help the ideas from another, and what yields clues as to what should change and how that might happen. Simultaneously, we're culling our clinical experience, setting our impressions alongside the information and ideas that we find from culling the research. The three of us have worked in and studied school districts in the United States, the United Kingdom, Canada, and several European, Middle Eastern, and Far Eastern nations.

When we meet and talk, we are amazed about the similarities in these presumably diverse settings. The structures of schools worldwide have a remarkable number of elements in common. If your ears were shut, you couldn't tell where you were.

In all these settings, we have worked in schools that work under horrendous conditions – no time for meetings, alienated parents, and indifferent district offices. We have worked in schools that have optimal conditions to improve themselves.

Inevitably, we develop lenses that we use as we peer at the problem we are trying to solve – how schools can live in an inquiring mode. Some of these lenses are pretty clear and give good resolution and magnification, some are rather murky, and others are just plain glass. They all become second nature and we're hardly aware that we're wearing them.

Periodically, we try to surface and count these lenses and examine their quality and consider whether they can be improved. Because we depend on them tremendously, and yet their imperfections limit us greatly.

Our common lens focusses on *structural elements*.

One example is particularly telling.

Research on site-based management (see the work by David and her colleagues, especially David and Peterson 1984) and on networks advocating collective (schoolwide) school improvement and action research (see Calhoun 1996) has uniformly reported that only a small percentage of schools can generate collective initiatives, unless they have very substantial technical assistance and greatly change their way of doing business. Frequently the problem is attributed to defects in the leadership of principals, and it does appear that those schools that make progress have extraordinary leadership by a combination of principals and lead teachers. Another explanation is that collective decisionmaking conflicts with the normative culture of the schools – the autonomous, privatistic culture so well described by Waller (1932, 1965) in the 1930s and Lortie (1975), Fullan (1982), Little (1982), Rosenholtz (1989), Hargreaves and Hopkins (1991), Deal (1993), and Fullan and Stiegelbauer (1993) in the last 25 years.

From our perspective there is considerable merit in those explanations, but our recent focus has led to a structural characteristic of the school that may influence leadership patterns and the culture of faculties and may deserve substantial attention as we contemplate school renewal.

In our studies three-fourths of the schools hold whole-school meetings once a month or less. About one in ten hold whole-staff meetings once every week or two and the remainder about once every three weeks. About one in three, mostly secondary schools, holds whole-school meetings only three or four times per year. The average meeting lasts about an hour.

Even if we assumed that the entirety of those meetings was devoted to school renewal, which is very unlikely, three-fourths of the schools would only have about nine or ten hours of whole-faculty discussions, which is too little to build a community that can take collective action.

To make matters worse, teachers and administrators frequently proclaim that they dislike whole-staff meetings and try to keep them to a minimum. The most frequent reasons are that the meetings are boring or that certain faculty members dominate the meetings with complaints of various sorts.

We have concluded that the time-structure for meetings is such that collective action simply cannot be organized unless time for active school renewal is built into the workplace. This is not the end of our story by any means, but its simplicity underlines the point that the structures of organizations, even superficially simple ones like *time to build community*, have enormous effect on the nature of the culture that emerges within them.

We have speculated about why so many instances of site-based management have failed to generate change significant enough to increase student learning even where principals, leadership teams, and faculties have had extensive Organizational Development training. The theory seems reasonable – yet the practice often doesn't bear out the theory.

The problem may lie in the nature of the workplace rather than in the reasonableness of the theory.

Thus we present a structure of school improvement that is centered on a substantially different way to conduct the business of education – a structure built by comparing the differences between schools that regularly generate unexpectedly high levels of student learning and those where student learning is normal.

In Chapter 1 the structure of hypotheses is the focus. In Chapter 2 supporting research is discussed, particularly in terms of how quickly school improvement can affect student learning. Chapter 3 consists of two case studies of schools and local education authorities that are struggling toward an evolutionary state.

1 Building the evolutionary school: looking for success in research and experience

We begin with some thoughts about the school and its place in the society, inviting your reflections.

On context

Richly connected to its social milieu, tightly clasped by tradition and yet the medium of modern ideas and artifacts, the school floats paradoxically in its ocean of social forces. It is a cradle of social stability and the harbinger of cultural change. Throughout history its critics have found it both too backward and too advanced. It falls behind the times and fails to keep up in simultaneous cadence.

Please think for a moment about the seemingly contradictory social currents in which the school swims. School, in this sense, is the system for educating children, rather than a particular place or a small unit in the overall system.

On mission

Its missions are quite clear to everyone, but agreeing on a single statement is quite difficult. Basic education is prized, but so too are creativity and problem solving; academic excellence is sought after, as are vocational skills, sometimes by the same people, sometimes not. Liberals and conservatives alike seek to make the school the instrument of social policy. It is the sword of the militant and the warm bosom of the humanist. Schools in the inner city and the rural hinterland and shiny suburban schools all grope for a coherent mission.

We, meaning all of us in the society, are simultaneously confident and unsure about what the school should pursue most strongly. Why is this? What confuses us?

On students

Students are varied – talents and handicaps mingle, sometimes in the same minds and bodies. Powerful self-concepts march through the front door of the school while timid souls slip in by the back stairs. Cultural differences are mixed together, with problems of identity and adaptation surfacing chaotically to be dealt with.

Variety within our species is a natural condition. Yet, to both education professionals and the public, that natural variety often is seen as a problem when it comes to the schooling. As Stevenson and Stigler (1992) have asked, why do we make a problem of individual differences rather than celebrating them and capitalizing on variety as a resource within the learning community?

On technology

Technologies strengthen the school's potential while threatening to replace it as the second biggest influence on the young. The high-technology forces of television and computer liberate our children while narrowing them to pop versions of knowledge and even leading them astray. On the way to school, children increasingly have to take a step down from the media-blitzed world of the home to adopt the sober pace of the classroom.

Clearly, the electronic age is upon us. New tools are ours for the learning. Do new missions come with the social change as well? Do we have to incorporate ways of working that were recently called "distance" learning but could now be a primary mode of teaching? Must the school as we know it change in order not to be submerged?

On teachers

Relatively speaking, teachers receive brief and modest training but are asked to manage one of the most complex professional tasks in our society. They have little status but awesome responsibility both for individual children and for the health of the society as a whole.

We believe the situation leads inexorably to a substantial change in the workplace – creating a better balance between instructional duties and study. We believe that about a half-day should be built into the paid time of teachers each week for staff development/school improvement work.

Essentially, teacher education has to become a career-long process. What do you think?

On innovation

Efficiency is highly prized, but innovations are watched with apprehension. Our societal patterns of schooling, established in the early 1800s, have become familiar and comfortable, and we want our children to have an education that has continuity with our own. Thus most citizens are cautious about educational innovation. People like the familiar as much as they criticize it. They tend to believe that current problems in education are caused by changes perceived as a "lowering of standards" rather than because the old comfortable model of the school may be a little rusty and out of date. The bucolic image of schooling is redolent in both our societies. In fact, society has changed a great deal since the days when those familiar and comfortable patterns of education were established, and many schools have become badly out of phase with the needs of children in today's world.

We conclude that very broad, formal involvement of parents, community members and institutions, and businesses (what we will call the Responsible Parties) is necessary to sustain attempts to improve schooling and create new ones. The school *will* be changing if it is to become more effective with respect to traditional missions and take on new ones. Involvement is the way to deal with the inevitable controversy that accompanies change in a fundamental social institution. What do you think?

FURTHER THOUGHTS

Because education exerts great influence on the young, society places great constraints on its schools in order that they reflect prevailing social attitudes and fit current views about how children should be trained. The very size of the system draws continuous attention, particularly in the educational systems where we work.

About 8 percent of the gross national product of industrialized countries is directly or indirectly consumed by the enterprises of education. In the United States, because the funding of education has shifted from local communities to the state level, education takes the majority of those state budgets. It is therefore unsurprising that the public watches its investment carefully, scrutinizing educational practices both traditional and innovative.

Effectiveness, as such, is not controversial. In our societies we may debate about what kind of education is best for our children, but there is total agreement that schooling should be rigorous and effective. Even people who are not particularly dissatisfied with the current state of education usually believe that schooling can be improved. How to increase

the effectiveness of schools is a more frustrating topic, and the more critical people are about the present state of schools, the more frustrated
they become.

Social institutions tend to deteriorate unless they are continuously
rejuvenated, and when patterns of education become routine, life in
schools becomes less vital. Schools need constant attention to revitalize
them and the lives of the children and teachers who live in them. The
public faces a continuing dilemma: to preserve familiar, traditional practices, making them as effective as possible, and yet keep up with the times
in order to meet the challenges presented by social change. The result is
that schooling exists in a social tug-of-war between proponents of tradition and proponents of change, and much that is known about what
makes schools more effective is not used unless the needs for both stability and change are reconciled.

THE STRUCTURE OF SCHOOL IMPROVEMENT

We take a broad look at the school and concentrate on how school staffs
and caring citizens can work together to make their local school better
and better. We try to weave together the best of what we have learned
from the literature of organizational change and research on curriculum
and teaching. We ask questions regarding the purposes of schooling and
suggest that the responsibility for improving the quality of specific
schools resides with what we call the Responsible Parties: those teachers,
parents, administrators, and community members who form a coalition
to create and maintain a learning organization.

What do we mean by the "structure of school improvement"?

The emphasis here is on the creation of a natural, organic evolutionary state where continuous efforts to make the school better are routine.
From this perspective, school improvement is a part of the ordinary
process of operating the school rather than a response to a belief that
things are terribly wrong or that there are dreadful problems that cry out
for immediate solution. Learning how to do things better and better is
just a way of life, and considerable attention is paid to the creation of an
environment where the adult caretakers of our children are in a healthy
state of study and learning. Creating this evolutionary state is the job of
all levels of the educational system: governmental policymakers, school
district leaders and support personnel, and everyone who works in the
school. Initiatives from every level need to be made with insight into the
nature of the complex processes of schooling and the complexities of
achieving implementation that is integrated into the overall curriculum.
Also, initiatives need to address the problem that caused them in the first
place. Instead of, say, adding programs for students who cannot read
very well, we might strengthen the curriculum in reading so that fewer
students fail to learn to read effectively.

Recently researchers and practitioners have taken a more holistic view
of the school (see especially Goodlad 1984; Glickman 1993; Stoll and
Fink 1996; Joyce *et al.* 1999) and how to improve it as a social organism

(Fullan and Stiegelbauer 1993; Joyce *et al.* 1993; Hopkins *et al.* 1996a; Schlecty 1997). There is a better understanding of the ecology of good schools and the structure or pattern of relationships among the various components of schooling which together have an effect greater than the sum of the parts (see Rutter *et al.* 1979; Mortimore *et al.* 1988). On these understandings we can begin to develop a new structure of school improvement.

As society changes and knowledge about curriculum and instruction increases, schools need to assimilate and accommodate many new realities. Schools need both to create a reasonable level of stability and constantly to be open and able to change.

The answer lies in the creation of a certain type of school culture, i.e. a set of organizational norms, expectations, beliefs, and behaviors which allow the establishment of activities fundamental to school improvement. This means that what must remain constant, what must remain stable in the life of the school, is the emotional and intellectual disposition toward improvement on the part of the Responsible Parties.

The good news is that there have been a considerable number of documented successful school improvement efforts, where student learning has increased a great deal; and their characteristics point the way to the nature of the structures that can enable any school to become a powerful self-renewing organization.

THE SCHOOL AS THE CENTER OF INQUIRY

The structure of school improvement, as we envision it, is built on a set of hypotheses generated from the study of successful and unsuccessful attempts to approve schooling. Each hypothesis deals with a dimension of a complex school renewal process.

Our approach to school improvement involves moving away from relatively isolated, highly targeted innovations intended to solve specific educational problems, and toward a fluid, continuous inquiry to make education better on a day to day basis. The aspiration is to make all schools into learning communities for teachers as well as students, making use of the best models of learning for both. To achieve this vision requires significant changes in organization, some structural and some procedural.

What we envision is a quantum leap toward the creation of a setting where inquiry is normal and the conditions of the workplace support the continuous, collegial inquiry that treats innovations as opportunities to study. The vision is of a "School as a Centre of Inquiry," (Schaefer 1997), where teaching and learning are examined continuously and improved in the course of engagement, where students are brought into the world of studying not only what they are learning in the "curricular" sense, but their own situation and capability of learners and the progress they are making. Hence the terms "constructivism" and "metacognition" come into the vocabulary of school improvement.

We hypothesize that, in time, a different culture of education will emerge. Relationships among teachers, between teachers and administrators, and between educators and laypersons will change quantitatively and qualitatively. Solutions will be hypotheses to be tested, rather than panaceatic creations which, once in place, solve the problem. Democracy will replace bureaucracy.

WORKING HYPOTHESES FROM THE STUDY OF CHANGE: THE CREATION OF THE EVOLUTIONARY SCHOOL

School improvement is a quiet rather than a noisy revolution, and the most radical of changed conditions are actually rather subtle. Rather than being a set of initiatives to replace one set of educational practices with another, school improvement is a redevelopment of the organization. Specific initiatives emanate from that organization. The core is the development of the conditions that foster continuous inquiry. These require some changes in the structure of the organization, the development of inquiring communities, a very different informational environment, and connecting the community with the nutrients available in the professional knowledge base. *The school is in an evolutionary state.*

As we present each hypotheses, we will identify optimal utilization of each of them – estimates based largely on our experience with school improvement programs.

From isolation to synergy: restructuring time

Synergistic environments – environments characterized by rigorous interchange – foster inquiry. Environments that separate people depress inquiry. Essentially, we need each other's ideas for stimulation and other people's perspectives to check our perceptions.

Schools were not designed to make it easy for colleagueship to flourish. The current organization of schools is really a loose federation of little schools (classrooms) and the minimum of interchange was built into the school as a workplace – almost the absolute minimum needed to keep the place operating. Schools were designed so that the beginning of the school year could be accomplished with just one or two days of meetings to get regulations clear and assign instructional spaces and duties. Then the teachers, brought together for just a few hours, fan out into the classrooms. The organization is designed for separate functioning, rather than for collegial inquiry and support. One can teach without really knowing one's colleagues or even what they actually are doing "next door." The scholars of the sociology of the school, such as Hargreaves, Woods, Waller, Lortie, and Rosenholtz, describe an environment that would be almost surrealistic, if it were not so sinister. Educators are assigned to instructional duties with almost no provision for collective work.

In such a structure, the making of curriculum, the creation of a common social climate, the collective study of students and what they are learning, are nearly impossible. As we examine the history of school reform movements we are amazed that, laboring under such isolating conditions, teachers have been able to keep the school as healthy as it is. However, school improvement has been an enormously frustrating business simply because time to study has not been part of the job. Our first hypothesis pertains to creating time for collective interchange.

Hypothesis 1: Restructuring the job assignments of educators so that time for collective inquiry is built into the workplace will increase school improvement activity.

The optimum condition is that the entire faculty can meet and work together for at least a half-day a week in one block of time that can be used for staff development, other forms of study, and preparation for work with the entire Responsible Parties group. This time needs to be within the workday and compensated accordingly.

Building community: the Responsible Parties

The tradition has been a loose federation of classrooms somewhat coordinated by principals and their assistants and a few central office personnel responsible for general administration and support. A "loose-coupled" mode (Baldridge and Deal 1975; Murphy and Hallinger 1993) has prevailed where classrooms are loosely connected to one another and to the school administration, and the school is loosely connected to local and national administrative structures. Central authorities create curriculum guidelines but have virtually no structure for communicating their intents thoroughly.

The community of the school carries the educational system, so let us structure it so that it can have the vigor and connectedness to do its work in an energetic, inquiring fashion. Let us legitimize a democratic governing body for each school, bringing the parents and other community members into the process. In a small school, let us include all the staff. In a larger school, let us elect representatives. Let the community also elect representatives. But let all major decisions be made with full participation of all the teachers, along with the elected representatives of the community. The head or principal will be the "executive secretary" of the Responsible Parties. Rather than being a traditional parliamentary governing group, our Responsible Parties will be an inquiring group, leading all members of the community in the study of the school, the students, and ways of making it continually better. Thus we come to a second hypothesis, elaborated in Chapter 4.

Hypothesis 2: Active, living democracy, including community members, engaged in collective inquiry, creates the structural condition in which the process of school improvement is nested.

Optimally, the fully developed Responsible Parties group meets every three weeks, the executive committee every week for about 90 minutes. Members include the school faculty, at least 30 parents (whatever the size of the school), and probably another 20 persons representing the school district, community agencies, and businesses.

We believe that people of all levels in the education complex need to develop an evo-lutionary stance, trying to create ever more vital schooling for the students and creating inquiring communities for themselves at the national, state, and local levels.

An information-rich community

Inquiry involves the collection and analysis of data and reflection on it. In an odd sense, schools have been both information-rich and informa-tion-impoverished. The richness has been in that much testing goes on in schools. Teachers teach, test, and assess the results. However, schools have lacked the reflective, experimental qualities that make assessment of learning lead to the study of ways of improving it. A few years ago we worked with a middle school where only 30 percent of the students met national standards by the end of each school year. Every teacher had information indicating that their students were failing to learn the pre-scribed material in their courses. Year after year they knew the students were failing. And yet, year after year the students failed. The teachers never met to reflect on that fact and change what they were doing. How-ever, a staff development program interrupted the situation by bringing the staff into the study of teaching. The students began to learn more, and within two years 95 percent of them were earning promotion with the same curriculum and the same tests being used to assess success. The data about student learning were being used differently – as part of a study to see if that faculty could help those students to learn more power-fully. The same information became richer because it became part of the material that a learning community used to build a better education for its students (Joyce *et al.* 1989; Showers *et al.* 1996).

Every school has large quantities of data available that can become part of similar inquiries (see Chapter 5), not only in the study of obvious problems such as low achievement, but into all aspects of the school environment and all learners. A set of schools whose students were acknowledged to be very high-achieving (in the top 5 percent of the nations' schools on standard tests) inquired into the teaching of writing and, within two years, the students were improving their quality of writ-ing several times more than they had in previous years (Joyce *et al.* 1996).

In both of these examples the teachers found that their own attitudes and beliefs became part of the inquiries. In both cases, they found that they had not really believed that the students could learn so much more effectively. And neither did the parents. Both groups found that the stu-dents could learn far more than they had been expected to learn. In Chapters 2, 3, 5, 7, and 9 we will examine other examples of the uses of information in inquiry-oriented settings.

Hypothesis 3: An information-rich environment will enhance inquiry.
Learning to study the learning environment will increase inquiry into ways of helping students learn better.
Optimally, progress in literacy is publicly reported monthly for the entire student body. Progress in achievement in all academic core areas is

reported monthly. Yearly summative data are used to confirm and make comparisons nationally and internationally. There are weekly reports on targeted areas. All data are public.

A community connected to the knowledge base on curriculum and teaching

Not only has teaching historically lacked provision for collective study, it has also lacked provision for study of the knowledge base. Thus many teachers have had to try to improve themselves without easy access to the accumulated knowledge of the profession. The study of teaching, curriculum, and technology has now created a substantial knowledge base that can help faculties think out solutions to problems (see Chapters 2 and 7). In our modern information world, access can be provided easily.

Hypothesis 4: Connecting the Responsible Parties to the knowledge base on teaching and learning will increase the development of successful initiatives for school improvement.
Optimum: The entire faculty and the members of the Responsible Parties Executive Committee study intensively the research on targeted areas. They use technical assistance to interpret the research and report it to the entire learning community. Decisions are made, or not made, in relation to the evidence.

Staff development as an embedded feature of the workplace

For teachers to use the knowledge base they cannot simply find out that something "has worked" in some other setting. They have to develop the skill to use that research in instruction so that they can conduct inquiries into the effects on their students.

Hypothesis 5: Staff development, embedded in the workplace, increases inquiry into new practices and the implementation of school improvement initiatives.
Again, the inquiry mode is important. Staff development has to be a regular event, but not in a "here is stuff that has been researched, so use it!" mode, but as an opening to new inquiries. Newly developed models of teaching (Joyce *et al.* 1999) are not static practices that one simply puts in place. They are models of learning that engender further study of the students and how they learn. Thus, a corollary hypothesis:

Hypothesis 6: Staff development, structured as an inquiry, both fuels energy and results in initiatives that have greater effects.
The content of staff development – curriculum and teaching – is organized so that as new practices are implemented, their effects are studied systematically (see Chapter 5).

Optimum: Time provisions, above, are related to this hypothesis. Essentially, all members of the faculty study common targeted areas regularly and rigorously.

The caring community – teams of problem-solvers

A major dimension of schooling is creating caring communities for children. The development of organizations that care for the professionals who work there has received much less attention, despite the existence of a large body of literature on the stresses of teaching, the liability to "burning out" and the characteristics of "adult learners." Yet the organization can be seen as a caring one. Simply building closer professional communities and developing democratic interchange and embedding the study of teaching can be hypothesized to have a considerable effect on the feelings of education professionals. Inquiry, as such, can be recommended for its effects on our collective mental health. Yet we can focus directly on the development of caring communities. Our assessment of the literature on organizations is that the caring dimension depends to a large extent on building organizations where small groups – often only three or four people – see themselves as not only working together to "get the job done" but also as having responsibility for seeing that each person receives support as human beings with human and psychological needs (Joyce and Showers 1996).

Hypothesis 7: Building small work groups connected to the larger community but responsible for one another will increase the sense of belonging that reduces stress, isolation, and feelings of alienation.
Thus, the building blocks of the larger community are small groups with tasks to do – parts of the inquiry – and also with responsibility for human connectedness in the organization.

Optimum: Faculties are organized into peer coaching teams of between two and four members who have great knowledge about what each person in the team is doing with the children and support one another in solving problems and implementing the new repertoire related to the school's initiatives.

Altogether, the seven hypotheses define a strategy for creating an evolutionary state – and maintaining that state will, we believe, require the exercise of all of them together – ensuring a homeostasis of change rather than a homeostasis of tradition. Some of the apparently simple structural changes, such as the provision of substantial amounts of regular time for collegial activity, are as essential as the overhauling of the informational, staff development, and governance components.

The structure of school improvement is based on the seven hypotheses: a multidimensional approach to school improvement that radically changes the way teachers, administrators, and others work together to make reasoned initiatives to improve education and live together as energized communities.

In the following chapters we will visit many schools that make refinements in existing practice, develop completely renovated curriculums, or redesign major components of their operation. We will find that schools starting virtually from scratch can do any of these – that the organization can learn rapidly how to make productive changes (see Chapter 2). Moving to a fully evolutionary state is a process that is never finished.

THE CREATION OF SCHOOLS: REASON AND PERSPECTIVE

> The world presses on us; even in the most benign circumstances we are not wholly free. When there is no pressure to move in any given direction, we often constrain ourselves by our lack of vision and resources, our sense of what is possible. In every human activity it takes an enormous effort and perspective and courage to back off from familiar patterns in order to achieve a philosophical awareness of where we are going and where we might be going.

In the case of a social institution such as education, we are further constrained because the basic processes of the society continually shape the function and character of schools. We are able – by dint of a mighty force of will, to be sure – to step back and observe ourselves, our society, and other schools. Once we gain perspective we can attempt, if we care enough, to create schools that will have deliberately selected goals: schools that will not only be produced by the society but will necessarily return the favor by benefiting the future course of the community.

It is difficult indeed for a society to create an educational system that deliberately pushes the young to generate unfamiliar ideas and institutions, and even more difficult to give children and adolescents the freedom to do something about those yet unborn notions. To do so requires a trust in growing youth, a belief that the evolving men and women will choose the best of their new ideas.

In the middle of the nineteenth century John Stuart Mill grappled with the problem of freedom and conformity and made a number of statements which appear as relevant today as they were when he penned them:

> protection against tyranny of the magistrate is not enough; there needs protection also against the prevailing opinion and feelings; against the tendency of the society to impose, by rules of conduct, on those who dissent from them; to fetter the development and, if possible, prevent the formation of any personality not in harmony with its way, and compels all characters to fasten themselves upon the model of its own.
> (Mill 1947: 27)

He states clearly the problem our society has with its schools: how much to use them to perpetuate the society as it is (or was) and how much to generate new forms of education which impel (and free) the young to rebuild their personal and social reality. Obviously we believe the dilemma should be faced squarely – that the curriculum should be made deliberately, whatever course is chosen.

In essence, our focus is on creating environments that promote continuous examination of school effectiveness at local sites so that specific, deliberated improvements can be made. Schools are social entities and, like the human spirit, require the challenge of improvement not only to soar but also to maintain themselves. Just as the body grows supple through exercise and fades without it, the growing edges of the mind are sustained by challenge. Without stimulus to change, the structure of schools and individuals slides into rigid postures, and values reach toward the status of commandments. School improvement thrives only as life in schools is infused by adventure and tested by challenge.

We opt for the evolutionary state, created through inquiry – a solid, purposeful structure of school improvement where learning by the Responsible Parties is centered around making learning better for the students.

2 Centering the school on student learning: imagining the possibilities

We reach for an evolutionary state because we seek an excellent education for our children and we are never satisfied that we are doing all we can for them. So we organize ourselves to study continually, examining our students and their progress, searching the literature for new developments, and making changes in the educational environment. In this chapter we study how long it takes to generate a sufficient level of change in curriculum, instruction, and school climate to see the effects on student learning. We look for the answer in a number of substantial studies where several of the hypotheses have been acted on in school improvement efforts. Thus these studies provide partial tests of the proposed structure of school improvement.

We conclude that intensive effort will make the changes that will accelerate student achievement abundantly within a year.

Creating a fully evolutionary school will take longer and the job will never end.

THE BASIC INQUIRY

We developed the seven hypotheses after a search for studies of schools and school districts that generated and implemented initiatives that affected student learning substantially.

Necessarily, we found a good many studies (most of the total array) where good intentions and intelligent activity did not succeed in making substantive changes in the learning environment or, if they did, the changes were ones that did not generate fresh or higher levels of student learning.

We sorted the studies and derived the hypotheses by comparing the more successful cases with the less successful ones. Incidentally, successful cases are not the rule. The massive testing programs in the United States and the cross-national studies of student learning report relatively flat levels of student achievement over the last ten years and even more. Searching for more effective schools, a study of more than 3200 California schools found that only 16 maintained above-average student achievement (controlling for the socioeconomic status of their students) three years running (Weil *et al.* 1984). In the state of Georgia a similar study of 700 schools located just 30 whose achievement was above average for three years running (again controlling for socioeconomic status) (Weathersby and Harkreader 1998).

However, there are a number of studies where student achievement was not just above average, but a *lot* above average *because of curricular/ instructional changes*. Those are of great importance to us.

We are primarily interested in the development of procedures that will enable schools to enter an evolutionary state, and we believe that acting on the seven hypotheses gives them a good chance. The critical test is whether they are able to generate initiatives that have the intended effect of improving student learning. (Success in building an inquiring collegial environment that couldn't improve the environment for students would not fill the bill.)

In addition, we searched for and conducted studies that would provide information about the strength of the hypotheses – whether progress would be made by employing them.

CURRICULUM, TEACHING, AND SCHOOL CLIMATE

We concluded without difficulty that just about all the reported programs that have documented student learning gains have made changes in the educational environment – in curriculum, instruction, or the social climate (the last generally follows changes in curriculum and instruction). We estimate that somewhere between 30 and 60 percent of the curriculum area associated with the gains was changed in order to achieve the intended results. In other words, the changes have not been just a matter of minor refining of the content or process of that curriculum area (see Chapter 6).

We need to note that schools that are in a less than full evolutionary state have made curricular/instructional changes that have affected student learning. They have done so by picking very strong and targeted approaches and accompanying them with sufficient and appropriate staff development to generate implementation *and* the careful study of student learning.

Eventually we arrived at consideration of the length of time that is necessary to make a promising change of a type and magnitude that affects student learning, and to see progress toward an evolutionary state.

We will confine the discussion to initiatives that affect the school as a whole. Clearly an individual teacher or a small group of teachers or a department can implement curricular and instructional changes that will increase student achievement in their classes, but action by individuals and small groups is not the scope of this book (see Joyce *et al.* 1997a) for an example of actions that can be taken by individuals, small groups, and faculties).

TIME FOR AN INITIATIVE TO HAVE SCHOOLWIDE STUDENT LEARNING EFFECTS

We need to mention the conditions that are created in successful projects. In order to make a schoolwide initiative that might affect student learning four conditions have to be met: a reasonable level of agreement by the staff and parents; an adequate amount of staff development to develop the necessary knowledge and skill; a related organization of the faculty (all staff) so that it can work together to achieve implementation; and, as we reiterated above, a focus on the learning environment. These are fairly obvious, but it is surprisingly easy to make time-consuming initiatives that appear sensible but do not make much change in the learning environment (see below), and a frequent error is to decide to renovate a portion of the school program but fail to provide adequate staff development. If regular staff development/school renewal time is not built into the weekly schedule, then *ad hoc* arrangements have to be made to provide the time on a temporary, initiative-related basis. Summer workshops are one way to capture some of the needed time, but time during the academic year is needed as well.

A reasonable level of agreement simply means that a large majority of the faculty are agreed to go forward and to engage in the learning that makes implementation possible. We and our colleagues use the same rule of thumb that the Success For All team at Johns Hopkins University uses: the staff needs to agree that if 80 percent of its members vote to go forward with a schoolwide initiative, then all will participate cheerfully.

Assuming that these four conditions are met, we will argue two propositions:

First, that even extensive renovations of the curricular/instructional complex can be made within the first year of an initiative.

Second, that student learning effects will occur during that first year. In fact, we have found no examples where a substantial change was not accompanied by student learning gains during the first year. If they don't happen then, they are unlikely to occur later.

HOW MUCH GAIN CAN BE ACHIEVED?

For support for these propositions, we turn to a number of recent studies. We have selected only studies where the size of gain was considerable. How much gain? Let's use as an illustration a small study that investigated the effects of introducing a single, albeit very complex, model of teaching into a social study course.

The model of teaching is Group Investigation, an intensive approach that combines elaborate methods for collaborative activity with scientific methods of inquiry. In this study, Shlomo Sharan and Hana Shachar (1988) illustrated how rapidly students can accelerate their learning rates. Their study focussed on a problem that exists in many societies: students whose families are regarded as socially and economically disadvantaged frequently display low achievement and receive disadvantaging treatment in the classroom from other students and from teachers. Sharan and Shachar prepared social studies teachers to organize their students into learning communities and compared the classroom interaction and academic achievement with classes taught by the customary "whole-class" method. In Israel, where the study was conducted, students of Middle Eastern origin generally belong to the "disadvantaged" population, whereas generally those of European origin are more advantaged. In this study, students from both origins were mixed in classes. The research design compared the achievement of the students who were taught using group investigation with students taught by the "whole-class" method most common in Israeli schools. In Table 2.1 the results are presented for the Middle-Eastern students under the two conditions.

Table 2.1 Comparison of achievement of Middle-Eastern students in Group Investigation and "whole-class" conditions

		Group Investigation (n = 47)	Whole class (n = 26)
History pre-test	mean	14.81	12.31
	SD	7.20	7.05
History post-test	mean	50.17	27.23
	SD	14.44	13.73
Mean gain		35.36	14.92

The Group-Investigation-taught, Middle-Eastern-origin students achieved average gains nearly two and a half times those of their whole-class counterparts. These normally disadvantaged students also achieved larger gains than did the European-origin students taught by the more typical "whole-class method" (35.16 to 21.05) and exceeded them on the post-test. In other words, the "socially disadvantaged" students taught by Group Investigation learned at rates above those of the "socially advantaged" students taught by teachers who did not have the repertoire provided by Group Investigation. The model had enabled them to become more powerful students immediately. The average gain by the Western-origin students was *twice* that of their "whole-class" counterparts. Thus, the treatment was effective for students from both backgrounds.

Nearly everyone would agree that these are sizeable gains. Later, as we consider options in curriculum and instruction, we will examine the concept of "effect size" that is used to calculate an index of magnitude of gain and ruminate on the relative sizes of gains that can be achieved through initiatives in curriculum and instruction. For now, let's continue our discussion by examining the example of several large-scale school improvement efforts.

LARGE-SCALE SCHOOL IMPROVEMENT PROGRAMS

Most of these programs are complex and brought about substantial changes in curriculum, teaching, relationships among teachers, staff development, community relations, on the way to successful implementation.

Success For All: combining curriculum, instruction, and tutoring

The Center for Research on Effective Schooling for Disadvantaged Students at Johns Hopkins University (Slavin *et al.* 1996) is beginning to report its efforts to improve primary education in the Baltimore schools. The Success For All program combines an intensive reading curriculum with close-order diagnosis of learning problems, immediate intervention with tutoring aimed directly at the problems, and family support teams. The focus is on preventing the onset of the downward spiral that so often begins during the primary years and leaves the students unable to cope with the ordinary demands of the upper grades. The program developers aim at bringing *all* students to satisfactory levels. They are very close to their objective. The multi-year effects of the program are very positive. Retention (where students repeat a grade) has been reduced greatly (from about 10 percent to 1–3 percent in the project schools). Gains in reading are considerable across a variety of tests, with effect sizes frequently reaching 1.0 or better, and fewer students are in need of special education services because their achievement is satisfactory.

In Nottingham, a collaborative effort by the Johns Hopkins team, a team from the University of Nottingham, and the Nottingham Education Authority generated the Success For All program in a family of schools in Nottingham. Using internal assessments of progress, they were able to report that achievement in reading during just the first term of implementation was twice the normal gains by students in those schools. Also, the team reported that gains by students was directly related to degrees of implementation in the schools as a whole. Understandably, there were considerable differences in initial implementation during this first year, among schools and among classes within schools, and the effects could be felt substantially in the degrees of gain that were achieved (Hopkins *et al.* 1998).

The Schenley Program: intensive, instruction-oriented staff development

In Pittsburgh a side effect of the development of an extensive district-wide staff development program was a test of what can happen if some of the most highly regarded teachers in a large district are concentrated in a high school whose lower socioeconomic status (SES) population has been achieving far below the national average. The Schenley School became a staff development center where outstanding teachers were brought together. Other district teachers rotated into the school, spending several weeks observing those teachers and studying instruction (Wallace *et al.* 1990). There was a very large rise in standardized tests in eight out of nine curriculum areas. In terms of the percentage of students scoring at or above the national average the rise in total language results was from 27 percent to 61 percent, in reading from 28 percent to 45 percent, in physical science from 21 percent to 63 percent, in biology from 13 to 41 percent, and in algebra from 29 percent to 73 percent. The gains were maintained or increased during the second year. As interesting as are the sizes of those improvements, it is equally interesting that they were so immediate. High schools need not feel hopeless about students with poor learning histories.

The Richmond County (Georgia) Models of Teaching Program

All of the teachers in 16 participating schools studied a set of well-researched models of teaching selected to increase the learning capacity of their students (Joyce *et al.* 1989; Showers *et al.* 1996).

In some of the schools the need for school improvement was urgent. For example, in one of the middle schools the students had such poor histories of learning that only 30 percent of the students achieved promotion at the end of the year before the project began. Scores on standard tests revealed that the average student in the school had gained only about six-tenths of the national average gain each year they had been in school. As the teachers learned to use models of teaching designed to increase cooperative activity, teach concepts, and teach students to work inductively and to memorize information, the learning rates of the students began to improve. By the end of the first year 70 percent of the students in that middle school achieved the standards required for promotion and 95 percent achieved promotion at the end of the second year. Judging from the standardized tests administered at the end of the second year, the average students in the school were achieving at a normal rate. Suspensions dropped from about 140 per semester (in a school of about 550 students) to about 35. The other 15 schools also had large gains in achievement, with average gains in 48 of 72 standard test comparisons being about half a year or more in grade-level-equivalent terms.

The Second Chance Program for secondary school students who are beginning readers

A pervasive problem in secondary schools is how to make provision for students who enter secondary school with poor literacy skills. They are doomed to failure if something is not done, but what to do?

In Chapter 3 there is an extensive description of a program that was implemented in the Samuel F. B. Morse high school in San Diego, California. Based on an extensive review of the literature on the teaching of "over age beginning readers" (see Calhoun 1997) an intensive program was developed to help a large proportion of the student body learn to read and write. Progress was several times the usual annual gain for students in their situation (Showers *et al.* 1998).

A FIELD STUDY IN HIGH-ACHIEVING SUBURBAN ELEMENTARY SCHOOLS

In recent years the study of learning to write has been subjected to exhaustive inquiry, and researchers for the National Assessment of Writing Progress (see NAEP 1992) have conducted large-scale investigations of student progress in quality of writing with good-sized samples of students drawn from various types of school districts across the United States. These studies provide an increasingly accurate picture of the magnitude of year-to-year growth in student's ability to focus and organize pieces of writing, and to establish and support themes or story lines, and in the complexity and correctness of the mechanics they use. Data are collected by providing the students with stimulus material, prompting them to write in several genres, and submitting the products to a content analysis. The grade 4 writing becomes a baseline against which the writing of the older students can be compared. When the writing of eighth grade students is compared with that of fourth grade students, the mean eighth grade score is about at the 62nd percentile of the fourth grade distribution and the variances of the grade 4 and grade 8 writing are similar. The grade 12 mean is about at the 72nd percentile of the fourth grade distribution. Smaller studies making grade-to-grade comparisons (fifth with fourth, sixth to fifth, and so on), and studies following students for several years, confirm that the annual growth at the mean is about 3 or 3.5 percentile points. Even in traditionally "high-achieving" suburban school districts, an annual gain of 5 percentile points at the mean is normal. (See pp. 84–5 for an explanation of the statistical terms.)

A growing community of researchers is attempting to generate models for the teaching of writing with the purpose of increasing several dimensions of quality.

In the nine elementary schools of a midwestern town we will call University Town (see Joyce and Calhoun 1996) all the teachers studied an adaptation of an inductive model of teaching (for a description, see Joyce *et al.* 1999) to help students analyze the devices used by published writers and incorporate those devices into their writing.

For many years standard tests have indicated that this town is one of the highest achieving in the nation, with means in all the curriculum area in the high 60th percentiles and even higher. About 60 percent of the graduates go to four-year colleges and nearly all the rest obtain some higher education. The teachers work in favorable conditions, supported by aides, rich instructional resources, even district-provided resources for their personal staff development and the resources of a major state university, and are accustomed to working with students who, in cultural terms, are relatively compliant and "easy to teach." Those teachers have had the opportunity to practice their skills in a setting where relatively high standards of achievement prevail.

What happened when they studied a research-based approach to the teaching of reading and writing and learned to use it?

Achievement prior to the intervention. Judging from the results of the analyses conducted during the 1991–2 school year over writing samples collected from all the fourth, sixth, and eighth grade students (n = 1200), the children in the University Town schools were progressing at an effect-size rate of about 0.14, or almost 50 percent above the national average. This translates to a gain, at the mean, of about 5 percentile points. Thus, in 1991–2 the average sixth grade student on the dimension "focus and organization" was at about the 60th percentile of the fourth grade distribution.

Achievement as a product of the inductive approaches to teaching and learning: grade 4 expository writing. Table 2.2 compares the means for the two periods (fall 1992 and spring 1993) for the three dimensions for which quality was assessed (focus/organization, support, and grammar and mechanics).

Table 2.2   Mean grade 4 scores on expository writing for fall 1992 and spring 1993

	Dimensions		
Period	*Focus/org.*	*Support*	*Grammar/mech.*
Fall			
Mean	1.6	2.2	2.11
SD	0.55	0.65	0.65
Spring			
Mean	2.8	3.2	3.0
SD	0.94	0.96	0.97

Effect sizes were computed for fall and spring scores: for focus/organization, 2.18; for support, 1.53; and for grammar/mechanics, 1.37.

All these are several times the effect sizes calculated for a year's gain for the national sample (0.10) and several times the annual baseline gains (ES = 0.14) estimated from the 1991–2 study in University Town. For focus and organization, the differences are so great that in the spring, the average student reached the top of the fall distribution, something that did not happen nationally during the entire time from grades 4 to 12.

To illustrate the magnitude of the gain, Table 2.3 compares the mean results for the spring fourth grade assessment with the fall sixth grade results.

Table 2.3 Mean grade 4 spring 1993 scores on expository writing compared with the mean grade 6 scores from fall 1992

	Dimensions		
Period	*Focus/org.*	*Support*	*Grammar/mech.*
Grade 4 spring Mean	2.8	3.2	3.0
Grade 6 fall Mean	2.11	2.90	2.87

The fourth grade students ended their year substantially ahead of where the sixth grade students were at the beginning of the year. They also finished the year with higher scores than where the eighth grade students began the year on the focus/organization (grade 8 mean = 2.32) and support dimensions (grade 8 mean = 2.95), and were close on the grammar/mechanics dimension (grade 8 mean = 3.32).

Studies over the following years indicate that the district continues, annually, to generate gains in quality of writing several times their annual gain prior to the initiative in language arts.

JUST READ: AN INTENSIVE PROGRAM TO INCREASE "AT-HOME" READING

First developed in the Department of Defense Dependants' Schools in Panama, Just Read takes the language arts program into the living rooms of the students. The program is a data-based action research process (see Chapter 5) wherein all students, teachers, the district, and the community study how much the students are reading independently and generate a campaign to increase at-home independent reading and study the effects on student reading and subsequent effects on their reading and writing ability. Although amounts of reading increased from kindergarten (reading to and with) through the twelfth grade, the initial research (Joyce and Wolf 1996) focussed on the fifth grades with respect to both effects on the number of books read (an average of 50 per year with a range of 15–100) and gains in vocabulary and comprehension and an indirect effect on quality of writing. The most important finding was that competence in reading increased, during one year, about one-and-a-half times what would have been expected for the students, given their learning histories, and competence in writing from two to six times more than their age cohorts. Again, the rapid growth is important to us in this analysis.

Although making large differences in student achievement through school improvement programs is hardly routine, the number of reports and variety of programs that have had considerable success suggests that the technology – the procedure for school renewal – for making rapid and significant change exists. The ones mentioned above are just a few of those the faculty discovered. For example, the more effective implementation of "Mastery Learning" programs (Bloom 1971; Block and Anderson 1975), Distar (a highly sequenced materials-based program for teaching reading and arithmetic) (Becker 1977) have generated large results. In the United Kingdom, the Improving Schools Project studied 12 schools that had demonstrated substantial improvement in examination results and discovered that the greater the inquiry into instruction, the better the results (Gray *et al.* 1999).

Many of the schools in the study chose to engage in efforts to raise exam results directly. It is an interesting feature of the English approach to assessment at the end of compulsory schooling that it "rewards" this kind of approach.

Many also worked on their policies for supporting teaching and learning. Only a small minority, however, had engaged in activities in relation to supporting classroom processes of teaching and learning, for example. As our subsequent analyses indicated, the most rapidly improving schools had probably found ways of doing all three of these things. They had managed to focus directly on aspects of pupils' achievement and on organizational policies supporting teaching, along with aspects of classroom culture and practice, at much the same time.

While almost all of the schools we studied in depth exhibited evidence of tactical approaches and several showed signs of strategic thinking, only two appeared to have moved beyond those stages. These two had a fairly sophisticated view of how to undertake change and "pull all the relevant levers" to enhance student achievement. They were knowledgeable about the problems to be faced, believed that they had engaged with issues of teaching and learning for some while, and were able to put forward fairly coherent rationales for the next steps.

What was interesting about these schools (and this marked them out from the others) was the extent to which they had shown a willingness to go beyond merely incremental approaches to change at some point in the not-too-distant past and engaged in some organizational restructuring with enhanced learning as an intended outcome. They had developed ways of being more specific about precisely how they wished to improve pupils' learning, were able to draw on colleagues' experiences to formulate strategies, and had found ways of helping colleagues to evaluate and learn from their own and other teachers' classroom experiences. In their quest for higher performance they showed a willingness to engage with a wide range of potential sources of advice by encouraging their staffs to pursue their own professional development, providing in-house opportunities for development and support, seeking out help from their LEAs as well as finding ways of bringing in people from higher education to support their School Improvement efforts.

Also in the United Kingdom, the Improving the Quality of Education for All (IQEA) group generates school improvement efforts focussed on both organizational and instructional change (Hopkins *et al.* 1996a).

UNLOCKING THE SHACKLES OF DEMOGRAPHY

One of the purposes of research in education is to increase the effects of the learning environment in comparison to demographic factors – ethnicity, language background, learning history (how well students have done in the past), and gender. The programs described above not only raised student learning in general, but in doing so greatly reduced the influence of the factors that place some students as being more "at risk" than others.

- Success For All targeted "Title I" students (economically poor students who qualify for augmented school programs) and made great progress with both boys and girls, and with children of every race and linguistic background.
- Second Chance targeted students of both genders and several ethnicities who had failed to learn to read adequately after ten years of schooling. Most of them profited greatly.
- Just Read substantially increased "at-home" independent reading with boys and girls alike from families having great variance in economic status, and students who were both good and poor readers in the past.
- The Pittsburgh Program targeted an urban high school where virtually all the students were in bad shape academically (virtually the whole place was "at risk") and turned student achievement around dramatically – for boys and girls, blacks and whites, and native speakers of several languages.
- The Ames Program showed how it is possible for a district that was touted for very high achievement, comparatively speaking, to accelerate the growth of those students dramatically in the literacy areas. The gap between boys and girls was reduced dramatically and poor achievers in that high-achieving district profited greatly as well.

In each of these cases large gains, several times the normal yearly gain, were made during the first year and made again, and often enlarged, during subsequent years as the faculties achieved better implementation.

In addition, the social dimension of the schools improved. Disciplinary actions were reduced. There were fewer referrals to special programs and achievement of the students with special needs rose, sometimes to the level of average students.

Many people are startled that effects can be achieved so quickly, but actually the phenomenon of first-year effects is not difficult to explain. *Essentially, students can respond very quickly to a new educational environment.* There is a very long history of research on curricular and instructional options that supports this contention; see specifically the studies by Joyce and Joyce (1968), Almy (1970), and Spaulding (1970). (In Chapter 6 we review part of the storehouse of research-based curricular and instructional options from which schools can choose.) In nearly every case the types of student learning that were the objectives were achieved to at least some degree as soon as the learning environment changed.

TIME TO REACH AN EVOLUTIONARY STATE

This is a much trickier question than the previous issue. Clearly, if a school can undertake one successful initiative, it ought to be able to make another one. If it can generate the necessary conditions for one, it has made progress toward using several of the seven hypotheses. And, having had success, should the community of educators, parents, and others not be impelled to even greater achievement?

The answer is "*not necessarily.*" For the full state to be reached continuous and sustained effort is needed. And it is easy to slip backward, particularly because, perversely, success does not breed support to anything like the extent that one might think it would. Levine has written passionately about how changes in districts have been accompanied by the dismantling of successful programs in favor of new initiatives that, not infrequently, do not pay off (Levine 1991).

Calhoun's (1996) extensive study of nearly 100 schools that selected action research as their door to school improvement (see Chapter 5) provides information about how easily schools can be derailed. Action research emphasizes the development of inclusive, whole-school democratic governance; the extensive use of objective data to study the students and their learning environment; the study of professional literature; and making initiatives to improve the learning environment and studying the effects of those initiatives. Sounds similar to our hypotheses, doesn't it? Of the 100 schools, only about ten actually succeeded in improving student learning. In the others, the process broke down somewhere along the way.

Some couldn't organize the whole faculty to work together. Some could, but couldn't figure out how to collect and organize data meaningfully. Some made initiatives that only reinforced the current curricular and instructional patterns, or were peripheral to the educational environment (see below). Some made initiatives that would have changed curriculum and instruction, but didn't organize the necessary staff development to generate implementation.

You can see why we emphasize the use of *all seven hypotheses* as the basis for a high-probability school improvement strategy, and how the loss of one of the dimensions can substantially weaken an otherwise sound effort.

Interestingly, all ten of the successful action research projects had extensive support from consultants expert in all phases of action research *and* in curriculum and instruction in the areas of focus. The successful faculties did the work, but needed help to enable them to start conducting business in a new way. More about this as we discuss the role of districts and other support agencies in the process of school improvement.

THE PERIPHERAL AND THE CENTRAL (THE PROXIMAL AND THE DISTAL)

Wang, Haertel, and Walberg (1993) have tackled the problem of sorting out what works in a manner somewhat similar to ours and their selection of studies overlaps with ours. They concluded that an important characteristic of approaches that make a substantial difference to student achievement is the focus on the learning environment. They distinguish variables that are *proximal* (close to the student) from those that are *distal* (at a distance from the student). In our terms, initiatives that affect curriculum, instruction, and the social climate or the home environment of the students are much more likely to affect student learning than ones that are directed at the periphery of the students' environment.

The proximal/distal distinction is useful when we try to explain why some very popular policies and initiatives have had such a poor track record, and why some modest and less-used ones have worked so well. For example, some state policymakers have attempted to raise student achievement in literacy by establishing testing programs accompanied with standards for promotion. Such a practice does not affect the learning environment, by providing instruction that gives students a better chance to achieve; it assumes that the threat of nonpromotion or nongraduation will provide pressure that will result in student achievement. Unfortunately, all that happens is that more students are retained, which for most students damages subsequent academic achievement and has a terrible effect on self-esteem. Suppose that, instead, the state had picked up, as Slavin and his colleagues did, on Bloom's finding that one-on-one tutoring by trained tutors dramatically increases student learning. The effect of the proximal initiative – a direct improvement of the learning environment – would have very positive effects for nearly all students.

Another example contrasts two approaches to the management of rule breakers: disciplinary problems. A distal approach is to make rules tighter and suspend more students, thus actually depriving them of instruction. A proximal approach is to create a cooperative learning environment (see Johnson and Johnson 1990) which has a fine track record for reducing misbehavior and simultaneously increasing student achievement, self-esteem, and cooperative, interdependent behavior. The distal will actually increase disciplinary problems whereas the proximal will reduce them.

The people of California have just voted to eliminate bilingual programs in favor of English-only programs for students whose primary language is not English. They will be disappointed, because either approach can work if enough teachers learn to use the best versions of it, but neither will work well if instruction does not improve – and California is undersupplied with teachers who can do either with the effectiveness of research-based approaches that are well documented in the literature.

Even some initiatives that "feel" proximal are too distal to make much difference in the ways students learn. Changing ways of reporting to parents, scheduling of classes, types of tests, nongrading and continuous progress schemes, all can make the functioning of the school smoother, but unless curriculum and instruction are also changed, little difference will be made to student achievement. Computers have thus far changed effects in very few schools because students have too little access (perhaps an hour a week in a lab) or the distribution of computers (one or two or three to a classroom) has not been accompanied by the type of training to make computers a major dimension of the learning environment.

As we will see, national, federal, state and local authority initiatives, such as the large categorical programs, will only make a difference if they provide the support in staff development and other terms to enable school faculties to make changes in the actual (proximal) environment the students experience. When a school receives external initiatives, it needs to be prepared to convert them into real improvements in the learning environment.

The message is "go for the proximal!"

REFINEMENT, RENOVATION, AND REDESIGN: DEGREES OF CHANGE

In the course of developing an evolutionary state, a school will make many initiatives that change the condition of curriculum and instruction and the social climate of the school. Some of these fine-tune or refine an aspect of the school; others renovate a curriculum area or other part of the learning environment; and others will redesign an aspect of the environment by providing a type of instruction or self-instruction not previously available to the students.

Refinement is a fine-tuning of an aspect of an ongoing operation. We refine things that we believe are going well but can be improved incrementally. For example, a fine graphic arts program can be refined so that the study of the history of art is incorporated. Such a refinement probably requires the addition of a gallery with renditions of art through the ages and/or the incorporation of computer graphics that serve the purpose of a gallery. Refinements are not technically difficult to make, but may require a broad level of consensus and a reallocation of resources. Generally speaking, all courses in all curriculum areas are optimally in a state of refinement. Importantly, refinements worth making are those that affect student achievement; they are not just cosmetic changes.

Renovation is an overhauling of an aspect of the program of the school. Sometimes we renovate in order to update content or incorporate more rigorous instructional strategies or models of teaching. Sometimes renovations touch all curriculum areas, as when intensive "writing across the curriculum" approaches are adopted by a secondary school. In several of the examples discussed earlier in this chapter, curriculum areas were overhauled substantially.

Redesign is a change in a major aspect of the school's operation, necessitated by an innovation in the learning environment that cannot be accommodated by the existing structures. High schools that develop intensive offerings through distance education generally have to make changes in scheduling, assessment of student learning, and home-study provisions that involve a considerable rearrangement of several features of the operation.

In the following chapters we will visit many schools that make refinements in existing practice, develop completely renovated curriculums, or redesign major components of their operation. We will find that schools starting virtually from scratch can do any of these – that the organization can learn rapidly how to make productive changes. Moving to a fully evolutionary state is a process that is never finished, but we will visit some places that are in wonderful shape.

COMMENTARY

While the road to school improvement is not a dangerous one, it is not completely paved and smooth and its surface is vulnerable to erosion. In a real sense, the community paves and repaves it in the process and neglect of any important factor will be paid for eventually. We watched a school that had made great progress, and documented substantial increases in student learning, begin to lose what it had gained because a new principal, unaccustomed to dealing with a learning community, unfamiliar with the new curricular elements, and preferring one-to-one relationships with faculty members, unilaterally cut the collective school improvement time and reduced faculty meetings to short monthly sessions. A dozen new faculty members were unable to study the new curricular and instructional patterns. The 30 experienced members became confused and angry. The new principal had the skills to maintain a "good old school," but the practices attendant on the seven hypotheses were new to her and she set about bringing the school in line with the practices she understood.

The district personnel office thought they had selected a new person who would learn from the vital school community that had been established. Now they know they were wrong, and what will happen now will depend on whether she will accept the support the district personnel can give her or whether she will stay in a low state of growth.

Meanwhile, in another district not far away, another new principal was busily setting up an evolutionary school, step by step. Beginning with the provision of weekly time, he organized an embryo version of the Responsible Parties, organized the faculty to study quality of writing in the school with the aid of a fine consultant, led the faculty into the study of the teaching of writing, and set up the peer coaching groups that would be the engine both for the caring community and for the implementation of the initiatives in the area of reading and writing.

In the first case the leader did not maintain a road that was in very good condition. The second leader knew something about how to build a road from scratch.

The structure of school improvement is centered around the *study* of students and student learning, rather than assumptions that we can proceed without learning more each time.

3 Studying evolving schools: watching the action

Let us look at two schools and reflect on our school renewal hypotheses as each school works its way toward an evolutionary state. These schools – an elementary school in the United States serving students ages 5 through 12 and an American city high school serving a multiethnic population of 1800 – have, in their own fashions, worked their way toward an evolutionary state.

CASE 1: SOUTHWOOD ELEMENTARY SCHOOL

Southwood is located in a town of approximately 32,000 residents in the Southwestern United States. Its student population is about 50 percent Caucasian, 35 percent Hispanic, and 15 percent black. The students come from a combination of middle-class and socioeconomically disadvantaged homes, with about one-third of the students receiving free lunch.

Southwood Elementary School serves kindergarten (age 5) through sixth grade students (age 12). This year, the school has 28 teachers and approximately 600 students. The Responsible Parties include all 28 teachers, 24 parents elected by the other parents, and four student–parent teams. The Executive Committee of 14 persons is elected from this group.

Leadership and collective inquiry

The Executive Committee often does initial organization of schoolwide data and gathering of information about curriculum and instruction from the professional knowledge base, but all Responsible Parties study the data and read key articles related to the school's student learning focus for the year.

For example, the district and its schools report student progress to parents on a quarterly and mid-quarterly basis. Southwood Executive Committee members take this information and organize, by grade level, tables that indicate the grades of all students (for kindergarten and first grade, the number/percent of students with performance indicators of "Excellent Progress," "Good Progress," "Needs More Work"; and for grades 2 through 6, the number/percent of students making As, Bs, etc.) At this same time, they share tables that depict the number and types of discipline referrals and absences by grade level and for the school as a whole. It has taken the Committee about two years to make this regular review of how students are performing and behaving, and what is happening to them in their learning environment, into a routine check on perceptions and a tool for identifying problems.

The Executive Committee is also responsible for keeping the work of the school connected to the external knowledge base, particularly in light of issues or problems that surface when the Responsible Parties analyze their school data and in terms of current schoolwide goals and initiatives being pursued. While the information on curriculum standards and the articles about what works to improve student learning contain much educational jargon, many parents in the Responsible Parties are as interested in the professional literature as teachers, and sometimes more curious about its implications for the learning environment. And because the Responsible Parties are engaged in continuous study, possible future initiatives are often identified while pursuing information about current goals.

Listen in on this discussion at a session of the Responsible Parties. Angela, a fourth grade teacher, is leading a public synthesis of an article on teaching writing: "Most of you felt the authors made a strong point for increasing teacher demonstrations of how to respond to written assignments. That we need to show kids how we would look for information and how we would write a response to assignments in social studies, science, and English."

Sam, one of the parent members, makes his observation: "Another point made was the need to give students something to write about, something they can all see or talk about. I think that would help me. I'm not much of a writer, but if I had something to look at and we were all talking about it, I'd at least have something to say."

Paula, a first grade teacher, signals for attention: "Remember that article we read a few months ago, by Gallo. He made a big point that professional writers use observation as a major source of ideas. This fits right with that."

The group discusses the idea of increasing demonstrations and the use of observation as a source for writing. Ideas include using pictures for helping young children with their group language experience stories, using more pictures in social studies as they study different regions and cultures, keeping records and writing about experiments being conducted, and even writing about changes in the classroom garden.

As the session concludes, Pauline, the Chair of the Executive Committee, says to them: "You have made it clear that you want to work on improving the quality of student writing next year. We [the 14 members of the Executive Committee] will take the notes from the two data-review sessions, the goal-setting session, and these two sessions on studying what works in improving student writing, and draft a school action plan. As always, time is a major variable to contend with. We'll build into the plan time and suggestions for studying student writing throughout the year and time and suggestions for supporting our staff development to increase teacher demonstrations of writing. We'll also check on the district initiative for next year and see how we might be able to use it to our advantage, either in data that might be available, staff development, or additional resources we might cadge. We'll have a draft plan ready for your review in about two weeks. This way, everyone will have time to study it and make recommendations before it's submitted to the district office."

Before a schoolwide initiative is built into the Southwood's School Improvement Plan, everyone has a sense of how the initiative will support student growth and why this particular initiative is a good option for them to try. The same is true if a program is rejected or an initiative is modified or discarded. At a minimum, the whole staff studies the conceptual foundations of a program and its student effect results. If the program does not seem well grounded or if its developers have not studied its effects on groups of students, the program is rejected. However, once a plan and its components are approved by the Responsible Parties, it becomes a public document requiring collective action and the use of resources.

Gradually, the school is learning to make data collection and use routine. The Executive Committee has played a big role in helping staff members come to reflect on and use both internal data about their students and external information from the available knowledge base. Committee members are still struggling to make routine the study of what is happening to the current student population that they are all responsible for. They have defined part of their job as keeping data about the status of current initiatives routinely available for study by all Responsible Parties. Next year, they plan to provide mid-quarterly, quarterly, and annual reports on student progress in Title I and the bilingual immersion classes.

Establishing time and content for collective work

In the Paularino School District, where Southwood is located, the students leave after lunch every Wednesday afternoon. From 1.30 p.m. until 4.00 p.m., the faculties throughout the district meet to study the effects of their current initiative. This regular collective worktime is the result of a negotiated district-wide agreement between the teachers' association and the school board.

The structuring-in of time for collective work occurred a year ago. We asked Carol, a Southwood teacher who was heavily involved in working with the community about this change in the school week, to tell us about it.

Carol: "I was a member of the district's ILT last year. We worked with Dr. Lin [the associate superintendent] all year. We tried to use a problem-solving approach in making structural changes at the district level that would support changes at the school and classroom level. At times, it felt like too many people trying to juggle too many balls."

We took a few minutes to find out what the ILT was, discovering it was a representative districtwide Instructional Leadership Team composed of 16 teachers elected from 16 of the district's 31 schools, 15 principals from the other schools, the district associate superintendent, and the district superintendent as an ex-officio member. Then we asked Carol to continue.

"We struggled with how to integrate district initiatives and better support school initiatives, with how to provide time for teachers to work together, and how to support long-term, substantive staff development. We knew we needed time for all teachers to work together as a staff if we were going to engage in an intensive program of learning for students and teachers. We couldn't improve student learning for all students if we just went with those teachers willing to stay after school, or with volunteers for staff development courses. We've done that for years and look at our student achievement, not the worst, we're better than you would think, but not as good as we would like it to be.

"We explored a number of different options for staff to have time to work together: pay for after-school time for all staff, building extra days into the school year, converting faculty meetings into study times. But we decided to go for the weekly, regular two-and-a-half-hour block because it best suited sustained work by staff, and we could include our paraprofessionals and teaching assistants in the work/study time. The superintendent and Dr. Lin worked with the school board, and some ILT members led a work session with school board members, outlining how the time would be used. Actually, the board seemed quite supportive of the idea from the beginning, once they knew it was not going to cost additional revenues. Then everything had to be worked out with the teachers' association."

Carol described for us both the process and the content of this restructuring move: While the association and board members were working out the details of the agreement, members of the districtwide Instructional Leadership Team were meeting with parent and community groups to discuss how the staff would be using the collective time.

The team planned the content of the public information sessions, providing ample time for questions and responses among participants. Presenting in groups of three or four (two or three teachers and one administrator), these teams illustrated how the staff worktime would be used.

Carol said team members tried to make their presentations as concrete and explicit as possible. They rehearsed them in school staff meetings, both as practice and also to help school staff get a clearer picture of what was being "promised" to the community. The content of the sessions included examples of the kind of state and national data that would be studied, as well as examples of district data and school-based data such as student writing samples and student procedures for solving math problems.

Team members even went so far as to share excerpts from and examples of key research articles and curriculum content standards that staff members would study to determine the best strategies or initiatives to pursue for improving student performance. They described the nature of the staff development that would be provided by the district to support the districtwide initiative of expanding the range of instructional strategies being used to improve reading at every level – kindergarten through grade 12 (ages 6 to about 18). They described examples of how school-selected staff development would operate: they explained how staff members would build lessons together, study their implementation of the instructional and curriculum strategies being developed, and how they would study student response to these strategies.

Carol said that talking with the community about the need to improve teaching and do a better job of studying student learning created mixed feelings for her. On one hand, she felt that teachers were doing an excellent job, better than most parents and community members realized. On the other hand, she believed that the common worktime and additional assistance in studying student performance were needed if major gains were to be made *schoolwide* for all students. When talking with community members during scheduled meetings and in informal settings, she articulated both perspectives. Most persons seemed to appreciate her honesty; however, she and others were occasionally challenged by those who bluntly said something like, "We thought that having a teaching certificate meant you knew how to teach." And a few who said, "Well, you folks have the summers off; the rest of us don't. Why not study together during the summer?"

Let's look now at what the Southwood staff members are doing this year and how they have organized themselves as a learning community.

Selecting a focus area for collective inquiry: improving the quality of students' informative writing

The Southwood staff members were concerned about student writing. They had ended the previous year by reviewing student results on the standardized test used by the district, results from the state writing tests, the grade/performance reports provided by the Executive Committee, and the new state curriculum standards. They were pleased with student performance in mathematics; they had worked for three years to strengthen the mathematics instruction they were providing. More than one-half of their students were performing in the top quartile of the district distribution in mathematics. They felt this was a good reminder of the power of instruction to affect student achievement.

The Responsible Parties were concerned about student performance in reading, for the school mean was about the middle of the district distribution. When they disaggregated the data, they were appalled by the number of young males who were not learning to read, but decided they would use the district initiative in reading to build capacity in this area.

However, it wasn't just the fact that their students were performing near the bottom of the state and district distribution in writing that led the staff to focus on improving the quality of students' informative writing, it was a combination of factors:

1 Several teachers were convinced that reading and writing could be improved simultaneously if the focus were somewhat weighted toward developing writing craft and audience awareness.
2 Several upper grade teachers were concerned about students' ability to read expository prose, the dominant genre in the textbooks and instructional materials they were using. They felt that students' comprehension of exposition would be improved if they understood more about how informative/expository prose was organized.
3 And when the teachers were reviewing the state content standards in language arts and thinking about their implications for instructional changes, they came to realize that they were not certain themselves about the different genres of writing students should become skilled in producing, much less how to teach them to produce higher quality pieces. As individuals and as a group, their understanding of the characteristics that define the different genres were often vague or unclear.

As they looked at the student writing results reported for personal narrative, informative, and persuasive/argument and studied the characteristics and major applications of each genre, they decided to focus on improving the quality of nonfictional, informative writing. Of interest is the fact that they did not select their "lowest area," persuasive writing, because they felt students needed to learn to write basic informative prose first. Nor did they select personal narrative, because their students were doing a relatively good job writing about experiences they had, because they felt they were providing at least some instruction in this genre, and because there was a good match between the state's curriculum recommendations and what they were currently doing to promote growth in this genre. Yet the teachers felt they had much work to do just to clarify among themselves what good informative prose looked like, and to figure out how to design instruction that would improve the quality of informative writing by all students.

Supporting collective inquiry and implementation

Listen in during the first afternoon of preplanning. Harry, Southwood's principal for the past four years, is ensuring that the formal social system supports staff study and the implementation of the initiatives selected.

Harry: "From your comments at the end of last year about working in peer coaching groups of two to four persons and my own observations about the support they provided when we were struggling to learn new teaching strategies in math, I suggest we use the same support system.

Select your partners, no group larger than four. Just for your information, I have already talked with Shana, our new kindergarten teacher, and Tami [a first grade teacher], we'll be a team this year."

Harry looks over at Rod, a fifth grade teacher and Harry's peer coaching partner last year, and says, "Of course, I know all of you would like me to be on your team, right Rod?"

Rod grins and responds, "Well, my kids probably had twice as many inductive lessons as they would have had. Not counting the fact that I had to keep practicing myself to continue the phases of the model because Harry and I rotated instruction every other day. Sort of put me on my mettle."

Many of the staff members smiled, some because they suspect Harry teamed up with Rod last year because he was concerned about Rod's willingness to engage fully with learning the inductive model. This was accurate, but Harry also did not want a whole class of fifth grade students to lose out on learning how to learn inductively. Last year, Harry spent about one-fifth of his time teaching; he plans to do the same this year.

Harry says, "Now don't scare Shana."

Harry also has leadership motives, other than simple support of the new teacher, for placing himself on her team. One is that the other two kindergarten teachers are gradually coming around to teaching reading skills appropriate to their range of 5-year-olds, gradually moving away from a wholly social and letter-a-week program, but it has not been easy for them. He does not want them to socialize Shana. And Harry has his own professional development motive: he wants to learn more about teaching young children.

Harry turns the staff meeting over to Laura, the teacher-chair of the Executive Committee for this year.

Laura: "If you look in the back of your teacher handbook, you will find implementation logs for us to record our practices in demonstrating written assignments and logs for use in recording practices with the picture-word inductive model. Like last year, we need you to turn the logs in to your Committee representative weekly.

"The district will be providing extensive staff development for the picture-word inductive model this year. Last year, the district cadre – including our own Ann, Bonita, and Roy – worked to learn how to use it from kindergarten through grade 8. You'll find much of the picture-word approach is similar to the inductive model we've been working with the last two years. Ann, Bonita, would one of you guys like to give us a brief description? I know some staff members are already familiar with the picture-word model because they 'stole' it last year when they saw what your kids were writing."

Bonita responds: "Well, we use large pictures. Last year, we built a file of about 25 photographs. My second graders used one picture about every three weeks. Once you have the picture you want to use, the students study the picture, then generate lists of words from the picture, classify those words phonetically or structurally or by content, and eventually write pieces about the picture using many of the words generated. The district's Instructional Leadership Team selected the model as one to support through districtwide staff development. It's intended to help improve reading and writing performance in kindergarten through second grade, and Roy used it with his sixth graders to improve teaching about other regions and cultures in social studies. At Southwood, we can use it to develop skill in informative writing for all grades! My kids really enjoyed it and the picture made a nice common 'object' to write about. Anyway, this summer I found about 20 more pictures we could use, some of them are great photographs of Southeastern and Northeastern towns and some are photographs of how the region around here used to look. I think they'd be great for the upper grades."

The year progresses. One Wednesday a month, the staff members participate in staff development sessions on the picture-word inductive model at their school, staff development that is provided by members of the district cadre and includes developing lessons. One Wednesday a month, they work on writing full and appropriate responses to written assignments and practicing the "think aloud" they will use when they present it to their students as a demonstration. One Wednesday a month, they bring samples of students' informative writing. Two peer coaching teams, working together, study the samples and decide what to work on next, or what to continue. Usually part of this session is used for the general review of data about grades, referrals, and the progress special-needs students are making. And one Wednesday a month, they gather information from an article or chapter on teaching writing that everyone reads, or look at videotapes made by the trainers and assess what they need to work on next to strengthen their use of the picture-word inductive model.

Celebrating progress: the satisfactions of inquiry

Let's drop in on an Executive Committee meeting around mid-May, as members are organizing the state writing results, the standardized tests results, and content analyses of writing samples the staff collected for study.

Laura has passed around copies of the results by school, grade, and class, including the distribution within the district. Committee members are poring over the reports, making comments, asking questions of each other. Laura, who looked at these data earlier with Harry, is so excited she can't stop grinning. She wants them to hurry up and get the big picture.

"Can you guys believe it? At fourth grade, we moved from number 30 out of 31 in informative writing to number 10 in our district – in just one year! I know we still have a long way to go, but look what we did. And our student performance in math is still near the top, and in reading we almost made it into the top quartile!"

Sam, one of the parents, bursts out with, "Did you notice how much difference there is between papers written in September and those written in April? I can't believe these papers were written by the same students. They seem so much smarter and better written. I know you share writing folders with us during parent conferences, but we're so focussed on our child, we don't see the growth that occurs across a whole class."

Sam, the parent co-chair of the Executive Committee, has been looking at the writing samples the staff collected on informative writing (one in early September, one in early February, and one in late April). Throughout the year, not only did staff members bring a set of samples to study one day a month with their work group, each teacher also studied three students of varying ability levels carefully, often interviewing these three students about how and why they wrote their pieces. Sam has been looking at these sets and at the teachers' reflections on what they learned about teaching writing this year.

And the inquiry continues . . .

CASE 2: A SECOND CHANCE: LEARNING TO READ AFTER THE PRIMARY GRADES

Success – in school and in life after school – is inextricably entwined with the ability to read at a reasonable pace and with good comprehension. Quality of life is enormously enhanced by reading, both through the pleasure and knowledge that comes through reading and, today, through access to the phenomenal resources of our technological world. Self-expression through writing – the communication of feelings and information – is utterly dependent on competence in reading.

In the middle and high school years poor competence in reading causes acute academic and social problems that are well known. Schools in the US are best prepared to teach children to read in the primary grades, but we know from the recent national studies (Mullis *et al.* 1993) that about 30 percent of our students leave the primary grades without the competence in reading to profit comfortably and fully from the upper grades and beyond, or to read recreationally for pleasure or information. Even in our highest-achieving school districts the proportion is substantial – rarely less than 20 percent.

And we know that we have not been well organized, after the primary grades, to provide the gift of reading to those children we have not yet reached. In the elementary schools, teachers have had at least some preparation to teach reading and have considerable experience trying to do it well. Upper grade, middle school, and high school teachers have not been well prepared to teach beginning readers, or readers who are beyond the novice stage but whose vocabularies and comprehension skills are not very well developed. Our secondary curriculums are not set up to teach reading. Our massive investment in special education, remedial education under Title I, and the teaching of English as a second language, a combination that sometimes represents 30 percent of our school budgets, has not solved the problem (McGill-Franzen and Allington 1991a,b).

The Morse context

In the Samuel F. B. Morse High School in San Diego, California, a group of imaginative administrators combined with a team of consultants to lead a school faculty in a straightforward approach to the problem.

Morse enrolls 1800 students in grades 9 through 12, of which nearly 40 percent are Filipino, about 30 percent are Hispanic of Mexican origin, 30 percent are African Americans, and a handful are of a variety of Asian nationalities (Laotian, Vietnamese, Thai, Guamanian, etc.).

The parent population is very supportive of education, particularly wanting their children to obtain a high school diploma. High school graduation is celebrated by family gatherings that rival weddings and funerals for elaborateness and family closeness. For many families a high school graduate is a first, and an important, milestone for the family. However, visions of higher achievement are less common.

Morse has a long tradition of generating effective innovations. Students have a number of options for connecting their academic studies to the world of work. For example, tourism is a major sector of the San Diego economy and the school has assembled a network of business partners from the hotels and restaurants in the area. Within that network several hundred students have the benefit of work-study programs, serving in a variety of roles in those hotels and restaurants, learning how those businesses operate and getting direct experience to prepare them for the workplace, whether they attend local colleges and need to defray those costs or whether they enter the world of work directly on graduation.

In addition, Morse has implemented technology to a degree that is exceptional. Benefiting from a grant from the National Science Foundation, the school has developed an extensive computer network and all the students have thorough instruction in computer use and courses are designed to organize the students for inquiry into both software-based and online information systems.

Thus the school is accustomed to collective action to extend and improve its program. While it doesn't have a Responsible Parties group as such, collective faculty action is well established, community involvement is extensive, and the leadership team is both strong and inclusive.

New energy to solve a long-standing problem

The literacy initiative rose directly as a side effect of the school-to-work and technology initiatives. Essentially, work opportunities and the ability to use computers effectively were functions of developed literacy – and reading and writing ability was not good for many students as they entered the school.

The Morse staff had studied reading achievement for several years. All ninth grade students had taken a short version of the Gates test as they entered the school. One-sixth were found to be reading at or below the level at which an average student exits the second grade. Another third scored at or below the level of the average exiting fifth grade student. At the other end, 10 percent scored above the average graduating high school student.

The awareness of the problem generated some courses for those students. Several members of the English department had offered courses to the students most in need, and school-district-sponsored programs were offered to others, but the needs for effective reading instruction were not satisfactorily met. The efforts over six years resulted in small but steady gains for this group, increasing by 8 percent the ninth graders scoring at or above the 50th percentile in reading comprehension at the end of the year. Unfortunately, for grades 10, 11, and 12 during the same six-year period scores remained stable or even declined.

Not surprisingly, competence in reading was related to other indicators of success: the poorer readers fail more courses, experience greater behavior problems, and are less likely to graduate than their peers with good reading skills.

The leaders decided that it was time to engage the technical assistance that could design and evaluate an intensive approach. They had come to realize that the students were beginning readers – over-age, to be sure, but novices in reading – and that they needed to be taught with the methods that are most successful with beginning readers of any age. To implement such a course the teachers involved would need extensive staff development, because the curricular/instructional pattern would be new to them and a rigorous, embedded study of implementation and effects would be needed. Thus time was set aside for about 15 days of training for the teachers for each of the first two years. Several teachers of English volunteered.

With extensive help from consultants a course was created and directed, first, at the ninth and tenth grade students whose reading competence was at the level of an average fourth grade student or below. Time was created in their schedule for daily attendance. Nine sections were offered during the first semester and 146 students were enrolled, half ninth and half tenth graders. The rationale was explained to their parents, including that the time for the effort would be created by reducing the students' elective courses by one. The parents greeted the initiative enthusiastically.

Connection to the knowledge base

The consultants made connections to scholars on the teaching of reading and writing to "over-age" beginners and made particular use of syntheses of the literature conducted with curriculum design in mind. Calhoun's (1997) review was particularly relevant because it was conducted with the specific objective of pulling together the many-sided literature to support designers of similar efforts. The review concluded that a multidimensional approach, with the components designed in accordance with the research, has a considerable chance of succeeding with many of these over-age beginning readers.

Design of the course and embedded evaluation

"What are the components that give students the best possible chance of learning to read?" Surveying the research leads to the conclusion that there is a fairly solid knowledge base: for the most part the research out-runs most contemporary practice. The approaches with the best track records are multidimensional. They do not depend on single aspects of the reading process, such as decoding, but generate several dimensions of learning simultaneously. Also, the teaching involves students in active inquiry – the students are taught to inquire into the process of reading – and so they develop metacognitive skills (Palincsar 1986; Pressley *et al.* 1995a).

What are these dimensions as components of the course?
Building vocabulary through natural language. Students dictate sentences daily and watch their words as they are written down and spelled by the teach-ers. The words are within their listening-speaking vocabularies so that meaning is not an issue. The new reading words are written down by the students on file cards and stored throughout the course. As the course progresses, the teachers learn to use the picture-word inductive model which capitalizes on natural language development and leads directly to the following components (see Joyce and Calhoun 1998; Calhoun 1999).

Building vocabulary through reading, classification, and cooperative learning. The development of a substantial "sight" vocabulary (words whose visual characteristics and meanings have been memorized) is a major dimen-sion of learning to read and write. Students need to learn how to acquire sight vocabulary as they read, and instruction needs to be focussed on the major techniques for doing so in reading narrative and expository prose. Words from the natural language component, from reading and "words of the day" (introduced by the teachers), are accumulated on cards in "My Words" boxes. Students list each new word on the front of an index card, write its meaning on the back, and file cards in a recipe box. During designated times, students band together to master the words in their files, and once weekly the teacher or an instructional aide test stu-dents (usually orally) on the new vocabulary they have collected. Stu-dents record the number of new words mastered each week on a record form kept in their reading folders. The bulk of vocabulary added is derived from the exercises devoted to mastery of context clues and the efforts of individual students in identifying and learning unknown words in the materials they read.

Reading in school and at home. Extensive reading needs to take place at the developed level. There is a rich children's literature, and students may at first be able to read only picture-story books, but they can learn from reading them. The students will have phobias about reading and writing and must learn to approach the feared material and profit from it. The reading can take place in and out of school. Parents are enlisted to help encourage reading at home. The students are taught how to select books at their developmental (recreational) level. Reading in class is at least 30 minutes a day and the students are expected to read at least that much at home each evening. The students find new words and add them to their "My Words" box. They bring words and sentences to class for study each day. Students are asked to set goals for the numbers of books to be read during each six-week period, and parents' help is solicited to support 30 minutes of reading per night at home. Students record all books read on a reading log kept in their reading folders, and teachers and students maintain wall charts displaying the numbers of books read by individual students as well as a class total.

Listening to reading by the teachers – further additions of vocabulary. The teachers model reading and also "talk aloud" ways of finding meanings for words and comprehending passages – modeling comprehension skills.

Daily writing. The students write daily, using their new vocabulary. Writing is primarily elicited by frequent, short assignments relating to comprehension of the materials being read. Dictated writing, modeled by the teacher with the entire class and with the assistance of students, is completed based on reading selections read by the teacher to the entire class.

Phonetic and structural analysis. Principles are learned through combinations of inductive analysis, where sight vocabulary words are classified until the phonetic and structural principles are developed, and the analysis of word families, where letters and combinations of letters are studied in relation to the sounds that are attached to them. Through regular use of the NAMES test, students and teachers study the combinations that have been mastered.

Instruction in comprehension. Figuring out the meanings of words, sentences, paragraphs, and the entirety of pieces is essential to reading. Conversely, clear writing defines words, and constructs the sense of sentences, paragraphs, and longer pieces meaningfully by structuring them appropriately. Data sets of sentences in which various types of comprehension devices can be used are presented to the students regularly, and they are taught the major ways of developing meaning from context. In addition, use of the dictionary and thesaurus is taught directly as the "words of the day" are explored. Cooperative strategies are focussed initially on lower-order comprehension (the factual recall of what is read). With increasing fluency, comprehension activities expand to include higher-order comprehension tasks (identification of main ideas/central themes, inference/interpretation, etc.).

Throughout, regular assessment of student progress, especially in the acquisition of sight vocabulary, is embedded to help students measure their progress and to provide diagnostic information to the teachers.

Thus, the multidimensionality of the approach is built on research on curriculum in reading, plus the use of models of teaching that have been shown to affect student learning positively.

The ambitious goal is to teach these students to read effectively and to make a start on their skill in writing.

The study of implementation and student learning

Implementation of the components was studied carefully. Throughout the first semester of 1996–7 the teachers studied how to implement the components of the course. The students learned to keep their word boxes and gradually learned to sort the words and look for similarities and differences. Importantly, many enjoyed the clarity of progress – they could see how many words they were learning. The teachers read to them regularly, picking short stories and articles of high interest and modeling comprehension from context. Developing data sets for teaching comprehension skills was a very new activity for the teachers, but with the help of the consultant (who spent about ten days with them each semester) they increased their skill and reduced their preparation time as the semester progressed. The students learned to read silently and to hunt for new words and try to figure them out. Whole-class instruction in comprehension skills occurred regularly – another new activity for the teachers – both with data sets and modeling by presenting sentences containing new words and contextual information and showing the students how to use context to discover word meanings. The dictionaries were in continual use when the students worked independently.

Not surprisingly, many of the students found independent reading very difficult, although there was a supply of books of varying levels of difficulty. It is not too much to say that these students had developed phobias about reading. They were vocal about "not wanting to read," even though they knew what a handicap poor reading was to them. Independent reading was the slowest and most difficult component to implement, even with substantial help from the parents.

The students had also developed serious aversions to test-taking. Unless testing sessions were monitored carefully, students had a tendency to "give up" on the test. The idea that valid test results depended on "best effort" was new to some of the teachers. They found that sometimes a student needed to be tested individually as much as two or three times before a valid result was achieved.

Assumptions were continually challenged. Several of the teachers had the long-held assumption that phonics was the chief problem of these students. They were surprised to find that many of the students had fairly good phonics skills – as long as they were dealing with one-syllable words. Structural analysis – breaking words down into syllables that could be attacked – was new to them. Also, the focus on the development of sight vocabulary was a new idea to many of the teachers. Some of them were quite suspicious of the formal knowledge base and were surprised at the consultants' knowledge about and skill in teaching reading and writing.

Perhaps most complex was the idea of studying student learning on such a continuous basis and in such a public fashion. Rather than teaching courses individually and assessing growth relatively privately, the teachers had to become a learning community that used the same tools for teaching and for studying student learning.

The study of student learning

As this book is written the team is concluding its fourth one-semester study of student learning. The following is a synthesis of some of the findings and the interpretations that were made.

Acquisition of sight vocabulary. "Sight" vocabulary is words that have become so familiar that they can be identified quickly by how they are spelled. During the first semester the average gain was about 100 words, with a range from about 75 to 125. Efficiency in this area rose with successive semesters until by the fourth semester the average gain was about 175 words, with a range from 125 to 225.

The teachers were unsure how to interpret this until the consultant connected them to research showing that the most common 1000 words make up 90 percent of the "running text" in English prose. The students began the course with several hundred of the most common words. Adding 400 or so in a year made a huge difference in their ability to read and express themselves in writing.

Phonics skills. The use of the NAMES test turned out to have great meaning. It permitted the identification of the phonics combinations each student knew and learned of the ones that were the most common bugaboos. By classifying their vocabulary words, the students made great progress. Nearly all mastered the fundamental phonics combinations within a semester.

Independent reading. This was the toughest component. During the first semester the average student finished only about a half dozen books. To be sure, these were the first books they had read in years, but since most new vocabulary is actually garnered through reading, the result was disappointing. Not until the fourth semester was the number as great as ten. Still not good, but 20 or more books per year where there were none read before is certainly a gain. More still to be done in this area, though.

Standard tests. Tests were administered at the beginning and end of each semester. The results were interpreted against the gains of similar students in the previous years and against their own growth as measured by district tests. Grade level equivalent scores are the most convenient comparison measure. Against an average previous gain of about 0.25 per semester, the average gain was about five times as much – 1.25 or more. Also, the gains were in the comprehension section of the batteries as well as the vocabulary section. As the semesters progressed, the number of students gaining several times their previous yearly gains increased.

Disaggregating the data generated some interesting findings and some clues about making the course more effective.

First, there were no systematic gender, ethnic, or racial differences in achievement; second, the distribution of grades in other courses rose each semester, and the longer students stayed enrolled in the course, the more their grades rose. The teachers recommended that the average student should expect to stay in the course for at least four semesters and that exit should only occur when their scores on the standard tests were at the national average for ninth grade students.

However, the study of students who gained the most and least from the course resulted in a real puzzle. The attendance was similar, as was the number of books read independently. They were equally positive toward the course. Their parents had similar views.

But, as the course becomes ever stronger, the number who profit greatly continues to increase.

Summary

Here we have a school with a history of collective action to generate some complex and important innovations. Its strong leaders connected the school to strenuous technical assistance, generated the time and resources for extensive staff development, and used the knowledge base on literacy to attack a problem that is driving many secondary schools to distraction. A curriculum was designed and implemented and the implementation and study of student learning was carried out as a formal inquiry – an exemplary action-research experience.

And as a result, several hundred students are reading better than before and increasing the probability that their quality of life will be satisfactory or better.

Did the effort in Morse produce an approach that might be replicated in other settings? Would it work as well in the UK as in the USA?

DYNAMICS

These cases will be referred to throughout the book, time and time again, as we elaborate the hypotheses and the overall structure designed to create evolving schools. In Part II we will present three extensive case studies of schools refining, renovating, and redesigning their learning environments and examine once again how the hypotheses work together in a comprehensive structure.

Part II   Elaborating the hypotheses: the detailed work of school improvement

The work of leading schools into an evolutionary state has several sides, each of which opens a door to the creation of the special culture that enables schools to pursue excellence as a natural part of the conduct of education. Establishing the Responsible Parties begins early (Chapter 4) and their tasks are defined by pursuing the hypotheses. An information-rich community is established – the students and student learning are studied routinely and, as initiatives are made, their effects are studied as the action-research process becomes routine (Chapter 5). The Responsible Parties lead the community in the continual study of educational research. They scan the knowledge base to learn the options in curriculum and instruction that are worthy of consideration in the quest to make the learning environment better and better (Chapter 6). Regular study (staff development) is built into the work of the faculty and of others working in the school on a paid or volunteer basis, and everybody concerned studies how to create better learning environments for the students (Chapter 7).

4 Establishing the Responsible Parties: organizing the decisionmaking community

Organizing the Responsible Parties begins at the beginning and continues throughout. They pursue the hypotheses, developing embedded time for the faculty to study and reflect, building an information-rich environment, embedding staff development, connecting the school to the knowledge base, and creating a caring community. All this is done in the process of generating initiatives small and large to improve the learning environment, and of studying the progress of their children.

BEGINNING

Most often, school improvement will be started by administrative and teacher leadership in the school, but citizens groups can be the instigators. In some cases it will be initiated by the local education authority (the school district), which wishes to see a school become a learning community or is opening a new school. However, schools can be operated by other entities as well. Private school corporations operate schools. As states make provisions for "charter schools," the possible nature of the initiators becomes much wider than it has been in the past.

Let's use the example of a school that is starting to move to an evolutionary state. What will the embryonic Responsible Parties look like and how will they function in relation to the school and district? First, if a Responsible Parties group is not already in existence in a school, then establish a group to fulfill this role/function. It can be titled anything – School Council, Leadership Team, Facilitation Team, School Improvement Team, Home–School Collaborative – but its function is to attend to the health of the student population and the school as a social and educational organization.

As early as possible in the renewal process (or, in fact, the development of a new school), district curriculum/instruction/staff development personnel should be given the executive functions necessary to support the school as it organizes the Responsible Parties and as it develops initiatives. In the case of a new school, the district personnel need to see the planning through and bring the school into existence, including finding the first principal or head and finding technical assistance to help with the planning.

- The district curriculum personnel and the school administrator and lead teachers need to become *pro tem.* Responsible Parties. They will need to add others fairly quickly.
- Teachers. The planning group needs to include several teachers who are interested in studying new and alternate educational forms and are interested in becoming faculty members in the new school.
- Technical assistants. Because it is unlikely that any local situation will contain all the expert knowledge that is needed, the Responsible Parties need to augment themselves with specialists in curriculum and instruction, educational technology, and staff development. They need to ensure that the knowledge base is available from the beginning of the process. One or two can be "official" members of our *pro tem.* Responsible Parties group.
- Parents and children. The Responsible Parties should also include parents and children from the projected catchment area or neighborhood that will be served by the school. Especially in large school districts, where school boards and other public representatives are likely to be quite remote, it is wise to make special efforts to include patrons in the planning process, but it makes sense in districts of all sizes. Children should not be involved in all aspects of planning. However, students can provide important perspectives in many areas. In secondary schools, student governments can handle certain matters such as helping to organize at-home reading progress such as Just Read. Also, the achievement and other characteristics of the children who will soon fill the school can be studied as a part of the planning process.
- Businesses and social institutions. Representatives of the business community, particularly from the neighborhood to be served, and community library and other relevant institutions need to be included as well, and early.

A CHANGE IN THE CONDUCT OF BUSINESS

Few would disagree that developing an evolutionary state requires considerable changes in the way most schools, school districts, and policymakers have conducted business since the common school was established. Essentially, the structures of the educational system were designed to maintain the organization in a steady state, with changes being few and gradual and undertaken with minimal disruption to the basic flow of organizational behavior.

The object of organizing the Responsible Parties is to build a community that can continuously rethink the purposes of the school, choose its most appropriate means, evaluate how they work, make adjustments, and, over time, repeat the cycle.

By providing ways that community members, teachers, and administrative staff can all participate in the creation of the educational program, the Responsible Parties can ensure that:

1 The school program is intelligible to everyone concerned.
2 Conflict over alternatives is resolved or at least dealt with so that disgruntled factions don't appear.
3 Debate is open and reasonable.
4 There is coordination among administrators, teachers, and community members right from the beginning.

In other words, the *pro tem.* Responsible Parties need to build a community that deliberately and openly builds, supports, evaluates, and rethinks the school program and which becomes the long-term Responsible Parties. A classic study (Berman and McLaughlin 1975) of federal initiatives to provide local communities with resources to improve their schools indicated the importance of including community members, teachers, and administrators in school improvement projects. It found that if administrators initiate change but do not involve teachers, no real change is likely to take place. If teachers generate ideas but the administration is uncommitted, the idea is likely to remain just that – a thought. If the community does not understand or approve of a change in the program, it is likely to be short-lived.

The solution is to build a continuous program-rethinking process which includes representatives of all three groups. This is not to suggest that the entire school program will be changed each year! Making changes generates a certain amount of stress even when there is broad involvement and firm agreement about what is to be done. As the Responsible Parties study the school they will develop priorities for change, and the efforts of any given year will be concentrated on the high-priority areas.

The practice of rethinking the school's mission and means has to become embedded in the life of the school and its community; the search for improvement has to become normal. The atmosphere has to encourage serious reflection and discourage excesses of advocacy. If fresh ideas are put forth dogmatically they will draw defensive reactions ("What's wrong with the way we are doing things now?") and positive governance will break down. Everybody needs to get accustomed to the idea of continuous effort to improve, and to continuous study and training. Until change processes are comfortably embedded into the organization, defensiveness is normal and need not be regarded as a disposition toward resistance or an unwillingness to take risks. Because renewal has not been a part of the organizational process in the past, people are likely to take proposals for change as personal affronts, as if they are being accused of wrongdoing or incompetence (see Muncey and McQuillan 1993; Muncey 1994 for an indication of how divisive this can be). The social workings of the Responsible Parties have to be open and supportive. It may well be that creating an environment where change is normal and cannot be construed as "blaming" is the most pivotal of the cultural changes that have to take place.

Also, innovations nearly always stumble at first. When a faculty brings new content into the curriculum they have to experiment with it. The first experiments are often awkward. If the climate is harsh and unforgiving of error, it will be nearly impossible for the period of trial and experimentation to function as it should, allowing new methods to be massaged into comfortable processes.

In the early 1960s, as the Academic Reform Movement propelled new mathematics and science content into the elementary and secondary curriculum, there was outstanding success when adequate support was provided in the form of staff development and formative assessment. Where support was weak and sporadic, implementation simply did not occur (Goodlad and Klein 1970).

None of this is mysterious.

During the awkward phase of using new instructional strategies both teachers and students can be uncomfortable. Parents worry that their children aren't learning enough, while administrators worry about discipline. All of these reactions are quite normal. The important thing, however, is what happens next, and that depends to a considerable extent on the social climate that is generated among community, teachers, and administrators.

If everyone understands what is going on, lends support, and helps the others over the rough spots, we can predict that the awkward period will yield to the teachers' efforts. They will become comfortable with the new approach, the students will respond, and the parents and administrators will relax. However, if the climate is harsh and unforgiving, if mistakes are not tolerated, if the atmosphere becomes heated with anxiety, then we can predict that discouragement and anxiety will prevail. Within such a negative atmosphere the new approach will soon give way to the old as teachers return to the safe and familiar ways that aroused few complaints. One reason why parents and community members have to be brought into the center of the process is that a certain number of people will respond to a proposal for change with anxiety, asking *"What's been wrong all this time?"* in a kind of nervous frenzy. Inclusion and calm discussion, with full explanations for the rationale behind even the most minor change, are the antidote.

During the 1970s the Rand Corporation study team came to similar conclusions. They found that organizations that successfully implemented agreed-upon changes developed vertical as well as horizontal integration. In terms of school organization this means that the school board, the central administration of the district, the building administrators, teachers, and community members must all be working in concert. A local school group working without the support of the central administration or the school board will soon get into difficulty. A school board and central administration which fails to include local community members and teachers in its organization will be equally doomed.

Although there is much emphasis these days on the contrast between "top–down" and "bottom–up" initiatives for change it appears that change can be initiated equally well from either level. Regardless of who presents the initiative, vertical integration of the various levels of the system is essential.

Creating a supportive organizational climate was also found to be vital. Innovation involves risk taking, and without a climate that supports risk-taking behavior, or at least avoids punishing experimentation, we can hardly expect that people will be encouraged to take the first fumbling steps that are essential as innovations are tried out.

THE HOMEOSTASIS OF CHANGE

Acting on the hypotheses we have teased out of the literature on school improvement adds up to the creation of what we can term a "homeostasis of change." The same types of forces that tend to prevent change will be employed to stabilize a condition of continuous study and collaborative effort. Let's revisit those hypotheses briefly again and consider them in terms of the dynamic whereby, put together, they can change the way the organizational game is played out in education and generate conditions that stabilize study and continuous improvement as a way of organizational life. The first two hypotheses, those relating to time and governance, need be addressed early in the process. Without time for collective inquiry by the faculty and other school staff, the Responsible Parties cannot mature. Without time for staff development, strong initiatives cannot be taken. Without a legitimized governing body, collective study cannot take place and no one – teachers, administrators, community members, school districts, or policymakers – can develop initiatives that will make a real change. The movement toward site-based or local management has been precarious from the start because time for establishing governance and study has not been established.

Starting the Responsible Parties

Hypothesis 1: Restructuring the job assignments of educators so that time for collective inquiry is built into the workplace will increase school improvement activity.
The school as originally organized (and, in most cases, as currently operated) was not designed to provide an evolutionary state. More than that, many of the familiar conditions of the workplace make it extremely difficult to generate a self-renewing situation *unless the conditions of the workplace are changed substantially*.

The lack of such time has prevented the collective action necessary to improve curriculum and instruction. Acting on this hypothesis changes the dynamic of the workplace so that communal study can occur. Yet building in the time for communal study does not destabilize the school – there is no threat to its operation. There is simply a recognition by policymakers at the governmental and district levels, and by the operational leaders of schools (the Responsible Parties), that educators need to be employed with the understanding that continual learning is an important part of the job of teaching.

The staffs of schools need to have from two to two-and-a-half hours a week dedicated to collective thinking, staff development, and related activities. Such an arrangement needs to be made without shortening the instructional week for the students, although one day might be shorter and the others lengthened proportionately.

Currently most school districts engage staff for a number of days over and above the instructional year. In the United States that number ranges from 10 to 20. Three or four of the days are scheduled just before and just after school begins. The remainder are scheduled for staff development and school renewal activities during the year. It is feasible to convert those half-dozen days into weekly time blocks devoted to school renewal/staff development, scheduled on the same weekday. Thus consistent study can be developed for all personnel. There is no budget increase in this plan. And little is given up. The periodic staff development days have not been very successful (see Joyce and Belitzky 1997 for an analysis in a large state) and are very unpopular with the public. However, if the staff is paid for regular time after the instructional day is over, there is little public complaint. *The public is in favor of school improvement.* Bruce just visited a school district where all the teachers were employed for one-and-one-quarter hours *each day* above the time that the students were in school. No one had thought to organize that time to shorten it a bit on four days and lengthen it on the fifth to provide the block of time we are talking about. Yet it was there to be had. One of our states employs the teachers for *18 days* more than the students attend and only needed to reconfigure that time to provide the weekly blocks.

However, providing regular time is not by itself powerful enough to create an evolutionary state by itself.

Hypothesis 2: Active, living democracy, including community members, engaged in collective inquiry, creates the structural condition in which the process of school improvement is nested.

The governance of schools has been loosely organized. Faculties meet occasionally and principals tend a host of logistical and public relations tasks that keep the organization running. Essentially, outside of the matters that keep the school running, there has been no legitimized governance body that can tend the academic and social health of the school by studying it and making initiatives to improve it. We suggest, from our search of schools and school district programs where initiatives to improve the educational environment has paid off in increased student learning, that a much stronger and more inclusive governance structure needs to developed.

As Henry Izumizaki put it to us (Joyce and Calhoun 1996), the traditional mode of organizational behavior in education results in a condition where there is hardly any organization worthy of the name. Creating a living democracy makes an organization. The combination of available time and the democratic, inclusive structure of the Responsible Parties sets the stage. Without the time, the study necessary for the faculty to prepare its part in governance cannot take place. Without the inclusive democratic structure there is no legitimate decisionmaking mechanism. A major reason why "site-based" policies have failed so abysmally is that schools have not really had a governance structure. Thus an early task for leaders is to pull together a group that includes teachers, parents, representatives of businesses and public community agencies, and district support personnel to create a governmental infrastructure for the organization. When making important decisions, that group – the Responsible Parties – needs to involve all the other members of the role groups it represents (like the faculty, when curriculums are being renovated, or like district representatives when standards and methods of assessment are being changed). (See Weiss 1978; David 1990; Glickman 1993; Muncey and McQuillan 1993.)

Yet time and democracy are not by themselves sufficient. Many schools operating under the site-based management policy have remained as "stuck" (see Rosenholtz 1989) as they were before that policy was initiated. And shared decisionmaking will not succeed by itself (Weiss *et al.* 1995). (Of course, some did not create the time-structure to permit the cooperative decisionmaking structure to emerge, or tried to govern through committees rather than establishing their Responsible Parties.)

We should pause on that old time question again. Many, many well-intended and otherwise well-engineered school improvement efforts have failed simply because the staff of the school could not meet often enough, either as an entity or with the other members of the Responsible Parties.

Hypothesis 3: An information-rich environment will enhance inquiry.
Learning to study the learning environment will increase inquiry into ways of
helping students learn better.
And now the Responsible Parties initiate the study of the students and the learning environment (see Chapter 5). The focus is on growth in student learning. The Responsible Parties involve the faculty in study of how successful are the components of the curriculum – all aspects of the learning environment. From this study come initiatives that change aspects of the learning environment, and the effects on student growth are figured.

The information dimension will result in the identification of more possible initiatives than can be made at one time: as the information is mined many attractive directions will be unearthed.

However, time, inclusive democracy, and information will not by themselves generate the evolutionary state. As Drucker (1989) and Toffler (1990) have reminded us in terms of cultural and organizational development, data and information are abundant, but understanding and use are rare. In the evolving school, they will be common.

Hypothesis 4: Connecting the Responsible Parties to the knowledge base on teaching and learning will increase the development of successful initiatives for school improvement.

Decisions need to be informed by the best available professional knowledge. The study of teaching, curriculum, and technology has now created a substantial knowledge base that can help identify solutions to problems. There is useful information about virtually every area of the school's operation. The Responsible Parties need to seek the most informed technical assistance they can find – people who can connect them to the knowledge base as areas for possible action are unearthed.

Yet even more has to be added. Individual knowledge of actions that may facilitate student progress, or the fact that such knowledge exists, does not automatically lead to changes in individual behaviors or to changes in how the organization operates.

Hypothesis 5: Staff development, embedded in the workplace, increases inquiry into new practices and the implementation of school improvement initiatives.

Hard work and continuous study are essential if changes are to be made in curriculum and instruction. The Responsible Parties are changing education in their school into a continuous study, and the faculty is changing from one that has worked in isolation to one that engages in continuous and collective study as a part of professional work.

Staff development has to be a regular event, but not a business of mechanical and unreflective study of new practice.

Hence a corollary hypothesis:

Hypothesis 6: Staff development, structured as an inquiry, both fuels energy and results in initiatives that have greater effects.

Time, the formation of the Responsible Parties, the study of student learning and the learning environment, and the use of the knowledge base come together in the acts of learning that change the learning environment, and in the inquiry to find out whether student learning changes as a result.

Finally, there is another aspect of the health of the community that needs to be considered by the Responsible Parties.

Hypothesis 7: Building small work groups connected to the larger community but responsible for one another will increase the sense of belonging that reduces stress, isolation, and feelings of alienation.

Professional educators and parents are not mere functionaries, mechanically doing their jobs and then going home to rest and have a life of their own. The tending of children is an endless and consuming task. Building little support groups throughout the school and an overall caring community are an important part of the responsibility of the organization to take care of its people. And the people who take care of children need to be regarded as precious and deserving of support in their own right.

A mutual-support, inquiry-oriented community is built with attention to the several dimensions that add up to a growing community. When we begin with a new group of Responsible Parties, we begin with the study of the hypotheses and gently start the process where TIME (the indispensable and insufficient factor) is created for all parties to come together and engage in the inquiry.

COMMENTARY: THE EDUCATION AUTHORITY/SCHOOL SYMBIOSIS

The loosely coupled organization simply has to be replaced with one in which district offices take direct responsibility for the health of the educational program of each of their schools and can exercise curricular and instructional leadership. (Large systems need decentralized organizations in order to create effective leadership that is close to the schools.) District (LEA) level units made up of professional curriculum developers, community members, and teachers need to insure that the Responsible Parties are thoroughly supported. The Responsible Parties must study current options in each curriculum area, make choices among them, and then make those choices happen.

The context of the district cannot be overemphasized (see Chapter 12). A district which provides encouragement for school improvement and the conditions that facilitate it will make the work of the Responsible Parties much easier. Furthermore, if any given school is not improving it is the district officers' responsibility to exercise their executive functions to help that school develop an organization of Responsible Parties and put them to work analyzing the educational health of the school and making plans to improve it. We will say over and over again that a school that is not improving is almost certainly deteriorating. The establishment of the conditions for school improvement require the direct assistance of the central office administration to provide the resources for staff development and training for Responsible Parties, and to ensure that the management team of the school clearly understands that the facilitation of school improvement, the creation of an evolutionary state, is the major part of its duties.

5 Information, information, information: the schoolwide action-research way of doing business

A school evolves slowly or rapidly, depending in large measure on its use of information to guide action and shape the learning environment. The school becomes an increasingly healthy setting for students and adults, as current practice is considered and future practice is guided by the thoughtful use of information.

As fits with our hypotheses – and the belief that all Responsible Parties need to study what is happening for learners in the learning environment of the school – the gathering and use of information are conducted to support collective inquiry. Internal and external information are blended in the ongoing study. Internal school-based data that indicate what is happening for students in relation to the goals of the school is combined with information from the external knowledge base that provides ideas for the expansion of learning opportunities. These two sources form the substance that guides school improvement. This substance must be organized in such fashion that the Responsible Parties can employ it to think simultaneously about students, goals, and time.

In this chapter, we address how the Responsible Parties clarify their collective knowledge of the student population and its current learning opportunities, select a curriculum domain or student learning goal for collective pursuit, gather information about student knowledge and skill in this domain or goal area, and study the learning environment being provided in classrooms across the school. As you read this chapter, think especially about Hypothesis 3:

An information-rich environment will enhance inquiry. Learning to study student learning and the learning environment will increase inquiry into ways of helping students learn better.

Let's look now at how the Responsible Parties build an information system that routinely guides their decisions and actions.

CLARIFYING COLLECTIVE KNOWLEDGE ABOUT THE STUDENT POPULATION AND THE STATUS OF STUDENT PROGRESS

We will begin with internal information, particularly data that are readily available in school records and can be organized so that everyone has an increasingly clear picture of the students and how they are doing – actually a moving picture of the students' progress.

We have divided the data sources that provide this information into three categories:

1 internal descriptive data,
2 internal indicators of progress, and
3 formal testing programs.

Internal descriptive data

These give the Responsible Parties a clearer picture of the composition of the student population, of student participation in the school setting, and of organizational programs and structures designed to support the education of this population. Basically, the Responsible Parties organize general school data to respond to these questions:

• Who are we working with and responsible for?
• How are the students responding, in general, to the school as an institution?
• What is our current organizational structure beyond the "regular classroom and curriculum," and how are these additional programs working?

Who are we responsible for? Looking at the student population. Data on population size, gender, and ethnicity will be needed. This basic information about the school population is essential for monitoring the progress of individual students and groups of students in a school. It can reveal inequities that may be invisible, but that have major implications for student success. The primary data sources are students: who they are, what they do, how they perform academically and socially, how they feel, what they know.

> How do the Responsible Parties begin to clarify their knowledge of the student population and of student progress within the school? They begin by gathering information about the student population; and this information gathering never ends. What they collect, how they collect it, and from whom they collect may change as their inquiry proceeds, but they unwaveringly gather information about their students and about what they are experiencing in the learning environment. This is how the Responsible Parties keep the school improvement lens sharply focussed on student learning.

Description

The primary data sources are students: who they are, what they do, how they perform academically and socially, how they feel, what they know. Socioeconomic, gender, and ethnicity data, as we will see, are very important.

For example, in American schools, to clarify the nature of the student population the Responsible Parties gather information about student characteristics such as ethnicity (for example Hmong, Hispanic, African-American, Native Indian), or native language (for example Mandarin Chinese, Spanish, English). Descriptions will lead to a wider inquiry to enrich comprehension of what is found. To understand the student body in a multiethnic population which contains ethnic groups not fully understood by the Responsible Parties, the latter will need to explore those cultures, reading about them and interviewing the students and their parents to develop a more complete picture of the students they are responsible for. They will enrich their own knowledge, and possibly correct some of their misconceptions. For example, a faculty in a school we know found that they did not know much about the culture of the Philippines, but a demographic shift in their neighborhood resulted in a population one-third of which had recently migrated from the Philippines. They were surprised to find that the Philippines are the third largest English-speaking nation in the world and that many of their students, who they had assumed were not acquainted with English, actually knew it pretty well, and their parents were fairly literate too. Another faculty found that children described as Hmong, who they had assumed were "really foreign" to them and insular as well, were from large, friendly extended families who were quite interested in participating in school activities and helping their children learn how to live and learn in the United States.

Socioeconomic status within the "native" English and American populations can take on new meanings as well. If the Responsible Parties study the vocabulary development of the students who are entering school, they will learn that there are socioeconomic differences in vocabulary development that need to be attended to, but also that individual differences are large. Some of the children of professional families will have relatively small reading/writing vocabularies, and some of the children of economically modest families will have relatively large ones.

The picture of similarities and differences will gradually emerge, and will have important implications for the nature of the curriculum that needs to be developed to ensure success for all students.

Internal indicators of progress

The Responsible Parties gather information about student progression through school, for example grade-level progression, such as the numbers of students in first grade, fifth grade, or participation in special programs, such as Chapter I reading, advanced algebra, German IV.

They also gather information about student progress in acquiring knowledge and skill within curriculum disciplines, such as the numbers of students receiving grades of A, B, C, D, or F in science, mathematics, social studies, language arts. In addition, they will examine how students respond to the environment by examining attendance, arrival in time for class, and the necessity for disciplinary actions.

Formal testing programs

The Responsible Parties gather information about student performance on standardized tests, such as "a grade equivalency of 3.7 in mathematical computations" or "at the 75th percentile of other tenth graders taking this examination." They gather information about how students feel about their progress in school and include these self-reports in their cumulative folders.

Operationally, most schools have done a far better job with gathering than with using this information. For example, many schools routinely collect most of the information described above, and some schools collect far more than we have mentioned. However, what few school staff or school/community collaboratives have learned to do well is to use this information: to keep the collective eye of the educational community on the progress of students through the school, and to guide collective inquiry into changes in curriculum and instruction.

Thus in order to use information to guide practice, the Responsible Parties must "break set" with the current normative use of data and develop routines for studying data about the student population.

The Responsible Parties organize data so as to regularly scan the student population and its progress

What data will the Responsible Parties need as they come to know and keep their collective eye on the student population? They will need to organize data about the nature of the student population, first by using existing internal data. They organize these data so they have an accurate description of the student population: size (how many students are they responsible for?); gender (what is the male/female distribution?); ethnicity (how many ethnic groups are represented?); native language (how many native languages are represented?); and socioeconomic indicators (what is the range of socioeconomic comfort and resources represented?).

The Responsible Parties use the multidimensional description of the student population to determine if they are successfully educating all students. Historically, in many state schools and school systems, these variables that simply describe student characteristics have become factors that predict how well students will perform academically. Here are a few examples: young males in the primary grades have a much higher failure rate than females, particularly in reading, which often influences their entire school career; African-Americans often have a

> much higher failure rate based on school grades and lower achievement on standardized test measures than do Caucasian and many Asian students; across all grade levels, poor students – those from "low socioeconomic" backgrounds – have greater difficulty making progress in school and have poorer academic records. Yet there are numerous examples of schools where these characteristics of students do not predict performance. When the learning environment is working optimally for all students, these variables do not predict attainment or lack thereof. In other words, looking at demographic variables is a quick "health screen." If there are large demographic differences in achievement, you know right away that some aspect of the school can be improved.

Thus the Responsible Parties organize data about the student population to answer these questions of equity about educational opportunity in their school:

- Is gender a factor in predicting a student's success or failure in our school? (See National Center for Educational Statistics 1994 for an analysis of our general concerns. Also, Sadker and Sadker 1994, Rop 1997–9, and the penetrating analysis by Tobias 1993.)
- Is ethnicity a factor in predicting a student's success or failure in our school? (See Slavin 1997/1998 for an analysis of this question.)
- Is native language a factor in predicting a student's success or failure in our school?
- Is socioeconomic status a factor in predicting a student's success or failure in our school?

SCANNING THE STUDENTS: DESCRIPTIVE INTERNAL INFORMATION

The Responsible Parties as individuals have a good deal of information about the students, information gained by living with them and working with them. The schools have heaps of statistics about the students. What we are talking about here is a shared clarification developed by organizing information more formally than usual and scanning it to see if it tells us anything about the health of the learning environment. Where do we begin? A good place is to organize information around characteristics that have been known to make a difference in educational progress. Counting students by gender, ethnicity, linguistic background, and socioeconomic background makes a good beginning because we know those demographic variables have affected progress in many schools, and because we know that they make very little difference in an optimal educational environment. The data need to be organized by grade or year and by enrollment in courses and special programs.

Let's see what some schools and districts have learned through such a simple counting operation.

Gender

We hope, of course, that no important differences will show up, but often they do. First, let's just look at enrollment by grade, including graduation. The enrollments by grade should be relatively equal in most circumstances.

Also, numbers of boys and girls in each grade in an elementary school ought to be similar. Let's imagine that they are. Let's then look at programs for students having special needs: special education for students with mild learning disabilities, support for students with limited English, support for students who are not achieving well and are from economically poor families. We look at enrollment in these programs because such a scan sometimes uncovers things that might need attention. Consider two schools with which we are well acquainted.

One school we know found that enrollments in those programs were relatively equal by gender – which is as it should be, because the genders have relatively equal learning ability.

Another school found that by the end of the second grade 20 percent of the boys and just 2 percent of the girls had been referred to special education for mild learning disabilities. That finding led to a further inquiry into the reasons why the students were being referred, and it turned out that the chief cause was that they were not learning to read adequately. Turning to external information the Responsible Parties learned that such a situation is not uncommon, but that the very best curriculum designs result in small, if any, gender differences in learning to read. Thus they had discovered a problem that is important, might be attacked squarely, and where the external information sources (see for example Calhoun 1994) indicate that curricular/instructional changes might make a difference.

The Responsible Parties from the first school found something to chew on also. Although their referrals to special education were equal by gender, about 15 percent of their students *were* being referred, and largely for problems in learning to read, which is far higher than necessary given the best state of the art. Just as serious, they found that very few of those students learned to read adequately during the next three years, which gave shape to another possible area of focus: whether to examine the curriculum in special education.

By counting enrollment in programs in special education and supplementary programs for economically poor students, a California school district that served 30,000 students found that 21,000 of the students just between grades 1 and 10 were enrolled in programs for students having special needs related to low achievement! Only 1700 (7 percent) of those students exited those programs during the year. The Responsible Parties of the district had to acknowledge that just organizing descriptive information carefully can lead to problem identification – or may not turn up anything problematical.

The use of data in secondary schools is similar.

A high school we are closely affiliated with learned that two-thirds of its graduating class were females! Everyone "sort of" knew that more females usually finished school there, but not by a ratio of two to one! Could that lead to an inquiry? Could the Responsible Parties now look at whether there was a drop in male enrollment in the ninth, tenth, or eleventh grades? Could they see whether other demographic factors were in the picture? Could they study whether there were gender differences in achievement far back in the grades?

Another school we know discovered that relatively few females enrolled in advanced mathematics and science, generating another possibility for inquiry into the reasons why.

Especially at the high school level, changes in enrollment by grade need to be examined closely. The state of Florida has discovered some interesting – and distressing – trends, simply by counting students by grade. Here is what they found for the school year 1996–7 (data taken from the 1998 "Profiles" reports generated by the State Department of Education):

Grade 9	193,000
Grade 10	161,000
Grade 11	128,000
Grade 12	105,000
June graduates	92,000

The state officials needed to learn whether the decline was a function of population change, asking whether there was a decline in the age groups of students who might have been attending school. The answer was no: there were about equal numbers of people in the state aged 14, 15, 16, 17, 18, and 19. Yet the grade 12 enrollment was only 54 percent of the grade 9 enrollment, and the number of graduates was less than half of the number of ninth grade students. The picture has been about the same for quite a few years!

Does that indicate the need for an inquiry by the Responsible Parties of the state? Surely so. Does it indicate a need by all districts and schools to find out if the same condition exists in their venue? Surely so, because a problem of this magnitude has to be shared by a great many schools.

If data are available about what students do after graduation, particularly whether they seek higher education, that is worth examining also (in Florida, about 60 percent of those graduates enrolled in colleges or technical schools).

Ethnicity, language background, and socioeconomic status

If many native languages are represented, data need to be organized to depict the languages and the number/percent and gender of students speaking these languages across the total population and within each grade level. Here is an example of a finding from a K-6 California school for those students who had reached the sixth year and had been in the school from kindergarten:

	Number	*Grade equivalent in reading*
Native English speakers	68	range 3.0–10.0
Native Spanish speakers	59	range 3.0–10.0

The good news is that the curriculum appeared to generate the same ranges for the two linguistic groups and very high reading achievement for some of the students. The bad news, of course, is that a considerable number were about to graduate from the elementary school with substandard reading skills.

If socioeconomic or income-background data are available (for example, the number and percentage of students receiving free school meals), this information would need to be organized across the total population, as a minimum. If the Responsible Parties feel the neighborhood or student population is changing rapidly, then these data would also need to be organized to present grade-level profiles. For illustration, let's continue to draw on the data by the state of Florida for a bit, even though our emphasis here is on the school. Let's organize the data to show the twelfth grade enrollment as a percentage of the ninth grade enrollment. The state organized its data in several categories of which the largest are "white, non-Hispanic," "black, non-Hispanic," and "Hispanic."

White, non-Hispanic	57 percent
Black, non-Hispanic	49 percent
Hispanic	50 percent

No group was immune to the terrible picture of declining enrollment through the high school years. Racial and ethnic differences had little if any "explaining value." The state schools as a whole need to worry about how to explain this picture for all three groups.

This exercise illustrates how descriptive data can be used and also how one question leads to another. If this picture was further broken down by gender, might anything show up?

Because nearly all the students in Florida who come to school with "limited English proficiency" are Hispanic, do you think a further breakdown by linguistic status will reveal anything more? We encourage doing it, but what might it show? Does the above picture give clues about what might be found? (About one in three Hispanic students are in programs for limited-English speakers.)

The most common descriptor of socioeconomic status is whether students receive subsidized lunches. That is true of 45 percent of the students in the state. What do you think will show up if the above data are further analyzed by that descriptor?

The Responsible Parties of any school might engage in these types of analysis, and we hope it is clear what kinds of inquiries might follow.

Let's now proceed to see what happens when we add indicators of student progress, again using data that are commonly found in abundance in school environments.

SCANNING STUDENT PERFORMANCE THROUGH USE OF INTERNAL DATA

We will concentrate, for illustration, on two types of data we find to be available in nearly all of the schools where we work. One is course grades or other indicators of achievement recorded by teachers on the records of the students. The other is disciplinary referrals or other actions recorded by the school management teams. The first is, of course, the school's primary internal measurement of students' academic progress. We have found that the second is a very good indicator of how the students are responding to the overall environment of the school. When the students are responding positively, there are virtually no instances of disciplinary action. Yet it appears that disciplinary actions are very common in many schools. In one of the larger states of the United States, we discovered that there were 240,000 suspensions in the school year 1996–7 from among the 1,200,000 students between grades 5 and 11! Now *there's* an unnerving statistic. If the state is having a problem of that magnitude, many schools must be having it too!

Grades and other indicators of academic performance

Let's begin with academic progress, first in the secondary school.

Clearly, the goal is excellence for all. In the perfect world, the Responsible Parties would smile a lot, because all the students would achieve the highest marks in all their courses.

Where to begin is a good question. In a school where 1500 students are each receiving grades in six or seven courses, we have nearly 10,000 data points each quarter and half-quarter.

The overall grade-point average. Suppose we begin by just looking at the overall grade-point average by year, gender, and demographic descriptors. Thinking of the examples we provided in the above section, we might get closer to the dynamics of achievement.

Here is the median year-end grade-point average for the ninth and tenth grade for males and females for the school that found the great disparity between males and females at graduation time (c = 2.0)

	Males	Females
Grade 9	1.8	2.4
Grade 10	2.1	2.6

Because half the students score above and half below the median, we are getting a clue. (We are a long way from a 4.0 for all students.) Pursuing the picture, we find that one-fourth of the males have an average below 1.5. Policy in the school is that no "credit" for graduation is given for grades of D or below. We have just learned that many of the students will not receive credit for half their courses or more – they will have to make up those courses somehow if they are to graduate.

In this school most courses are year-long. So let's find out how well first-quarter grades predict the final grades. We learn that almost all the students who received a failing grade at the end of the course received one at the beginning. In other words, we have an early diagnosis if we choose to act on it.

The "gatekeeper" courses. In American schools, grades in the important ninth and tenth grade courses in English, Mathematics, Science, foreign languages and Social Studies are very useful because success in those courses so much affects what students can do later. Students who do poorly will avoid the later, more difficult courses, or if they are required to take them will often do poorly if the later courses build on the earlier ones. Aggregating the grade distributions for those courses can point to areas where instruction might be strengthened or lengthened. Practice helps: it might be that two-period courses for some students would make a difference.

Grades and promotion. In the Richmond County program described in Chapter 1, a middle school discovered that only two-thirds of its students were earning promotion each year: the average student was taking five years to get through the three-year middle school curriculum. A figure like that is so striking that it will get the attention of any Responsible Parties, and it did in Richmond County. The intensive study of curriculum and instruction resulted in a change to a situation where over 90 percent of the students were earning promotion *using the same standards as before, standards used throughout the school district.*

Literacy as a diagnostic area. Ability to read and write is so critical to self-teaching ability that it is almost always useful to take a look at those areas. An extended example is the development of the "Second Chance" program described in Chapter 2. Once the school found out the reading levels of its entering ninth and tenth grade students, it had found a focus for what became a very successful action-research project. Shortly we will revisit the Southwood School for an analysis of how it used data on quality of writing to ground its initiatives.

Special studies of highly successful students. Careful analysis of the grades and other performance indicators can help understand the characteristics of the most successful students and the degree to which they are being challenged. Some schools have developed the practice of giving "pre-tests" to outstanding students to ensure that they have not mastered the course content before the course begins! The National Assessment of writing progress has helped some schools identify areas for study that have been very useful in some cases. In Ames (see Chapter 1) the finding from the National Assessment that quality of writing improves very little during the secondary years caused a closer look at the quality of writing there, with the result that strong initiatives were developed to improve performance for all their young writers, including those who had made the most progress before the initiatives were made.

Little bits of data can lead to problem identification. Here is an extreme-case example from a secondary school in California of around 1100 students, approximately one-third white, one-third Hispanic, and one-third African-American. The school leadership team, with the assistance of an external consultant, organized a picture of grade distributions for grades 9, 10, 11, and 12, by gender and ethnicity. Then the team organized the grade distributions by department and by courses within each department, by gender and ethnicity. A number of areas to investigate surfaced. We'll share one that had been going on for several years.

Approximately 30 percent of all African-American females were failing physical education in grades 9 and 10. This was greatly disproportionate to the failure rate of white or Hispanic females, and of males. These Fs were averaged into each student's grade-point average. Would you like to make a guess about the reasons for this data picture?

Briefly, students were required to take first-level swimming courses in grades 9 and 10. Classes were segregated by gender. Females took swimming in periods one, two, and three. Many of the young African-American females did not want to get their hair wet at the beginning of the day, and some did not want to get their braids wet at all. Gradually, a power struggle had developed between a couple of staff members and the students. Making this struggle public was not easy on the social system of the staff. Again, there was much discussion about "not lowering standards" and "students must meet the requirements of the course."

The leadership team worked with the physical education department and with the students. Several changes were made, the major one being to reverse the order of male and female swimming classes. Simply having females take their classes in the afternoon helped. Then individual swimming caps were provided for those who wished. A small matter in the operation of the school as a whole; a large matter in the kind of place a school is for its students.

When Responsible Parties study the grade distributions or student progress designators schoolwide, by grade and by course, they almost always find something that needs to be changed by the adults in the system. It may be that a disproportionate number of young males are entering special needs programs at the beginning of second, third, and fourth grade and never exiting. It may be that 25 percent of the students who take Spanish I do not take Spanish II – whereas the intent of introductory language courses is partly to develop students' confidence that they can learn the language. Or that 25 percent of the students who take Algebra I do not take another advanced mathematics course, thus limiting their chances of higher education without these gatekeeper courses as part of their high school credential. (Meaning also that these initial courses are not only serving as gatekeeper courses to more advanced work, but are also automatically screening or tracking students, sometimes paired with a notion of "we cannot lower our standards.")

Instruction in public schools is intended to be criterion-based, not norm-referenced. If the learning environment of the school is working, the grade distribution ought to show extreme kurtosis: almost all grades ought to be skewed to the high end (As, Bs) of the distribution. The grades students receive, despite variations in grading procedures from teacher to teacher, are the major currency of success in schools; they, more than any other indicator of performance, reflect a student's progress through the school. Therefore, grade distributions and retention/promotion data provide critical information that the Responsible Parties need to scan regularly.

Now let's examine a few examples in the primary school.

Literacy. Progress in quality of reading and writing is so important to the success of the elementary school that it is difficult to imagine that the Responsible Parties would avoid the area. The Success For All Program described in Chapter 1 was created in response to studies by inner city schools indicating that as many as half of their students were not exiting the third grade with the competence to handle the upper grade curriculum and beyond. The fact that that initiative, and similar ones, are available to schools offers great promise to students who are really struggling.

The study of writing can be very revealing. Clearly, competence in reading is important to development in writing; but it is not the only factor, as Ames (Chapter 1) reveals, and some of the best writers can make great improvement when well-designed initiatives are made.

Special programs need attention in these areas also. We suggest that Responsible Parties pay particular attention to the progress in reading and writing of students described as having mild learning disabilities, and to the number of students who reach levels of competence where little further special help is needed. In the school mentioned in the above section, curricular and instructional changes were made that virtually eliminated the need for special support within a year.

Here the Responsible Parties begin to organize data about the number, nature, costs, and student effects of special programs. These programs have been added to the school in an attempt to support the education of those students whom we decide cannot receive an optimal education in the "regular classroom environment."

The intent of these programs is that they go beyond "regular classroom instruction" and

- remedy student performance: for example, compensatory programs in reading;
- add knowledge or skills essential to success within the school: for example, immersion programs to teach the English language;
- enhance and provide enrichment beyond the regular classroom curriculum: for example, classes for those labeled as "gifted"; and
- provide an education, to the extent possible, for students whose mental ability severely limits their participation in regular classroom instruction.

What data do the Responsible Parties need as they begin to inquire into these special programs? They will need data that help them clarify the role of these programs in the school as a whole and data that help them clarify the effect of these programs on student progress.

Let's look first at data collection related to the breadth and impact of these programs on the school as an organization and its total student population. The Responsible Parties can use an organizer such as this to depict the number of programs currently in place in the school, for example, Title I reading, tutoring programs, mathematics labs, science, bilingual programs, English immersion programs, programs for gifted students. The table can depict who these programs are designed to serve and the number/percentage of students being served; when these programs were initiated; the total cost of these programs (including salaries, materials, staff development and support, and space); and their general impact on student achievement.

Now let's have the Responsible Parties look more closely at the effects of these programs on the student population. The Responsible Parties can depict the total number of students served in each program, their ethnicity and gender, and the number and percentage of students for whom remedial programs or booster programs, such as English immersion, have been successful (indicated by the number and percentage of students redesignated into regular classroom instruction).

The Responsible Parties need to establish regular scanning of the effects of these additional programs. In many schools, these programs include a large portion of the student population and consume a large portion of total school expenditure. Too often, once a program has been put in place to serve the special needs of students, we tend to assume we have "taken care" of these students. The Executive Committee of the Responsible Parties will need regularly to present data that help everyone understand the general effects of these programs: on the educational progress of the students being served, on the health of the organization, and on the relationship of these programs to both research on practice and to the goals of the school.

PERFORMANCE AS RESPONSE TO THE SCHOOL

Here's a question that requires a real openmindedness from the Responsible Parties: *Do students want to be in our school and our classrooms? Looking at general indicators of student response to the school.*

Here the Responsible Parties organize data on school attendance and on disciplinary actions. Most of these data have been accumulated already, either at the request of the local education authority or for use in completing school improvement reports. What the Responsible Parties have to do is organize these data into easy-to-read charts that communicate how the student population, and groups within that population, are responding to the school as a place to be.

To break set with the current normative practice of accumulating these data and storing them in the school archives, we need to step back and think about their implications. Let's think about attendance first. At the schoolwide level, we are accustomed to thinking about student attendance in terms of fiscal and *in loco parentis* implications. Fiscally, many school staffing levels are based on the average daily attendance of students or on projections of the average daily attendance. So in one sense the size of the school staff and additional resources depend on maintaining a high level of student attendance. We are also accustomed to our legal and moral responsibility for students, because the school "stands in" for the parents or guardians as caregivers during the school day and is legally responsible for the well-being of all children enrolled.

Now let's look at disciplinary actions. Data about discipline referrals are accumulated by most schools. Data sources include records of disciplinary actions, such as who is referred to the principal/head or counselor's office, for what reasons, and the number of incidents; and the consequences of these referrals, such as individual counseling with students, conferences with parents, placement in in-school suspension, after-school suspension, suspension from school for a number of days, placement in programs for behavior-disordered children, placement in an alternative school, expulsion from school, or relinquishing students into the care of law enforcement officials. While these data on disciplinary actions are accumulated routinely in many schools, they seem to move immediately into the school archives, with little reflection by the staff on what they mean for the educational progress of the student population.

Conceptually, there are four other major reasons for looking at attendance and disciplinary actions. One reason is that schoolwide and by class or course, they are powerful indicators of the school's social climate. Over time, they tell the Responsible Parties whether students feel that the school (or class or course) is a positive environment. And pushed a little farther, they reveal much about the staff's ability to radiate a firm, but caring and just, persona individually and collectively, and about the acceptance by each member of the staff of the responsibility to teach all who come in at the classroom door.

Another reason for a closer look is that these data allow the Responsible Parties to calculate the degree of absence from instruction. It's extremely difficult for most students to make good educational progress if they are not present for instruction. Whether students are missing prime instruction because they are not present in school or because they are sitting in in-house suspension, their likelihood of feeling successful in school or of learning the curriculum offered by the school is decreased.

There are natural pressures from citizens working within the school and from citizens outside the school grounds for operating the school as a safe and orderly environment. These pressures have tended to increase the range and severity of consequences for students who disrupt the learning environment. Almost everyone wants students to remain in school at least long enough to receive the minimum basic education necessary to participate as citizens and survive economically. In the United States, this school-time credential is represented by the high school diploma. We often feel almost virtuous in establishing in-house suspension programs and alternative schools because at least we are keeping our youth in school. Yet the overuse of disciplinary actions that remove students from their heterogeneous social group and lead to a "send them down the hall or across town" solution may be extremely unhealthy for the maturing of students and for the self-esteem of the staff.

A third reason for looking at these data, especially the disciplinary referrals, is to confirm or disprove perceptions among the staff or community about student behavior and to pinpoint problems with settings or with current disciplinary procedures. Time and again, we have worked with teachers who were convinced about the prevalence of some aspect of misbehavior, only to have a careful look at their data disprove the belief. Another common occurrence when staff members disaggregate their disciplinary referrals by incident and location of incident is to pinpoint certain sites in the building or on campus where more adult presence is needed.

Sometimes school disciplinary codes can have unintended negative side effects. For example, look at these data for another school within our acquaintance. This secondary school had a disciplinary code with these consequences: if a student was tardy (more than five minutes late) for class three times, she or he was placed in in-school suspension; if placed in in-school suspension three times, she or he was suspended from school for three days. The number of tardies was large, and came from all grade levels and from all ethnicities. The school was a large multi-building facility; students had four minutes to change classes. What do you think was a major contributing factor to the problem of "students just don't get to class on time; they must learn to be responsible"?

Here are the highest three categories of the 1067 disciplinary incidents that were looked at for a student population of 780 students for a four-month period during which attendance at the school was over 95 percent (almost all the remainder were absences for illness and other unavoidable reasons):

1 unexcused absence from class – 205
2 late to class – 240
3 no-show to a "teacher detention" (where the teacher requested the student to "stay after school" for any of a variety of reasons) – 58.

The total of these three items is 503, almost half of the incidents.

The 14 members of the Facilitation Team (school staff size: 50) were taken aback when they organized these data schoolwide and looked at the cumulative effect of their disciplinary code on instruction. Many of them had been major developers of the code, and they felt their classrooms were quieter, more peaceful places as a result – and they were correct. They decided that during the next five school days, they would collect some additional information about the absence and lateness problem. They decided to take the first 15 minutes of their planning periods for a week and simply walk the halls; when they found someone tardy, they would escort that person to her or his class, interviewing them on the way about why they were late.

As you probably guessed earlier, the major reasons for lateness had to do with bodily functions: toilet time and the need for water. Both the number of water fountains and the number of toilets were limited in relation to the size of the school body. The academic areas were grouped together, i.e., mathematics for all grade levels, English, sciences, etc., meaning almost all students had some distance to travel in their four minutes. Also, there were indications that some of the students in this predominantly middle-class setting were simply using the disciplinary code's sequence of tardies-to-suspensions to get out of class; it was their way of beating the system and making a bit of a game out of the process.

The Facilitation Team shared the results of their analyses of discipline referrals and their interview data with the whole staff. At first they encountered resistance to change, but as they pressed colleagues for suggestions and encouraged them to take a look at the school setting as a humane environment, good ideas for actions began to surface. The fact that many staff members expressed many of the same feelings of frustration, disbelief, and "so-what" that some Facilitation Team members had expressed when they first looked at the data was useful in discussing the implications of the discipline code.

The staff decided to ask the Student Council to make recommendations. Council members came up with a range of actions that could be implemented immediately, and with some actions for the future (for example, one thing the students wanted was easier access to water). One student recommendation that surprised the staff was to add 15 minutes to the school day, to be used to provide a ten-minute class-changing time after second period and after fourth period and add an extra minute to the other between-class times. When presented with that recommendation, the staff had to grapple with its beliefs about allowing "teenagers" so much time not directly supervised. Again, the implications of such seemingly innocuous data – when pulled from the school archives and studied with interest by Responsible Parties – surprise many school improvement teams.

The fourth reason for Responsible Parties to inquire into attendance and disciplinary data is to identify groups of students who may be at high risk because of absence from instruction, or because of behavior patterns that are common to a group. Are African-American, Caribbean, Hispanic students over-represented in disciplinary referrals? If they are, why? What types of infractions are most common? Are there general schoolwide patterns? For example, are males over-represented in terms of discipline referrals? If so, how early does this begin? Kindergarten or Level 1? Are there instructional implications?

What about classroom patterns, patterns common to individuals? Now we move into the dangerous social territory of violating the norms of adult privacy. However, schoolwide data are accumulated class by class, teacher by teacher. For example: Do some elementary school teachers routinely have a high number of referrals of African-American males? Are there some female teachers who routinely have a high number of referrals of Hispanic males? Are invisible adult prejudices at work, yielding unnecessary inequities among the student population?

In the school we were discussing just above, a number of items were related to relationships between the teachers and students. These included

4 leaving class without permission – 52
5 insubordination – 124

6 refusal to obey reasonable request – 28
7 disruptive behavior – 146
8 offensive behavior to teacher – 11
9 vulgarity or profanity – 33.

This group adds up to another 394 incidents or another third, leaving about 15 percent for a large number of other categories of incident which ranged from the mild (such as eating in an unauthorized place – 7) to the more serious, like forging notes from parents (30), and then to more worrying items like "fighting" (26 incidents). The Facilitation Team discovered that 90 percent of the incidents in the categories from 4 to 9 occurred in the classrooms of just a half-dozen teachers and that none occurred in the classrooms of 25 of the faculty members.

What could they make of that? Another avenue of inquiry?

The challenge for the Responsible Parties – as they look at data on disciplinary actions and what these data mean in terms of absence from instruction and effects on student membership in the school community – is to form a reasonable balance when considering changes in instruction and changes in the learning environment, along with use of the more common disciplinary actions listed above when student behavior is disruptive to student progress. Delicacy, astuteness, and bravery are all required when prying meaning and utility from these seemingly innocuous data.

Also, when consulting the literature we find that curriculum and instruction are important factors in reducing or eliminating referrals. In the Richmond County program described in Chapter 1, the same middle school that had the horrendous non-promotion rate had an equally disturbing suspension rate (27 percent of the students per semester), which dropped to 7 percent in the first semester when cooperative teaching/learning strategies were studied and used by the faculty.

THE FORMAL TESTING PROGRAM

In the United States *standardized test results* provide the Responsible Parties with one more source of information about their student population. While the results of these tests are indicators of student performance, they are separated from those listed above because teachers have little to do with the selection of content and skills evaluated on these tests and with the assignment of scores or performance levels. Thus in one sense these tests provide an "independent" measure of the school's curriculum and learning environment.

Standardized test results may be from norm-referenced tests or from criterion-referenced tests. The word "standardized" simply indicates tests that are uniform in content and scoring and with common guidelines for administration. Here, we address specifically norm-referenced and criterion-referenced tests that have been standardized for national, statewide, or district-wide administrations.

Norm-referenced achievement tests are based on the assumption that levels of student performance on the content being measured will resemble a normal curve, with most students' scores falling in the middle of the distribution, and other students' scores thinly but evenly distributed on either side. In these tests, standards of performance are relative, i.e. whether a student score indicates high achievement, average achievement, or low achievement is heavily determined by how the norming group responded to the items on the test. Norm-referenced test results allow Responsible Parties to compare their students' performance to that of other students who took the same tests.

Criterion-referenced tests may also be standardized for content, scoring, and administration. These tests are designed to measure specific objectives and/or skills within a discipline or skill area. In contrast to norm-referenced tests, the standards of performance are absolute, i.e. whether a student score indicates high achievement, average achievement, or low achievement is not determined in relationship to how other students scored, but is dependent on his/her mastery of the content/ skills being measured. Criterion-referenced tests can be used to measure the effects of instruction on student knowledge.

If the school has standardized test results available, the Responsible Parties begin by looking at the typical summary data provided to schools – as Southwood did. These reports indicate the average (the mean) performance, within an academic area, by grade level, of those students who took the test. They may indicate the numbers and percentage of students performing at different levels by percentile rank or stanine.

While these summary reports provide some information, their visual presentation and interpretation tend to keep their meaning arcane and productive *use* of the data almost impossible. Without study by the staff, the test results reported will remain distant from the classroom and mask what is happening for many students. Thus to provide useful information for guiding collective action, the Responsible Parties will need to disaggregate these summary data to provide information about the levels of performance for all members of the population tested, as well as disaggregating by gender, ethnicity, and special-program participation. At some point, the Responsible Parties will need to look at these test results across several years, both for the total population and for a sample of students who have been in the school for several years.

Southwood gives us an example of the use of the formal testing program and also how data collection and analysis evolve naturally into an initiative.

SELECTING A FOCUS OR PRIORITY AREA FOR COLLECTIVE INQUIRY

How do the Responsible Parties select a curriculum area or student performance for collective inquiry? Let's revisit Southwood Elementary (see pp. 32–40), then discuss what they did in detail.

The Southwood staff members were concerned about student writing, and had ended the previous year by reviewing student results on the standardized test used by the district, the state writing tests, the grade/performance reports provided by the Executive Committee, and the new state curriculum standards.

The state writing test used a six-point scale, with 1 being low and 6 high. It was a criterial test of writing quality that could be used to compare growth in the quality of student writing across grade levels. When staff members organized the writing data by genre and grade level from the state test, these are the mean scores they saw:

Fourth grade

Narrative writing:
content/plot – 2.8; support/character development – 3.0;
    grammar/mechanics – 3.4

Expository/informative writing:
focus/organization – 1.6; support – 2.2; grammar/mechanics – 3.2

Persuasive writing:
focus/organization – 1.2; support – 1.4; grammar/mechanics – 3.1

Sixth grade

Narrative writing:
content/plot – 3.2; support/character development – 3.5;
    grammar/mechanics – 3.6

Expository/informative writing:
focus/organization – 1.8; support – 2.5; grammar/mechanics – 3.6

Persuasive writing:
focus/organization – 1.4; support – 1.8; grammar/mechanics – 3.5.

As they looked at the student writing results reported for personal narrative, expository/informative, and persuasive/argument genres and studied the characteristics and major applications of each genre, they decided to focus on improving the quality of nonfictional, informative writing. Of interest is the fact that they did not select their "lowest area," persuasive writing, because they felt students needed to learn to write basic informative prose first. For a variety of reasons, they did not select personal narrative as their inquiry focus: because their students were doing a relatively good job writing about experiences they had had, because staff members felt they were providing at least some instruction in this genre, and because there was a good match between the state's curriculum recommendations and what they were currently doing to promote growth in personal narrative writing. Yet, the teachers felt they had much work to do just to clarify among themselves what good expository/informative prose looked like, and to figure out how to design instruction that would improve the quality of informative writing by all students.

What did the Responsible Parties at Southwood do in selecting their collective focus? They were concerned about student writing in general, and could have simply decided to study student progress and how their current learning environment supported the development of writing among their students. However, they scanned the student population, its progress, and the curriculum: they looked at standardized test results in reading, language, and mathematics and disaggregated these test results by gender. They also looked beyond the summary reports that provided the "mean" student scores and disaggregated these data into perform-ance profiles (in this case, the number of students performing in each quartile).

Southwood's Responsible Parties looked at student grades and progress reports. They looked at the criterion-referenced test results from the state's assessment of writing. They had writing test results and scores for grades 4 and 6. These results indicated the quality of students' nar-rative, expository/informative, and persuasive writing, based on three samples of writing from each student. Once they decided to focus on expository/informative writing, the Responsible Parties charted these scores by gender and discovered that the males were performing, on average, about 0.50 to 0.60 of a scale score point below the females.

They knew how significant this difference was, because when studying the attributes of the different genres they had found the National Assess-ment of Educational Progress reports on writing. These reports had indi-cated very gradual growth in the quality of writing across genres between grades 4 and 12, approximately 0.10 to 0.16 of a scale score point per year.

As they studied the knowledge base and looked at their students' writ-ing, they decided to concentrate the development of lessons and their work during early release days for the first few months on the domain of focus and organization. Look back at the data. These data about student performance in the domains scored – i.e. for informative/expository prose, focus/organization, support, and grammar/mechanics – con-flicted with teachers' perceptions. They strongly believed that their stu-dents' weakest area of writing was grammar and mechanics. As they studied more, they came to see that one of the major skills they needed to help students develop was the ability to announce their subject and main idea clearly; and the students needed to learn that the domain of focus and organization was the domain that carried the main message for the reader or audience. Until students could learn to present their major point with some skill, their writing competence would be limited.

While reviewing the state's new curriculum-content standards, staff members were also thinking about their current school curriculum and areas that might need strengthening. Here, the knowledge of several teachers about the use of the reading/writing connection to support stu-dents' development as readers and as writers; the awareness of upper grade-level teachers of the difficulty many students have with reading expository prose; and the acknowledgement by many teachers that they were not as knowledgeable as they wished about writing or about teach-ing writing – all helped in determining Southwood's focus area: to improve the quality of students' expository/informative writing.

(The knowledge of the Responsible Parties will continue to expand as they study the external knowledge base and simultaneously study student learning in their school, moving their collective expertise beyond the initial study described in Chapter 3.)

Let's move on from how Southwood selected its focus on informative writing to some considerations for any staff or Responsible Parties in selecting a focus for collective inquiry. Here are some ideas to hold in mind, comprising our best recommendations for the attributes of focus areas/student learning goals to guide whole-staff study:

- Select an academic student learning goal in a curriculum area. Determine what student knowledge and performance would describe a continuum of development for this goal or curriculum domain.
- Select a goal or performance area that encompasses all students: one for which almost all teachers and parents would say, "Yes, all students must become highly knowledgeable/skilled in this area."
- Select a goal or performance area that is vital for future work within a discipline (such as computation) and/or has a cognitive and skill continuum whose development will yield benefits throughout school and beyond (such as mathematical problem-solving).
- Select a goal or learning performance that staff members want students to become very accomplished in and that they want to become very proficient in supporting.
- Select a focus for inquiry that is broad enough to embrace a critical student performance domain; narrow enough to focus study, but not too limiting.
- Substantive study and substantive changes in practice take time. If the focus area is too broad, a staff can only engage in shallow collective study. Enter a few areas within a discipline with depth; if well done, these areas will give a lead across the discipline, forging connections (almost like synapses) that form the discipline and making these connections visible for curriculum and instructional planning.

GATHERING, ORGANIZING, AND STUDYING INFORMATION ABOUT A FOCUS AREA

The Responsible Parties now begin to inquire with greater depth into the focus area selected. They look more closely at student knowledge and performance in their focus area; they look at how, and to what extent, students are being taught the continuum of knowledge and skills that comprises the focus area; they continue to study the external knowledge base; and they continue to study student performance in the classroom and develop lessons to enhance this performance.

Let's move now to a brief generic review of what any school would need to do as it gathers, organizes, and studies information about its focus area:

The staff will need to study information about student knowledge and performance in the focus area.

The staff will need to study information about how the learning environment in its school supports student development in the focus area. In developing their picture of the current learning environment, teachers will need to look at how the focus area or goal is being taught in classrooms, what content is being used to develop student knowledge and skill, what materials are being used, and how much time is allotted for teaching.

The staff will need to study information from the external knowledge base about how students develop in the focus area, and ideas about how the learning environment could be designed to support student development in the selected area. Staff members will seek information in the professional knowledge base about pedagogy, curriculum, materials, and amount of time necessary for development among learners of various needs and abilities.

The staff will continue to gather and study information about student performance and come to a sharper collective understanding about how students develop cognitions and skills in the focus area.

From their increased understanding of student performance and their interaction with others who have studied student development in the same focus area (through their collective inquiry into the professional knowledge base), teachers select actions that can be implemented immediately and actions that can be implemented over time to improve the learning environment.

THE ACTION-RESEARCH WAY OF DOING BUSINESS

Inquiry, by definition, means seeking a better understanding. However, a clearer understanding of student learning and of the learning environment of the school is only part of the purpose of collective inquiry. Inquiry into the nature and goals of an organization carries with it the notion that increased clarity and additional information may lead to changes in behaviors and/or attitudes by members of the organization, in other words, changes in curriculum and pedagogy.

The primary goal of evolutionary school improvement is enhanced student learning; however, a healthier workplace for adults often evolves. The Responsible Parties structure a continuous collective study of what is happening for learners in the learning environment of the school. This collective study, when accompanied by changes in curriculum and instruction, can yield immediate student-learning benefits. In terms of benefits for the adult community and the culture of the school, over time, the continuous collective study of the learners and the learning environment becomes part of the work norms of a school and reduces the feelings of isolation or loneliness in supporting student development.

We refer again to the action-research paradigm that was worked out in the middle of the twentieth century to help organizations move into a self-renewing state. In colloquial terms,

• everyone is involved;

- the state of the organization and its productivity and processes are studied;
- an area of functioning is identified and focussed on;
- external information relevant to that area is gathered and organized;
- an initiative is made to improve that area;
- implementation and effects are studied carefully;
- either that area is the subject of a modified or new initiative, or
- another area comes into focus.

The inquiry continues.

6 Connecting to the knowledge base: finding curricular and instructional options

One of the important tasks of the Responsible Parties is to survey the knowledge base as areas of focus are identified, and this task requires some study of how to approach it. The reason is simply that continuous, collective study of the knowledge base is relatively unusual in schools, school districts, and state and national departments of education. The study, which connects the inquiry to the relevant knowledge base, occurs as a curriculum area has been identified as a focus for inquiry. The Responsible Parties are searching for curricular and instructional options that might make a difference to their students.

THE CONCEPT OF "EFFECT SIZE"

To select a teaching strategy or curriculum procedure for schoolwide study and implementation, the Responsible Parties need to know whether it has a history of yielding student achievement in other settings. And they need to have an estimate of the degree of student achievement they can expect if the strategy is implemented with fidelity. The concept of effect size will help them select innovations for schoolwide pursuit.

Estimating the size of the effects of an educational procedure requires a base of investigations relevant to the procedure. Optimally, investigators conduct a controlled experiment, take measures of the students at the beginning; assign the students to control and experimental groups on the basis of pre-tests; expose the groups to the procedures; and measure again at the end of the treatment and possibly at intervals thereafter, comparing the distribution of scores of the two groups. A statistic known as "effect size" (Glass 1982) is then computed. By repeatedly computing the sizes of differences in effects with each study that is conducted, we can arrive at a reasonable picture of the effectiveness of various teaching and curricular procedures.

To understand the concept of effect size, we have to understand a number of other concepts that enable us to describe and compare scores on various measures. For example, we describe distributions of scores in terms of *central tendencies*, which refer to the clustering of scores around the middle of the distribution, and to variance, or the dispersion of these scores. Terms describing central tendency include the average score or arithmetic *mean*, which is computed by summing the scores and dividing by the number of scores; the *median* or middle score (half of the scores are above and half are below the median score); and the *mode*, which is the most frequent score in the distribution – graphically, the highest point in the distribution. In Figure 6.1 the average, the median, and the mode are all in the same place because the distribution is completely symmetrical.

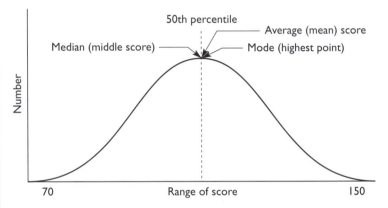

Figure 6.1   A sample normal distribution

The *dispersion of scores* in a distribution is described in terms of the *range*, the distance between the highest and lowest scores; the rank, frequently described in *percentile* (for example, the twentieth score from the top in a 100-person distribution is at the 80th percentile because 20 percent of the scores are above and 80 percent are below it); and the *standard deviation*, which describes how widely or narrowly scores are distributed. Standard deviation describes the position of a score in relation to the *mean* of a continuum of scores; and effect size describes the differences between *means* of procedures as a proportion of standard deviation.

In Figure 6.2 the range is from 70 (the lowest score) to 150 (the highest score). The 50th percentile score is at the middle (in this case coinciding with the average, the mode, and the median). Standard deviations are marked off by the vertical lines labeled +1 SD, +2 SD, and so on. Note that the percentile rank of the score one standard deviation above the mean is *84* (84 percent of the scores are below that point); the rank two standard deviations above the mean is 97; and three standard deviations above the mean is 99.

When the mean, median, and mode coincide as in these distributions, and the distribution of scores is as symmetrical as the ones depicted in

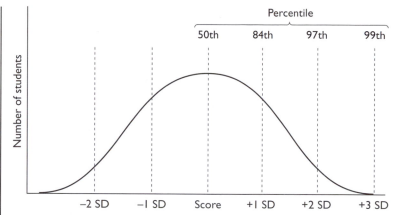

Figure 6.2   A sample normal distribution with standard deviations

these figures, the distribution is referred to as *normal*. The concept of normal distributions is very useful in statistical operations, although many actual distributions are not symmetrical, as we will see. However, to explain the concept of effect size we will use symmetrical, "normal" distributions.

As part of learning how to select curricular and instructional innovations, the Responsible Parties study effect size. They explore the concept of effect size using a recent study of a complex model of teaching, Group Investigation, an intensive approach that combines elaborate methods for collaborative activity with scientific methods of inquiry. In this study, as mentioned in Chapter 2, Shlomo Sharan and Hana Shachar (1988) illustrated how rapidly students can accelerate their learning rates. Their study focussed on a problem that exists in many societies: students whose families are regarded as socially and economically disadvantaged frequently display low achievement and receive disadvantaging treatment in the classroom from other students and teachers.

As part of the study, Sharon and Shachar prepared social studies teachers to organize their students into learning communities and then compared the classroom interaction and academic achievement in the classes using group investigation with the levels of interaction and student achievement of classes taught by the customary "whole-class" method. In Israel, where the study was conducted, students of Middle Eastern origin generally belong to the "disadvantaged" population, whereas generally students of European origin are more advantaged. In this study, students from both origins were mixed in classes. The research design compared the achievement of the students who were taught using group investigation with students taught by the "whole-class" method most common in Israeli schools. In Table 6.1 the results are presented for the Middle-Eastern-origin students under the two conditions.

The Group-Investigation-taught, Middle-Eastern-origin students achieved average gains nearly two and a half times those of their whole-class counterparts. These normally disadvantaged students also achieved

Table 6.1 Comparison of achievement of Middle-Eastern students in Group Investigation and "whole-class" conditions

		Group Investigation (n = 47)	Whole class (n = 26)
History pre-test	mean	4.81	12.31
	SD	7.20	7.05
History post-test	mean	50.17	27.23
	SD	14.44	13.73
Mean gain		35.36	14.92

larger gains than did the European-origin students taught by the more typical "whole-class method" (35.16 to 21.05) and exceeded them on the post-test. In other words, the "socially disadvantaged" students taught with Group Investigation learned at rates above those of the "socially advantaged" students taught by teachers who did not have the repertoire provided by Group Investigation. The model had enabled them to become more powerful students immediately. The average gain by the Western-origin students was *twice* that of their "whole-class" counterparts. Thus the treatment was effective for students from both backgrounds.

Let us see what the results look like in "effect size" terms. Figure 6.3 compares the post-test scores of the low SES students in the "whole-class" and "Group Investigation" treatments. The average score of the "Group Investigation" treatment corresponds to about the 92nd percentile of the distribution of the "whole-class" students. The effect size is computed by dividing the difference between the two means by the standard deviation of the "control" or "whole class" group. The effect size in this case is 1.6 standard deviation using the formula

$$ES = \frac{\text{average of experimental group} - \text{average of control group}}{\text{standard deviation of control group}}$$

$$\frac{50.17 - 27.23}{13.73} = 1.6$$

The utility of the concept of effect size is that when reading a report of research, one can concentrate on the relative size of the impact of a given procedure on the students.

Now back to our Responsible Parties and their challenge of selecting innovations that will facilitate student learning. In a district we know the members were amazed as they sought articles and research about their focus area. Very few authors reported student achievement effects for groups of students. Many authors discussed the importance of the area they were writing about and students' difficulties in the area, but few authors discussed how the teaching strategy or curricular approach related to the curriculum framework of the discipline as a whole. Most authors did an excellent job describing use of the teaching strategy, and some did a good job in discussing materials to use and describing how

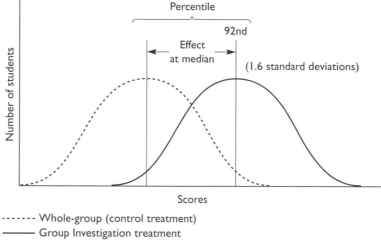

Figure 6.3 A sample effect size

different individual students might respond. However, few authors talked about how to learn the teaching strategy or to support oneself while learning it.

Nonetheless, the Executive Committee finds several articles that do report achievement effects for students by group. They select three that seem to be especially clear in describing the strategies, student effects, and curriculum implications. All Responsible Parties receive a copy of these three articles; each peer coaching group reads and discusses the articles. As they share their reading and responses with their peers, they discover that there are several instructional procedures that can generate powerful effects, and a number of curriculum approaches that do so. They begin a more extended inquiry. They are pleased to discover that quite a few models of teaching promise to increase student learning substantially. Let's look at three of them.

RESEARCH ON MODELS OF TEACHING

Mnemonics

Mnemonics is a good place to start, because the model-builders in mnemonics attempt to teach students learning skills that can be applied to a range of school subjects. In many of their studies they measure outcomes of the sort that make the recitation popular.

Although research on memorization and mnemonic strategies has been conducted for more than one hundred years, until a few years ago most of the yield for school practice offered few and very general guidelines, such as advice about when to mass and when to distribute practice. Little research had been conducted on the learning of school subjects. In the mid-1970s a productive line of work was begun by Atkinson (1975) at Stanford University – a line that has been greatly extended by Pressley and Levin at the Universities of Western Ontario and

Wisconsin. They have developed a series of systems for organizing information to promote memory and have given particular, although not exclusive, attention to one known as the "link-word" method. Atkinson applied the method during experiments with computer-assisted instruction in which he was attempting to increase students' learning of initial foreign-language vocabularies. He experimented with what he called "acoustic" and "imagery" links. The first was designed to make associations between foreign pronunciations and the sounds of known English words. The second was used to make the connection vivid (Atkinson 1975). In one early study the link-word method produced as much learning in two trials as the conventional method did in three. The experimental group learned about half as many words again as the control group and maintained the advantage after several weeks. He also found that the method was enhanced when the students supplied their own imagery.

Further developmental work included experiments with children of various ages and across subjects. Using a link-word system in Spanish vocabulary learning, second and fifth grade children learned about twice the number of words as children using rote and rehearsal methods (Pressley 1977). In later work with Levin et al. (1982), Pressley employed a "pictured-action" variant of the method with first and sixth grade children, who acquired three times as much vocabulary as did control groups. With Dennis-Rounds (1980) he extended the strategy to social studies information (products and cities) and learned that with instruction, students could transfer the method to other learning tasks. Pressley, Levin, and McCormick (1980) found that primary school students could generate sentences to enhance memorization. The results were three times as good as for students using their own methods. Similar results were found with kindergarten and preschool children (Pressley et al. 1981a). With Levin et al. (1981) the work was successfully extended to vocabulary with abstract meanings. Levin and Levin (1990) have also extended the application to abstract prose and conceptual systems from the disciplines.

It was important to learn whether better "natural" memorizers, with practice, develop their own equivalent methods. Pressley, Levin, and Ghatala (1984) asked whether students, with age and practice, would spontaneously develop elaborated methods for memorizing material, and found that very few did. The better performers had developed more elaborate methods than the majority, who used rote-rehearsal methods alone. However, the newly developed mnemonic methods enhanced learning for the best memorizers as well as for the others. Hence it appears that the method, or an equivalent one, can be very beneficial for most students.

The consistency of the findings is impressive. The link-word method appears to have general applicability across subject matters and ages of children (Pressley et al. 1982), and can be used by teachers and taught to children. The effect sizes reached by many of the studies are quite high. The *average* for transfer tasks (where the material learned was to be applied in another setting), was 1.91. Recall of attributes of items (such as towns, cities, minerals) was 1.5. Foreign language acquisition was 1.3, with many studies reporting very high outcomes. Delayed recall generally maintained the gains, indicating that the mnemonics strategies have a lasting effect.

The community of scholars who are studying mnemonics have developed considerable interest in the area of metacognition, and their work has given rise to the theory that helping students to inquire into themselves as learners and develop cognitive control over learning strategies can increase the capability of learners to learn.

Scientific inquiry

Models taken directly from the sciences have been the basis for curriculums for both elementary and high school children. The results of the research indicate that the scientific method can be taught and has positive effects on the acquisition of information, concepts, and attitudes. More narrowly defined studies have been made on inductive teaching and inquiry training. Beginning with Taba's (1966) exploration of an inductive social studies curriculum, periodic small-scale studies have probed the area. In 1968 Worthen provided evidence to support one of its central theses – that induced concepts would facilitate long-term recall. Feeley (1972) reviewed the social science studies and reported that differences in terminology hampered the accumulation of research, but that the inductive methods generally lived up to expectations, generating concept development and positive attitudes. Research on Suchman's (1964) model for teaching causal reasoning directly supported the proposition that inquiry training can be employed with both elementary and high school children. Schrenker (1976) reported that inquiry training resulted in increased understanding of science, greater productivity in critical thinking, and skills for obtaining and analyzing information. He reported that it made little difference in the mastery of information per se, but that it was as efficient as didactic methods or the didactic-cum-laboratory methods generally employed to teach science. Ivany (1969) and Collins (1969) examined variants in the kinds of confrontations and materials used and reported that the strength of the confrontation as a stimulus to inquiry was important and that richness in instructional materials was a significant factor. Elefant (1980) successfully carried out the strategy with deaf children in an intriguing study that has implications for work with all children.

Currently the clearest evidence about the potential effects on students comes from the study of the academically oriented curriculums in science and mathematics that were developed and used during the 20-year period from 1955 to 1975 and from the experience with elementary curriculums in a variety of subject areas (Rhine 1981; Becker and Gersten 1982). The theory of the academic curriculums was relatively straightforward. The essence of the position was stated in *The Process of Education* (Bruner 1961) and Schwab and Brandwein's *The Teaching of Science* (1962). The teaching of science should be as much as possible a simulation of the scientific process itself. The concepts of the disciplines should be studied rigorously in relation to their knowledge base. Thus science would be learned as inquiry. Further, the information thus learned would be retained well because it would be embedded in a meaningful framework and the student would possess the interrelated concepts that make up the structure of the discipline.

In the academic reform movement of the 1950s and 1960s, entire curriculums in the sciences (for example Biological Sciences Curriculum Study biology), social studies (for example "Man, A Course of Study"), mathematics (for example School Mathematics Study Group), and language (for example the linguistic approaches) were developed and introduced to the schools. These curriculums had in common their designers' belief that academic subjects should be studied with the tools of their respective disciplines. Most of these curriculums therefore required that students learn the modes of inquiry employed by the disciplines as well as factual material. Process was valued equally with content and many of these curriculums became characterized as "inquiry oriented."

Much curriculum research resembles the experimental studies of teaching, but the unit under study is a configuration of content, teaching methods, instructional materials and technologies, and organizational forms. In the experiments any one of the elements of the curriculum may be studied separately or in combination with the others, and the yield is expressed in terms of whether a curriculum produces predicted effects. Research on curriculum depends heavily on training in the content of the curriculum and the teaching strategies needed to implement it. Following training, implementation is monitored, either by classroom observation or by interviews. Effects are determined by comparing student outcomes in experimental and control classrooms. In a few studies (for example Almy 1970) combinations of curriculums are employed to determine effects on cognitive development and intelligence.

In reviewing the studies, El-Nemr (1979) concentrated on the teaching of biology as inquiry in high schools and colleges. He looked at the effects on achievement of information, the development of process skills, and attitudes toward science. The experimentally oriented biology curriculums achieved positive effects on all three outcomes. The average effect sizes were largest for process skills (0.44 at the high school level and 0.62 at the college level). For achievement they were 0.27 and 0.11 respectively, and for attitudes, 0.22 and 0.51. Bredderman's (1983) analysis included a broader range of science programs and included the elementary grades. He also reported positive effects for information (0.10), creativity (0.13), and science process (0.52), and in addition he reported effects on intelligence tests where they were included (0.50). From these and other studies we can conclude that it is possible to develop curriculums that will achieve model-relevant effects and also will increase learning of information and concepts.

In England the "Cognitive Acceleration through Science Education" project has emphasized problem-solving and developing the students' capacity to find their own solutions and increase their awareness of how they reached these solutions. Adey and Shayer (1990) report that they are able to reach 25–50 percent of the students and that gains are made on the traditional measures (passing the science tests) as well as on measures of problem-solving and metacognitive understanding.

Also, vigorous curriculums in one area appear to stimulate growth in other, apparently unconnected areas. For example, Smith's (1980) analysis of aesthetics curriculums shows that the implementation of the arts-oriented curriculums was accompanied by gains in the basic skills areas. Possibly an active and effective curriculum in one area has energizing effects on the entire school program. Hillocks's (1987) review of the teaching of writing revealed similar effects. His conclusion indicated just how closely the way we teach is connected with what we teach. Essentially, the inductive approaches to the teaching of reading and writing produced average effect sizes of about 0.60 compared to treatments that covered the same material, but without the inductive approaches to the teaching/learning process.

Inquiry into cooperative learning models

There have been three lines of research on ways of helping students study and learn together, one led by David and Roger Johnson at the University of Minnesota, a second by Robert Slavin at Johns Hopkins University, and the third by Shlomo and Yael Sharan and Rachel Hertz-Lazarowitz in Israel. Grasping the research is difficult because the term "cooperative learning" is used to refer to a considerable variety of teaching strategies and there is a very large body of literature that is quite variable in quality. Further, various forms of cooperative learning are designed to accomplish quite different objectives. A model to teach students how to solve conflicts will be tested in relation to that objective, whereas another model may approach academic learning directly.

Among other things, the Johnsons and their colleagues (Johnson and Johnson 1974; Johnson et al. 1981, 1990) have studied the effects of co-operative task and reward structures on academic learning. The Johnsons' (1975, 1981) work on peer coaching has provided information about the effects of cooperative behavior on both traditional learning tasks and the effects on values and intergroup behavior and attitudes. Their models emphasize the development of what they call "positive interdependence," or cooperation where collective action also celebrates individual differences. Slavin's extensive 1983 review includes the study of a variety of approaches where he manipulates the complexity of the social tasks and experiments with various types of grouping. He reports success with the use of heterogeneous groups with tasks requiring coordination of group members on both academic learning and intergroup relations, and has generated a variety of strategies that employ extrinsic and intrinsic reward structures. The Israeli team has concentrated on Group Investigation, the most complex of the social models of teaching.

What is the magnitude of effects that we can expect when we learn to use the cooperative learning strategies effectively? Rolheiser-Bennett (1986) compared the effects of the degrees of cooperative structure required by the several approaches (Joyce et al. 1989). On standardized tests in the basic curriculum areas (such as reading and mathematics), the highly structured approaches to teaching students to work together generated effect sizes of an average 0.28, with some studies approaching half a standard deviation. On criterion-referenced tests the average was 0.48 with some of the best implementations reaching an effect of about one standard deviation. The more elaborate cooperative learning models generated an average effect size of somewhat more than one standard deviation, with some exceeding two standard deviations. (The average of the students in the experimental group is above the 90th percentile student in the control group.) The effects on higher-order thinking were even greater, with an average effect of about 1.25 standard deviations and effects in some studies as high as three standard deviations.

Taken as a whole, research on cooperative learning is overwhelmingly positive: nearly every study has had from modest to very high effects, although some have had no effects on academic learning. The cooperative approaches are effective over a range of achievement measures. The more intensely cooperative the environment, the greater the effects: and the more complex the outcomes (higher-order processing of information, problem solving), the greater the effects.

The cooperative environment engendered by these models has had substantial effects on the cooperative behavior of the students, increasing feelings of empathy for others, reducing intergroup tensions and aggressive and antisocial behavior, improving moral judgment, and building positive feelings toward others, including those of other ethnic groups. Many of these effect sizes are substantial – one or two standard deviations is not uncommon and one is as high as eight. Hertz-Lazarowitz (1993) recently used one of the models to create integrative interaction between Israeli and Arab students on the West Bank! Margarita Calderon has worked with Lazarowitz and Jusefina Tinajero to adapt a cooperative integrated reading and composition program for bilingual students, with some very nice results (Calderon *et al.* 1991). An adaptation in higher education that organizes students into cooperative study groups reduced a dropout rate in engineering from 40 percent to about 5 percent (Bonsangue 1993). Conflict-resolution strategies have taught students to develop integrative behavior and reduced social tension in some very divided environments in inner-city schools (Johnson and Johnson 1994).

The teaching/learning of writing

In another district with which we are acquainted, some members were surprised by Hillocks's interesting review (1987) of the effects of various approaches to the teaching of writing. They learned that the intensive study of grammar and mechanics by itself has virtually no effect at all (in studies conducted as far back as one hundred years!). Modeling of writing devices had an average effect size of about 0.22, with "sentence combining" at 0.35 from the intermediate grades on. The highest effect size (0.57) was from well-implemented "inquiry" approaches to the teaching of writing. The inquiry approaches required more staff development for a good implementation, which helped the faculties grapple with the relationships among curriculum implementation, needed staff development, and the focus of school improvement energy when the more effective strategies were selected.

The Southwood School (Chapters 3 and 5) made good use of this work when it approached the problem of increasing student learning in the area of writing.

THE CORE CURRICULUM AREAS

It is far beyond the scope of this book to provide adequate references to the literature in all the curriculum areas. The previous section, on instructional options, provides an idea of what can be found. There are ample books and journals in each curriculum area that can provide frameworks for looking at the curriculum areas, and an increasing number of analyses from government sources that are designed to help schools and school districts find promising programs to study (see for example Slavin *et al.* 1994a, and Herman and Stringfield 1997). In the United States the National Organizations representing the core academic areas provide "standards" that are backed up with extensive bibliographies on the research and thought on which they are based.

Schools (and school districts and governmental agencies) can generally use help as they approach the task of digging into the literature. The knowledge base is complex and the answers are not simple. Also, there are important problems that have not been "solved," but where the knowledge base can be assembled to develop promising approaches.

An example is the problem of creating literacy curriculums for secondary-level students with poor literacy skills. In the following section we provide excerpts from a paper written for a state department of education to help that department think about – and help its schools think about – literacy for beginning readers and writers in the secondary school. These excerpts are included here because they provide an example of the kind of analysis of the literature that is often needed and the type of commentary that is provided by an expert in the area of concern.

Paper Generated for a State Department of Education

Emily Calhoun

SECTION I: PURPOSE AND PROCESS

The inquiry into the knowledge base reported herein was a search for information about

- the extent and nature of the literacy problem among secondary school students and

- promising approaches to ensuring literacy for all secondary school students.

The overall objective was to gather adequate information to design a program based on the best available knowledge about literacy education. Thus, this concept paper contains

- the results of a search of the literature on literacy education,
- guidelines for the construction of an intensive program for secondary students, and
- the design of a program that we will call LITERACY FOR ALL.

(The name owes its origin to the very effective program for primary students, "Success For All", that was developed at Johns Hopkins University under the leadership of Robert Slavin. See Slavin *et al.* 1996.)

The level of literacy among many secondary school students is a serious problem with serious consequences. In the United States, more than eight million students now enrolled in grades 6 to 12 do not have the level of literacy to profit fully from current secondary education programs. Close to a million and a half leave school or even graduate without the education that will enable them to participate fully in their society, most dramatically in the economic dimension (Mullis *et al.* 1993).

Nearly three decades of extensive programs, such as those for the economically poor, for students having special needs, and for students whose primary language is not English, have failed to alleviate the problem significantly despite the efforts of hundreds of thousands of hard-working and purposeful teachers.

One question asked in this inquiry was whether research on literacy education would provide guidelines for improving the literacy levels of secondary students most in need of assistance. Thankfully, the answer to that question is affirmative; there is considerable research on how to teach reading, a knowledge base that can be used in designing curriculums that will reach secondary students with low levels of literacy and help them move forward into a more literate world.

As part of this inquiry into the knowledge base, reading research and research related to literacy development in general, particularly works published in the last 15 years as well as seminal works from earlier years, were reviewed. About 50 books synthesizing the research were consulted and about 200 studies were examined directly. The findings were sorted for the most reliable descriptions of the nature of the problem and guidelines for curricular and instructional design. These guidelines were synthesized into the Literacy For All program components.

[The paper begins with a discussion of the nature and extent of the literacy problem and an analysis of the reasons the extensive remedial programs have not met their goals. Next, the literature on the nature of literacy and on literacy education is summarized. Third, guidelines synthesized from the research are presented and the components of a research-based literacy-acquisition program are described.]

SECTION 2: COMPETENCE IN LITERACY: THE GOAL AND DIMENSIONS OF THE PROBLEM

[This section presents basic literacy goals for secondary students and an overview of the reading performance of United States secondary students at present.]

Goals

Literacy is defined as using printed and written information to develop one's knowledge, to achieve one's goals, and to function in society. It is one of the ways people make sense of their world both by the acquisition of information and ideas from others and through the process of expressing themselves. Thus literacy involves doing something, not just knowing something. Literate persons can understand and make sense of what others have written, and can communicate well through writing.

Although reading and writing will be given the major emphasis in this paper, literacy has meanings beyond sheer competence in reading and writing. Literacy creates access to opportunity within schools and beyond, and the capability for full participation in a democratic society. Without skill in language use – both oral and written – one's exercise of citizenship is endangered.

Competence in reading is a striking example. Secondary students must be able to read proficiently if they are to proceed successfully through the middle and high school years, if they are to learn through and with the materials used at these levels, and if they are to have full access to educational opportunities after high school.

In terms of the "grade levels" of written materials, high school students need to be able to read effectively the materials that are typical of at least grade 9. At that level they can, with appropriate assistance, productively attack and learn to read materials at higher levels. If students arrive at the middle school with competence much lower than that required to read grade 6 material, they will struggle seriously.

The National Assessment of Educational Progress "Basic Level" for grade 12 states the needed level of competence as follows:

- When reading *informational text*, students should be able to explain the main idea or purpose of a selection, use text information to support a conclusion or make a point, and make logical connections between the ideas in the text and their own background knowledge.
- When reading *practical text*, students should be able to explain its purpose and the significance of specific details or steps.
- When reading *literary text*, students should be able to identify and explain the theme, support their conclusions with information from the text, and make connections between aspects of the text and their own experience (Mullis *et al.* 1993).

Problems in student performance

National reports on the number of adolescents who cannot read at a basic or a proficient level document a massive problem in the general population of secondary students, with even greater deficits for black and Hispanic youth and for the most economically deprived (Mullis *et al.* 1993; NCES 1994).

Poor interpretations of "test scores," particularly percentile ranks, have concealed the magnitude of the achievement problem in reading. For example, if the average percentile rank of students in the sixth grade is at the 50th percentile, about 30 percent of the students are reading at the level of the average fourth grade student or below. Effectively, that means that the instructional materials normally used at grade 6 are beyond their reach for adequate comprehension.

Unless secondary students can read and write effectively – comprehending the textbooks, resource materials, and computer resources that are essential to the curriculum and to expressing themselves in lucid prose – they slowly strangle academically. They feel great frustration and their self-esteem is, figuratively speaking, bombarded. The side effects are terrible in terms of feelings of alienation and attempts to find dignity within the walls of the classroom or school.

While all social woes in the United States cannot be attributed to inability to read, failure to learn to read is still a major predictor of who will drop out of school (Lloyd 1978; Slavin *et al.* 1996; Garnier *et al.* 1997), with all the negative real-life connotations that stigmatize the "dropout." Depending on methods of calculation, the national drop-out rate ranges from 10 to 40 percent. But the sheer number of students lost is more gripping than percentages: in 1990, approximately 1,700,000 persons in the United States aged 16 through 19 had not completed high school and were not currently enrolled in a school program. Also there were 3,900,000 persons aged 16 through 24 who had not graduated from high school and were not enrolled in any form of schooling (Kaufman *et al.* 1992). Around one-third of these dropouts will find jobs, and these jobs will be low-skill, minimum-wage positions (William T. Grant Foundation 1988); few will become productive citizens in today's knowledge-driven society (Banks 1997). Lack of basic literacy and dropping out of school are highly correlated, with the negative consequences of dropping out ranging from limited job opportunities to unemployment to welfare dependency to criminal behavior (Garnier *et al.* 1997).

For an even more dismal perspective on the "outcomes" of the current educational system and the effects of current methods of instruction, take a look at the literacy level of adjudicated juvenile delinquents (Gemignani 1994); or at the literacy rate of youths residing in juvenile centers in Georgia – a rate that averages six grade levels below that of their peers (Atlanta Journal and Constitution 1997); or at the adult prison population where one-half of the prisoners have literacy rates that exclude them from the current labor market, even at the lowest wage levels (Barton and Coley 1996). Students in bleak inner-city backgrounds have to use literacy to climb out of their predicament. Politicians complain about their lack of a "work ethic," but it is almost impossible to develop one when you cannot get a job.

What about those students who do not drop out? How many students remain in school for 12, 13, 14 years and receive their diploma or certificate, but still exit high school without basic literacy skills? Looking at the reading performance of twelfth graders in 1992 on the National Assessment of Educational Progress in Reading, 25 percent of these predominantly 17 through 19-year-olds were reading "Below Basic" on a scale that includes "Advanced, Proficient, and Basic" (Mullis *et al.* 1993), with the 1994 results significantly lower (NAEP Executive Summary 1996). Many of these students who do leave high school with a credential become trapped in minimum-wage jobs and have little inclination or opportunity to pursue advanced training or education. Even for these students who make it through the educational system, a huge self-defeating cycle is at work: the results of the education they have received create an adverse reaction to "schools" or "schooling" of any sort. Unless they improve their literacy and problem-solving skills their social and economic mobility is capped, and they are cut off from productive participation as citizens (Drucker 1989, 1994; National Center on Education and the Economy 1990).

For all large urban districts, two well-documented national trends are of grave concern. First, US schools have been least successful in teaching children from low-income families to read (McGill-Franzen and Allington 1991b; Cooley 1993). Second, of the black youth who remain in school through grade 12, 46 percent cannot read at a basic level; 39 percent of Hispanic youth cannot read at a basic level (Mullis *et al.* 1993). Moving back a few grades to the middle-school level, the National Education Longitudinal Study of eighth graders (National Center for Educational Statistics: NELS 1990, 1991) reports that 6.8 percent of its eighth grade cohort had dropped out of school by 1990. Hispanic and non-Hispanic black students dropped out of the cohort at a rate twice that of their age-peers. The most common reasons cited for dropping out were school-related: "did not like school" (51 percent) or "was failing in school" (40 percent). The only major reason for dropping out that was not school-related was that one-third of the female dropouts from this eighth grade cohort indicated they had dropped out because they were pregnant.

Summary

Without elaborating further, there is clear evidence that the literacy problem is massive. Evidence about reading was emphasized here, but clearly people who cannot read well cannot write well, either, and growth in both goes together.

Also, when such a large proportion of students cannot read well, we can be fairly certain that the rest of the students have not reached the levels of literacy that we desire. To forecast a finding that will be reported later in the paper, programs that change the picture, reaching the students we have been talking about, also dramatically improve the reading/writing complex for all students.

SECTION 3: PROBLEMS WITH CURRENT AND PROPOSED PROGRAMS FOR IMPROVING READING ACHIEVEMENT

Perhaps the most amazing aspect of the massiveness of the reading/writing problem at present is that it exists despite 30 years of effort by federal, state, and local agencies to combat it. We need to examine those attempts and to ensure that current proposals are more effective than past initiatives have been.

We will emphasize the studies of the large-scale efforts to ensure student proficiency in reading.

The large-scale initiatives: what went wrong?

A paragraph from *Opportunity to Learn: Issues of Equity for Poor and Minority Students* (Stevens and Grymes 1993) summarizes the results concisely:

> States have tried graduation course requirements, accountability indicators, student competency testing, teacher competency testing, teacher certification, curriculum revisions, and adoption of new curriculum frameworks. Many states expended tremendous sums of money to implement their reform solutions. Unfortunately, despite all the reform efforts, academic achievement continues to be low for poor and minority students.

We have massive evidence that the many national- and state-funded compensatory programs funded through Chapter I/Title I and special education provisions have not succeeded in teaching a large portion of the school population to read (Allington and McGill-Franzen 1989; Magner 1991; Allington 1994). And district and school-initiated programs have not done any better. A handful of schools have done fairly well, but have not developed transportable solutions.

Why have the enormous federal and state initiatives not done better?

One hypothesis questions the curriculum content and instructional strategies used in many of the compensatory and remedial programs. A number of serious questions have been raised:

- Instruction in many of these programs has been influenced by "the legacy of 'slow it down and make it more concrete'" (Allington 1991).
- Another is the oversimplification of content such that the instruction actually impedes literacy learning (Roehler 1991).
- The time available for students to engage in reading in these remedial programs is often less than that available to their peers because of the emphasis on skills-based instruction instead of reading and on learning reading strategies (Johnston and Allington 1991).
- Instruction for good and poor readers frequently varies: Poor readers

often experience lessons with far less emphasis on the final
performance (reading), much more drill and/or many materials
focussed on fragments of literacy performance, and reinforcement of
their old, less effective strategies, while better readers are being taught
more effective reading strategies (Allington 1983; Applebee *et al.* 1988).

• The less responsive students are to the curriculum and instruction they
are experiencing, the greater the tendency of the educational system to
fragment their curriculum and daily lesson content, focussing
instruction on the lowest-level subskills and losing sight of the student
performance goals of reading and writing as communication (Pearson
1992: 1080).

• Essentially, remedial programs have taken a "synthesis of skills"
approach, teaching phonetic and structural analysis, comprehension
skills, and "vocabulary" on a piece-by-piece basis with the idea that the
students will at some time be able to "put the pieces together" and
read and write. The better students are given more opportunity to put
all the pieces together as they read material at their level, and more
opportunity to build the concepts necessary for word recognition and
comprehension.

• Instruction in writing is subject to the same criticism. Middle-school
and secondary students who cannot read or cannot read proficiently
have difficulty communicating through writing also. Looking at the
nature of instruction and feedback for the least proficient writers, more
of the instructional feedback for these students appears to emphasize
grammar and mechanics, not the message the student is trying to
communicate (Applebee *et al.* 1990; Gentile 1992). And as in reading,
low-performing students have less time to write (Applebee *et al.* 1994).
The program for the more proficient students tends to be more
balanced, with more time to write and an emphasis on communicating
the message as well as using standard grammatical conventions.

In sum, the analysts of the large-scale programs believe that these
programs have not utilized the large quantities of reading and writing at
the developmental level of the student that are necessary for the
development and consolidation of literacy skills. When students are
placed in remedial programs, the amounts of reading and writing they do
are often actually reduced in favor of an unbalanced emphasis on skills
taught in isolation from the acts of reading and writing and, worse,
taught in a piecemeal fashion.

Present proposals to improve these programs

As educators from the state department to the classroom struggle to find
ways of teaching more students to read well, the historical tendency has
been and continues to be a recurrent move toward curriculum
documents and instructional programs that focus on tangible aspects of
the conventions of language instead of focussing on learning how to
communicate through reading and writing.

Federal education officials are as stuck as state department, district, and school staff. They are concerned about the fragmentation of programs, services, and the student day; about the limited responsibility many school staff take for student progress in these programs; and about the limited effects on academic achievement of most remedial and compensatory programs. However, the efforts to reconceptualize large-scale federal programs are yielding recommendations and descriptions of programs that are very similar to what is not working now (Commission on Chapter I, 1993; US Department of Education 1993) and what has not worked in the past. The current federal shifts to *collaboration* and *inclusion* (Allington and Cunningham 1996) are not likely to yield student-achievement benefits unless instruction from both "regular" classroom teachers and "special" teachers changes, which seems unlikely despite the renewed federal emphasis on staff development for teachers working in these programs (1994 Reauthorization of Title I).

Under different labels in the last two decades, collaboration (*coordination*) and inclusion (*mainstreaming*) were heralded as operational solutions to improving student performance for students in remedial and/or special programs. In the late 1970s, as part of the effort to improve student achievement for Title I students, many districts held work sessions for school staff to learn how to "coordinate" curriculum and instruction between regular classroom teachers and special teachers. Many meetings and much documentation ensued, but little changed in terms of student performance in reading.

The current rationale surrounding inclusion sounds much like that for its predecessor, "mainstreaming": a healthier social environment for students (least restrictive, heterogeneous) and improved achievement for students believed to have special needs. In addition, many district and school personnel see it as a way to reduce class size, and many people – both educators and members of the general public – seem to automatically equate smaller class size with improved student achievement. However, there is much evidence to indicate that reducing class size by itself leads to small gains in student achievement, gains that could easily be surpassed by implementing a structured reading program or by expanding the range of instructional strategies used by teachers.

For example, the frequently cited Tennessee statewide study reported the largest class size effects ever found: at the end of third grade (after four years of small classes of around 15 students), the effect sizes in reading were 0.24; in a follow-up study at the end of the fourth grade, the effect size was 0.14. A similar statewide study in Indiana found far smaller effects at the end of third grade, a reading effect size of 0.06. Most other studies – South Carolina, New York City, and Austin, Texas – found effect sizes similar to Indiana's. There may be other reasons for reducing class size, such as improved teacher morale; however, in many settings it is unlikely to improve student achievement in reading, while implementation of a structured reading program accompanied by staff development and on-site support, such as Success For All, yields effect sizes in reading of 0.43 at the end of third grade (Slavin *et al.* 1994b).

There is another problem with inclusion as a solution to poor achievement in reading. If it is implemented as a way to avoid "pull-out" programs for students in remedial reading classes, many students will simply be returned to the same curriculum and the same methods of instruction that were unable to prevent their poor performance in the first place. And while class size may be reduced schoolwide, the classes for many of these students will be larger than their remedial classes.

Inclusion is probably a good idea socially. However, for students who are in special programs primarily for reading deficiencies, the classroom instruction they return to needs to be strong enough to help them make regular progress into the world of literacy. Currently, this is unlikely, for quality instructional delivery is missing in too many classrooms (Sirotnik 1983, 1987; Stevens and Grymes 1993), and the use of research-based practices in the teaching of reading comprehension appears to be extremely limited (Richardson *et al.* 1991; Lloyd and Anders 1994).

Something similar is happening at the primary level with the renewed emphasis on "phonemic awareness" (Adams 1990; Copeland *et al.* 1994) and on teaching students letters and letter sounds before teaching them words. If the hierarchy-of-subskills approach is followed rigidly, the instruction students are receiving may well inhibit literacy development (Pearson 1992).

What is the probability that the renewed emphasis by federal education officials on staff development will improve the reading achievement of at-risk students? The 1994 Reauthorization of Title I allows schoolwide programs to benefit all students and can be used to provide extensive professional development for all staff on site. The idea is to expand teachers' knowledge of content and the range of instructional strategies they employ with these students.

The flexibility of using more funds for staff development and of providing staff development for everyone has great potential for improving student performance in reading . . . if district and school personnel will design high-quality staff development focussed on improving student and staff learning. The current likelihood of this occurring in most settings is infinitesimal. Although much is known about designing staff development for student achievement (Joyce and Showers 1995), little of this process knowledge is implemented at the school or district level (Goldenberg and Gallimore 1991; Richardson and Hamilton 1994).

Whether we look at the results of these compensatory and special programs (and the millions of dollars and thousands of people they have added to school districts across the country) or to the stability of instructional methodology in high-school reading programs over the past 50 years (Barry 1997), what we are doing is not working for a large portion of our school population.

Altogether, too many of the current reform initiatives are based on old "solutions" with poor performance histories, simply renamed or extended; or based on good ideas unlikely to be implemented with fidelity in most schools and school districts. While some would call this "same old, same old," or "complacency with how things are done" (Stedman 1995), the current operation of education in most districts and schools tends to domesticate any initiative (Huberman and Miles 1986). Such domestication tends to keep instruction at the recitation or lecture/recitation level and to keep student–teacher interactions similar across decades and across reform movements. In a sense, regardless of the reform movement of the moment, the interactions between teachers and students and the results from "behind the classroom door" look much the same.

A large part of what keeps the achievement of at-risk students so low may well be

1 the stability of the educational system as it operates in most schools and districts, so that new programs and initiatives have cosmetic impact but in reality are simply absorbed into present school and classroom practices;
2 the lack of knowledge about teaching reading, particularly at the secondary level;
3 the lack of quality instructional delivery;
4 the ideological battles engaged in by the "experts" in the fields of reading/language arts;
5 the tendency to simply "buy a person" or program that has value for students who are not responding to instruction in the "regular" classroom; and
6 the lack of immediate, professional horror that after one to 13 years, of five- and six-hour days, 180 days a year, at least 25 percent of the students in most large school districts still have difficulty with basic literacy.

In sum, we have a massive classroom, school, district, and nationwide problem. We have to overcome a condition that is well documented:

• If students do not learn to read effectively by the end of the primary grades, most are not reached by present remedial curriculums or the most commonly used instructional strategies, even the provisions made through established ESL (English as a Second Language) and Title I/Chapter I programs that provide for the services of teachers who can work with them in small groups and as individuals.
• About 30 percent of middle-school and high-school students are in serious difficulty with respect to reading.
• Fewer than half of all students read daily outside of school; 30 percent of fourth, eighth, and twelfth graders report never reading to reading something "monthly" (Foertsch 1992).

We need to make strong and skillful attempts to help all children learn to read well enough to handle the materials they encounter in school and the materials they will encounter if they are to be productive citizens after they leave school. We know very early in the schooling experience of most children those for whom the system is not working. We generally know by the end of first grade those students who are not learning to read, or in other words, those students who are not responding to the instruction the system is providing (Juel 1988); and we know that the correlation of their reading performance with the probability they will drop out of school is significant at the 0.001 level (Garnier *et al.* 1997); we are certain by the end of third grade (Lloyd 1978; Juel 1988); we see the cumulative results of this lack of literacy at the beginning of middle school; and we see the tremendous number of students who drop out in grades 9 and 10.

Operating as we are with current educational and instructional practices, the approximately 4,500,000 adults working with 41,000,000 students in US public elementary and secondary schools do not interrupt this dismal picture (Snyder and Hoffman 1992) – a picture that has been clear since the middle of first grade. The fault does not lie in these children. They do not come to school as "failures"; but the system has clearly allowed them to become such by the time they leave sixth grade.

We need powerful literacy instruction for our "at-risk" secondary students, and this instruction needs to be different from what they have experienced the previous six or seven years and intense enough to change their learning history. Regrettably, there is no simple, easy-to-implement, self-instructional program for students who cannot read and write effectively (or, for that matter, for those who can read effectively and need to extend their competence). And there are very few schools that have solved the problem and can be emulated (Allington and Cunningham 1996; Slavin *et al.* 1996). Attacking the problem requires that we go where few have gone and, if we succeed, develop an approach that can be used in many settings. Our task is defined by the need to build generically effective programs that can be used with a wide spectrum of students.

Constructing a better future

There is a considerable knowledge base available on which we can design programs that are very likely to reach those secondary-education students who have low levels of literacy. In these next pages we examine the literature, identify dimensions of the acquisition of literacy for secondary students, and suggest the structure of a course that is built on the current research.

SECTION 4: GENERAL PRINCIPLES AND STRUCTURE

We now turn to the process of generating more promising hypotheses from the research, attempting to design a curricular/instructional approach with a higher probability of success.

Importantly, constructing a fresh attempt has to begin with an acknowledgment that there is a problem and a belief that curriculum and instruction can solve it. Thus, we recognize that about one-fourth or more of middle-school and high-school students are having serious problems in reading. Something must be done immediately because the consequences of lack of literacy are severe. Also the major federal, state, city and district initiatives to help these students make progress in literacy are not working in most settings. Moreover, the secondary schedule was not designed to teach reading; the secondary curriculum has not been set up to teach reading; and very few secondary teachers are prepared to teach developing readers.

Within that context we have to develop a practical solution – a substantial literacy effort at the middle-school and high-school levels. In the long run, all teachers probably should be prepared to teach literacy, not just for these "developing" readers but for all readers, and to teach each subject from a literacy stance. In the short run, we probably need to design a substantial course with a sharply focussed literacy curriculum that will develop skill in and regular use of reading and writing.

How much time is needed for a substantial course?

At least a double-period course is needed. Time is an important variable, as is practice, which cannot occur unless there is enough time for it.

Time

To consider time as a factor, we draw heavily on John Carroll's (1963, 1977, 1989) model for student learning that was based on intensive studies of measures of intelligence and achievement. A major variable in the model was the provision of adequate time for learners to master any given set of objectives. Our problem becomes one of estimating the time that a course for beginning or low-developmental readers will need to maximize its chances for success.

The very effective Success For All program in the primary grades is a very good source (Slavin *et al.* 1996). We recently had contact with its implementation in a school that is generally regarded as fairly good in a district that is also well thought of. One of the dimensions of Success For All is an uninterrupted period of 90 minutes per day devoted to the study of reading. The curriculum is designed to avoid "busywork," and to ensure that each student is reading, receiving instruction, or working with instructional materials requiring reading during the entire period. The principal of the school in question studied the extent to which the study of reading was affected by the institution of the 90-minute period. She reported that the increase in time was threefold for the average student compared with the customary curriculum that was being followed before Success For All was implemented. Slavin and his colleagues make similar estimates in the schools where they have implemented Success For All.

Such an increase in time is not by any means the only dimension of that program. But it is a reasonable assumption that the tripling of the amount of focussed instructional time devoted to a curriculum area partly accounts for the outstanding success it has enjoyed.

If a well-articulated curriculum using 90 minutes per day worked for "at-risk" primary students, are there implications for such a course for adolescents? We believe there are. The adolescents will have larger listening–speaking vocabularies, despite their difficulty in learning to read. Counterbalancing that advantage, they will have the disadvantage of having developed aversions to reading and writing. We estimate that a course of 90–135 minutes per day will give many of them (assuming a powerful curriculum) the time necessary to learn to read adequately within about a year.

Naturalistic research on teaching supports the importance of time to a considerable extent. There was surprise by some when Brophy and Good (1986) recommended that teachers employ "whole-class" teaching in the core academic subjects. However, their observation came from their research, which indicated advantages in student learning *because*, they speculated, many teachers who used small-group methods did not know how to organize the students for productive learning activities when they were not working directly with them. Thus, eschewing the fact that effective ways of organizing students for productive independent work exist, the fact remains that there was an increase in instructional time in many classrooms when "whole-class" teaching was employed. The results were not nearly the dramatic ones achieved by Success For All, but they were there.

Practice

Time is obviously related to opportunity to practice using new knowledge and skills. What is not generally understood is that effective practice is not simply the mechanical repetition of skills or rote enunciation of knowledge at the same level at which they are first learned. Effective practice elevates and consolidates skills. Skills in reading are a clear example of skills that need elevation and consolidation through practice that follows instruction. When students are first introduced to the skills for identifying meanings of words through contextual analysis, they need to apply those skills through considerable amounts of reading, delving for meanings across a variety of contexts and, when those contexts fail, turning to reference materials. Research on Just Read, a program that increases out-of-school independent reading, illustrated the effects of practice: gains in comprehension were nearly doubled in schools that established an "at-home" reading habit as compared with schools that increased amounts of reading to a lesser extent (Joyce and Wolf 1996).

The area of writing is another example. First, wide reading appears to be essential to the development of skill in writing. Quality of writing in Just Read schools provides an example, for gains in scores on quality of writing were twice the national average (Applebee *et al.* 1990), even without an intervention in the writing curriculum. Second, practice in writing is as essential to the consolidation and elevation of skills as is practice in reading. If, say, the study of metaphoric expressions is to be incorporated in writing, that transfer cannot be accomplished simply by learning the definition of metaphor and learning to recognize examples. The students have to transform that knowledge into skill through considerable amounts of practice in writing and in analyzing the metaphoric content of material that is read. In the course of that practice, knowledge will be elevated and skill will increase.

In a recent project on writing, it was discovered that students in the 150 elementary classrooms of one district were being asked to compose an original piece only about once every three weeks – about ten times per year, aside from free writing in journals. During the project, the teachers studied how to help students learn literary devices and grammatical conventions inductively, but they also greatly increased the amounts of writing done by the children to five or six times the amounts before the project began. Gains in quality of writing ranged from two to six times higher than expected from the baseline year's growth (Joyce *et al.* 1996).

Thus time and opportunity for practice in many ways go together, but it is not simply a matter of practice: it is practice with the clear goal of consolidation and elevation of skills and knowledge.

How can time be provided? A block of time, the equivalent of two or three instructional periods (90–135 minutes), needs to be provided each day for the students in middle schools who are reading below the fifth grade level and students in high school who are reading below the eighth grade level.

There are two sources for this time. One is time currently being used for electives; this time can be consolidated into a daily block and devoted to the Literacy For All course. Such a solution is practical in all settings and can easily be arranged administratively. The other is to waive courses that are currently required but are not among the core academic subjects. This solution is also administratively feasible. In some settings, the use of "elective" time will suffice. In others, there may have to be a combination of time sources.

Guidelines to the structure and process of the course

The research and the major analyses of research in the literacy field provide a number of principles that can guide the development of the course:

- a multidimensional approach: teaching several aspects of literacy simultaneously and using multiple teaching/learning strategies;
- an inquiry orientation: teaching students how to learn and how to construct knowledge;
- a collaborative orientation: teaching students to learn together and support one another's efforts;
- a formative-assessment orientation: building an assessment system that provides teachers, students, and parents with regular information about progress and programs so that goals can be clarified, achievements celebrated, and diagnosis of problems understood;
- explicit instruction: use of modeling and demonstration to build knowledge and skill;
- metacognitive control: developing students' knowledge and use of their own cognitive resources.

Let us consider each of these in turn.

A multidimensional approach to literacy development

The research on how people learn to read and write indicates that the process of learning to read and write entails several dimensions of learning. Each dimension leads toward an aspect of competence that is integrated with the others, but has to be addressed specifically during the time when the student is moving toward literacy. Thus teachers or program developers, when selecting what students will do and what processes they will engage in, think about both the learning dimensions and the competencies they are seeking to develop. The results of these decisions yield the curriculum content students will experience during the year or course, and this content determines how class time will be used.

While there is much debate in the field of education on how to develop literacy (Chall 1967/1983; MacGinitie 1991; Dreher and Slater 1992; Smith 1992), the focus in this report is on helping students become more skilled readers and writers and on helping them use reading and writing skills as learning tools in school. With these performance goals in mind, the curriculum needs to reflect a balanced or integrated approach to developing literacy (Tiedt *et al.* 1989; Shanahan 1990; Heller 1991; Fielding and Pearson 1994; Moore *et al.* 1994; Weaver, in press; Winograd and Bridge 1995): students engage in and develop increased competence in reading, writing, speaking, listening, and thinking, all simultaneously.

A streamlined, but broad-based, literacy acquisition curriculum for this course would address the following dimensions of literacy acquisition:

- reading extensively at the developed level, nonfiction and fiction;
- building sight vocabulary for reading and writing;
- learning to use phonetic, structural, and contextual analysis to identify and form words;
- writing extensively to apply language skills, to share ideas, to think, and to consolidate information;
- developing skill in and understanding of comprehension and composition processes.

This course relies heavily on the teacher, not on materials or commercial programs. Much interactive instruction will be needed as teachers work to bring these students into the world of literacy: instruction that involves almost continual modeling and demonstration of learning strategies, and the use of print and continual formal and informal assessment of student performance in reading and writing. As we look at the dimensions of literacy instruction, the importance of teacher–student interaction will become more and more apparent.

Developing language literacy through inquiry

Inquiry-oriented, inductive approaches to learning in reading, writing, and other curriculum areas have been effective in generating long-term knowledge and skills (Brophy and Good 1986; Hillocks 1986, 1987; Sharan and Shachar 1988; Carpenter *et al.* 1989; Brophy 1992; Joyce and Calhoun 1996; Joyce and Weil 1996). Applying the information from our collective knowledge base to this literacy development program means that instruction must be designed so that students become active inquirers: seeking materials of interest to read; identifying words they do not know; studying the writing of "expert" authors and their own writing, and identifying qualities and literary devices they wish to acquire; building their reading comprehension skills; using multiple sources of information; using reading and writing as learning tools. The structure of lessons should minimize passive participation and maximize students' participation in their own progress.

Developing collaborative learning communities
The development of each class group into a cooperative disciplined community inquiring into reading, writing, and its own thought processes is supported not only by the research on cooperative learning for social benefits and improvements in student achievement (Johnson and Johnson 1981; Sharan 1990; Slavin and Madden 1995) but also by the social context of reading and writing as communication (Bloome 1987; Shanahan 1990; Tierney and Shanahan 1991; Myers 1992) and by the sociocognitive nature of reading and writing, i.e. "that language learning is ultimately an interactive process, that cognitive factors are influenced by context, and that they, in turn, affect the meanings that are produced" (Langer 1986).

Collaborative learning communities generate more learning than do isolated individuals who are not part of cooperative communities; however, most students will need to be taught how to inquire together. Organizing students into study teams whose members strive together for achievement has been effective in increasing student achievement, particularly with students who have had little success and display low academic self-esteem in an area. Teachers on this course or program will need to develop cooperative communities, large and small, that strive for high achievement and will need to establish structures that encourage individual students to strive for high achievement. For students with poor learning histories, instructional design that engages students in exploring literacy and building a literate community has much promise (Alvermann *et al.* 1996).

Frequent assessment of growth in reading and writing and immediate use of the results to select content and design lessons
Assessment operates as an inquiry into language literacy. Teachers and students engage in formative diagnostic study of student skill in reading and writing, the assessment of reading being more formal and frequent.

In successful reading improvement programs whose results have been published and that have a record of transferability (they work across school sites, districts, and geographical regions), and whose emphasis has been on working with students who are "at risk" in the current educational system, assessment of performance is frequent and the results are used by teachers and students to plan the next moves (Pinell 1989; Pinnell *et al.* 1994; Slavin *et al.* 1994a, 1996). The effective schools' research also indicates the need for awareness of current level of performance, clear articulation of immediate and long-term goals, and the design of instruction to turn those goals into reality (Levine and Lezotte 1990; Levine 1991).

To implement a rapid literacy development program, teachers and students need to live a continuous cycle of studying performance and designing actions that facilitate individual and group progress. In fact, both teachers and students work much like good action or applied researchers. For example: what is the current status of reading performance? What is the reading level and what does it need to be? Which comprehension skills need work? Are there word recognition skills that need to be mastered? The traditional instructional-unit cycle of identifying current performance, setting goals, engaging in actions to attain those goals, and assessing performance again is spinning continuously at the whole-class level, the small ad-hoc group level, and the individual level.

This way of thinking about instructional design is not new. Most teachers in the United States studied this instructional-design cycle as content in either curriculum or instruction courses during their undergraduate or graduate programs, or both. Nevertheless, the college/university instruction did not yield performance in the field, for in most classrooms, data are not used formally and formatively to design instruction on a daily and weekly basis (Sirotnik 1987).

However, frequent assessment, even frequent "authentic" assessment, will not lead to student achievement unless the results are used meaningfully by the teacher in the design of lessons and activities. (This is not true for highly active self-learners who can and will teach themselves anything, but few students in this program will be active academic self-learners.) Over the years, many commercial programs marketed to "remediate" students in reading and math have been designed using the principles of continuous formative assessment for identifying objectives, materials, and activities. (For example, Hoffman Reading Program; P.K. Yonge; High Intensity Learning Systems in Reading and Math, HILS; using old and current NDN catalogs, the list could be a page long.) The results of these programs have been variable, and many students have not become successful readers even after several years of participation.

While the assessment stance recommended here is well grounded, there is debate among language-arts authors and specialists, measurement specialists, and educators in general about how to assess literacy. The same muddy water that exists in the recommendations about how to teach reading exists in the recommendations about how to assess progress in reading. While the current movement toward authentic or alternative assessment has potential for bringing teachers to better use of assessment results, there is a lax and "anything goes" approach in many alternative assessment proposals that make them unlikely to generate better instruction or better achievement, although they consume massive amounts of teacher and student time (Harp 1991; Tierney et al. 1991). In "Authentic Assessment of Reading and Writing," Calfee (1992) stated the dilemma succinctly: "The situation has the makings for a battle royal."

Much of the rhetoric and evidence surrounding "authentic assessment" sounds similar to that surrounding the move in the 1980s to "whole language": with authentic assessment, the teacher and students can do what really needs to be done; this is much more real; student achievement will increase. As with whole language, authentic/alternative assessment has potential for instructional improvement accompanied by increased student achievement, but it is a low probability shot as it is currently supported and implemented in most schools.

Our best bet (and belief about the best use of time) is to make assessment a natural part of daily instruction. For optimal progress, both teachers and students need a mindset of live inquiry into current performance.

Except for formal, somewhat standard checks on progress in reading and writing, most of the assessment that occurs should simply be a part of daily instruction, with both teacher and students observing or "noticing" areas of difficulty or areas of performance that are ready to be elevated to the next level. For example, in terms of difficulties, the teacher notices that many students are confusing interesting details with the main idea, or that many students do not know how to announce their topics in informative writing; or a student notices a key word whose meaning s/he does not know and records it for study in her or his vocabulary file, and the teacher notices in scanning many of the students' vocabulary files that most students are having difficulty with the same three or four words; a student realizes that he is not putting in enough reading time to improve his performance.

For areas that are ready to be elevated, the teacher may notice during discussions that many students are able to identify the topic and have some sense of the main idea in informative passages from textbooks or tradebooks ("real books"), but they are not able to see or use the organizational devices the authors have provided to make the relationships among these ideas clear, as in text structures that use cause and effect, comparison and/or contrast, sequence, explanation followed by a series of examples; or a student who has gathered information from three or four sources and is pleased with what she has discovered, recognizes she is struggling to consolidate her ideas in writing.

In sum, using assessment to help improve the reading and writing achievement of at risk students works best

1 when teachers, students, and parents know as clearly as possible where the students stand with respect to performance,
2 when progress is studied continuously,
3 when results are used for individual, group, and self-instruction, and
4 when results have meaning in terms of acquired skills and knowledge and are celebrated as such.

The role of modeling in developing knowledge and skill
As in the use of formative assessment to guide individual and group instruction, modeling and demonstration are old ideas based on good

learning theory. Essentially, instruction in complex skills needs to include demonstration to be effective.

Looking at learning theory (Gagne 1975; Gagne and Briggs 1979) in relation to complex cognitive tasks, such as reading or writing, some major instructional moves are missing from instruction in many classrooms (Sirotnik 1983), just as they were missing from the commercial programs described above. These moves include modeling of the tasks and its processes, discussions and explanations that raise the level of cognitive processing, and practice with interactive analysis of performance. Modeling or demonstrations without the discussions and without practice and reflection is far less effective, for the cognitive processes of the skilled reader or writer will still be invisible to many students. At first, the teacher does most of the modeling, leads the discussions and teaches students how to participate in focussed discussions, and serves as the coach in analyzing performance; eventually, if the instruction is working, students will perform many of these "teaching roles" as they help themselves learn.

For full implementation of this principle, teachers will need to model their use of specific instructional strategies in their own learning. When teachers continuously demonstrate and explain their use of the same teaching/learning strategies as they are teaching students, they provide a sharp example of the utility of course content. In the context of language arts, students can "see" how a literate person functions and how increased literacy can expand one's life and perspective.

Developing students' knowledge and use of their own cognitive resources
Many secondary students who have not learned to read and write well are resourceful persons in their daily lives inside and outside of school; one of the aims of a rapid literacy-development program is to have students use their natural cognitive resources for academic purposes.

Research on a variety of models of teaching in several curriculum areas (Johnson and Johnson 1990; Pressley *et al.* 1995a) and research in reading and writing indicate that students learn more when they have an understanding of the learning process and how to use it (Palinscar and Brown 1984; Heller 1986; Garner 1987; Pressley *et al.* 1987; Englert *et al.* 1991; Guthrie and Pressley 1992). In other words, student achievement is enhanced when learners are made "insiders" to their own cognitive processes and can intentionally direct their efforts toward knowledge and performance goals.

A major difference between good and poor readers lies in their understanding of their own comprehension processes: poor readers are less likely to understand lapses in comprehension, and when they do detect them, they are less able to repair them (Palinscar *et al.* 1993).

A major difference between expert and novice writers is their ability to draw on knowledge-telling and knowledge-transforming strategies; in other words, the latter do not know how to scaffold or present their message (Bereiter and Scardamalia 1987a; Englert *et al.* 1989; Flower 1989). For example, to meet the demands of written communication at the secondary level, students must select appropriate and sufficient content; employ suitable text structures to convey that content; build on what is known and reflect such construction of meaning; engage in cooperative discourse with an indeterminate audience; and constantly monitor the message they are developing (Rubin 1984). Novice writers do not have these cognitive processing skills.

These metacognitive processes are similar whether students are native English speakers or English-as-a-second-language speakers (Langer *et al.* 1990; Fitzgerald 1995).

Better readers, who also tend to be better writers, are fundamentally better thinkers throughout the reading and writing processes; they have the cognitive control that the poorer readers need. Although poor readers and writers do not have metacognitive control of the processes of reading and writing, they can acquire this control – and must do so to advance rapidly and be equipped to learn on their own. Instruction in metacognitive skills needs to be taught explicitly, modeled continuously, accompanied by much practice (Heller 1986; Duffy *et al.* 1988; Hermann 1990; Dole *et al.* 1991; Englert *et al.* 1991).

In sum, these six principles together lead to the structure and process of the course: a multidimensional program that addresses the dimensions of literacy through multiple teaching/learning strategies; an inquiry-oriented approach to literacy learning; a collaborative orientation whereby a learning community is developed; frequent assessment that shapes instructional actions; modeling complex processes; and using student knowledge and developing metacognitive control of the learning process. Essentially, we are trying to stack the instructional deck for student achievement: implementation of any one of these six principles will elevate the probability of student learning; implementation of all six increases the odds accordingly.

COMMENTARY

The above excerpts are only about a third of the complete report, not including a bibliography of well over 100 items. We hope they illustrate how much energy is needed for thorough connection to the knowledge base. And you can see that the report is leading toward a solution that will depend on considerable staff development and the kind of formative evaluation described in Chapter 5. Very few secondary teachers have been prepared in preservice education to teach beginning readers and writers, and when they appear, much learning is in order.

Teachers solve all the instructional problems they can with their existing repertoire of teaching/learning strategies. When there is a serious problem that affects a whole school, serious study and new repertoire are indicated. And in this case, the problem is a virtual plague that affects many, many schools.

7 Embedding staff development: living in a state of learning

In this chapter we review the history of staff development and the design of training to support changes in classroom practice. Then we offer our best current recommendations for establishing the embedded study of curriculum and instruction: thoughts about the design of the workplace and the content of staff development and thoughts about the use of peer coaching to support staff and student learning.

As you read this chapter, think especially about Hypotheses 5, 6, and 7:

Hypothesis 5: Staff development, embedded in the workplace, increases inquiry into new practices and the implementation of school improvement initiatives.

Hypothesis 6: Staff development, structured as an inquiry, both fuels energy and results in initiatives that have greater effects.

Hypothesis 7: Building small work groups connected to the larger community but responsible for one another will increase the sense of belonging that reduces stress, isolation, and feelings of alienation.

A HISTORY OF STAFF DEVELOPMENT

When the common school was created in America, there was no vision of creating a workplace for teachers or administrators that ensured life-long learning or a collaborative, collegial, self-renewing culture in schools. The teachers were, for the most part, the oldest unmarried literate women in the community. They "heard lessons" in every grade and subject. After a few years they started their families and were succeeded by other young women until, in their turn, they married and their places as teachers were taken by the next in line. Teaching was not a career and the idea of continuing study by teachers was not an issue.

In the middle of the nineteenth century in the United States preservice teacher education began to develop, largely in "normal" schools. These offered one-year training courses, later extended to two years. Their curriculum followed the common curriculum of the schools and consisted of courses and practice designed to help the prospective teachers teach the curriculum as it existed with the methods then being used – largely recitations and presentations. About the same time schools became larger, but the conditions of work changed little. After a very short period of preservice education, teachers were assigned to classrooms where they worked in virtual isolation, albeit under a shared roof. Instructional duties were to consume the day. No time was set aside in the workday for either staff development or collaborative planning, let alone school renewal. Implicitly, the society envisioned a barebone, static curriculum that would change very little over the course of a career in education, so continuing education of teachers was not in the consciousness of the planners, and teaching was considered to be an individual pursuit rather than a collective activity. Various reform-minded educators, particularly Horace Mann and Henry Barnard, disagreed and believed that the schools were out of date and needed to change radically. They made some difference in particular settings, but mainstream practice continued uninterrupted for the most part, except that corporal punishment was gradually reduced and psychological and philosophical orientations toward students were gradually incorporated into the normal school curriculums.

For many decades efficiency was viewed as a problem of the capability of the students rather than the educational system. A third or more of the students did not learn to read and write effectively and dropped out, or waited out the years until they could do so. The children of the economically poor often left school to contribute to the family income. The more effective and affluent students could aspire to higher education, but before World War II only about 10 percent received any form of higher education, including those enrolled in one- and two-year programs in fields such as teaching and nursing. Teaching was not considered to be a profession, even after teacher education became available. Nor was entry into normal schools selective. Teacher education was so ineffective that a major study in Pennsylvania showed that the academic level of graduating teachers was approximately equal to that of graduating high school students. *Half* of the teachers scored lower than the students they were about to teach.

Not until the end of World War II was it generally accepted that teachers should have a college education, and even then continuing education was a matter of taking a couple of courses every five years to renew a certificate. Not until the late 1960s did the last of the normal-school graduates retire, and all teachers have baccalaureate degrees. In Canada, elementary school teachers were prepared in "grade 13" programs (one year after high-school graduation) until the 1970s.

About 25 years ago policymakers became aware that without some investment in staff development and school renewal, societal changes would – in fact, already had – outrun the capability of the schools. It was clear by then that the 20 years of investment in curriculum development designed to modernize content and teaching approaches had largely failed for lack of staff development (Goodlad and Klein 1970). Efforts began to stimulate staff development through school systems and universities. These efforts were initially led at the federal level through Teacher Corps and the Teacher Centers program. States gradually began to fund districts for staff development that was largely, but not entirely, connected to specific curricular interests, as in the case of instruction in reading in the inner cities. A few school districts, such as Montgomery County, Maryland, invested local funds in staff development and school improvement, but those districts were the exception. In nearly all school districts, federal and state resources were a far larger part of the staff development budget than were local resources in nearly all districts.

We can see the last 25 years as a first-phase effort in the staff development area, and the effort is reminiscent of a steam locomotive trying to get started, except that the social-policy engine driving staff development was much less muscular than was needed. A full conceptualization of a thriving system of support for individual and staff growth did not exist, and the partial conceptualizations that were available (Joyce *et al.* 1972) were largely ignored. Lightly funded, piecemeal efforts were plentiful, many directed at pressing problems, such as discipline, classroom management, drug prevention, and safety. Categorical programs, establishing special services for the economically poor and underachieving, were initiated, but the basic structure of the schools remained unchanged; teachers still worked in isolation and little time for individual and collective professional development was provided within the paid days of teachers. The caretakers of most initiatives, including those generated in schools, had to struggle against the constraints of a workplace where the education of educators was (and largely remains) a foreign entity.

All times are good times to assess where we are and build on what we have. The current period is particularly propitious. Through awareness and thoughtful actions, we can re-create the workplace of educators, creating evolutionary schools that will serve society as a model of continuing education.

A STAFF DEVELOPMENT SCENARIO: LEONARDO HIGH SCHOOL

What kinds of support do teachers need in order to implement new curriculum plans? Let's examine another scenario. A team of teachers is learning Synectics – which trains students to use analogies to seek solutions to problems and to rethink concepts – as a new teaching strategy for their department.

The eight members of the English department of Leonardo High School are studying new teaching strategies which they are considering using in some of their courses. The current model of teaching on their agenda is

Synectics (Gordon 1961), designed to stimulate metaphoric thinking. Several members of the department think Synectics will be useful both to encourage creative writing and in the study of fiction and poetry. They began their exploration by reading W. J. J. Gordon's book *Synectics* (1961) and then a trainer skilled in using Synectics came to the school, demonstrated the strategy several times, and held discussions with the teachers.

They also watched a videotaped lecture of Gordon explaining the theory behind Synectics, and visited a school in Stockton where two teachers had been using Synectics for the last two or three years. They then planned lessons based on the Synectics procedure and tried them out on one another. They taught each other lessons in creative writing and in the analysis of poetry. They examined the use of metaphor in Ionesco and Stoppard plays.

Each teacher practiced the teaching strategy several times with the other teachers before trying it out with students. Then, working in teams of two, they began to try it out, first with the most able students in their elective writing classes. One team member taught and the other offered constructive criticism; then they switched places. Sometimes they taught together. Each teacher practiced several times with the "coaching partner" present to reflect on progress and to offer suggestions about how to improve the next trial.

Then, still working in teams, they began to work the teaching strategy into a couple of their courses, selecting places where they thought that it would be the most productive and where they were highly likely to have success. Not surprisingly, they found that the hardest part of using a new model of teaching was less in learning what to do as a teacher than in teaching the students to relate to the model. For example, parts of the Synectics strategy ask the students to generate "personal analogies" such as being a snowman, tennis ball, dinosaur, lawnmower, toothbrush, etc. A few of the students were puzzled by the instruction to "be a toothbrush and describe how you feel and what you think about your users." It took time before some of the students responded smoothly to the procedures and became comfortable with them. Also, some of the variations on the Synectics model asked the students to share their writing publicly – at best an uncomfortable procedure for some of the students.

As time passed, the Leonardo team found it useful to reread parts of Gordon's book and to study the videotapes made by the trainer and other teachers who were more experienced users of Synectics. They obtained the consultative services of the Synectics trainer for another day. She reviewed the theory and gave them some tips for practicing and coaching one another.

The Leonardo team are engaged in the serious study of expanding instructional repertoire (Joyce and Showers 1995; Joyce and Calhoun 1996; Joyce and Weil 1996; Joyce *et al.* 1997b), and are using training procedures which are virtually guaranteed to bring almost any approach to teaching within their grasp.

Over the years, a number of research reports on how teachers learn to integrate a new teaching approach into their active repertoire has been accumulated (Joyce and Showers 1995). Studying theory, observing demonstrations, and practicing with feedback are sufficient to enable most teachers to develop their skills to the point that they can use a model fluidly and appropriately when called on to do so. Skill development by itself, however, does not ensure transfer into classroom practice. Relatively few people who obtain skill in new approaches to teaching will make that skill a part of their regular classroom practice unless additional instruction is received following the workshops. Not until the coaching component is added into the equation, and used effectively, will most teachers begin to transfer their new model into their active instructional repertoire.

One message from this research is very positive: teachers are wonderful learners. Nearly all teachers can acquire new skills that "fine-tune" their instructional range. They can also learn a considerable repertoire of teaching strategies that are new to them.

The second message is more sobering, but still optimistic. In order to improve their skills and learn new approaches to teaching, teachers need conditions that are not common to most staff development settings, even when teachers participate in the governance of those settings.

The third message is also encouraging. The research base reveals what conditions help teachers to learn. This information can be used in designing appropriate staff development activities.

COMPONENTS OF TRAINING

What exactly does effective "training" look like in the context of staff development? What happens during training that makes a difference to whether the content and skills being taught are transferred into classroom practice?

Most of the training literature consists of investigations in which training elements are combined in various ways, whether they are directed toward the fine-tuning of teaching styles or the mastery of new approaches to curriculum and instruction. Each of a number of training components that have been studied intensively, alone and in combination, contributes to the impact of a training sequence. When used together, each component has much greater power than when used alone. The five major components of training in the studies reviewed by Joyce and Showers (1982, 1995) were:

1 *Presentation of theory*. Studying theory can provide the rationale, conceptual base, and verbal description of an approach to teaching or instructional technique. Readings, lectures, films, and discussions are among the most common forms of presentation. In many higher education courses and staff development workshops, it is not uncommon for presentation of theory to be the major, and in some cases the sole, component of the training experience. In research, it is frequently combined with one or more of the other components.

Level of impact. Whether for fine-tuning of teaching style or mastery of new approaches, presentation of theory can raise awareness and increase conceptual control of an area. It is rare, however, for the presentation of theory and rationale to result in skill acquisition or the transfer of skills into the classroom (although there are some people who build and transfer skills from theory presentations alone). On the other hand, when theory is used in combination with other training components it appears to boost conceptual control, skill development, and transfer. Alone, it is not powerful enough to achieve much impact beyond the awareness level, but when combined with other components, it is essential to building skillful use of new teaching strategies.

2 *Modeling and demonstrations.* Modeling involves enactment of a teaching skill or strategy either through a live demonstration with children or adults, or through television, film, or other media. In a given training sequence, a strategy or skill can be modeled any number of times.

Level of impact. Modeling appears to have a considerable effect on awareness and some effect on knowledge. Demonstration also increases the mastery of theory. We understand better what is illustrated to us. Many teachers can initiate demonstrated skills fairly readily, and a number will transfer them to classroom practice. However, for most teachers modeling alone is unlikely to result in the acquisition and transfer of skills unless it is accompanied by other training components. A fairly good level of impact can be achieved through the use of modeling alone where the fine-tuning of style is involved, but for mastering new approaches it does not have great power for many teachers. All in all, research appears to indicate that modeling is likely to be an important component of any training program aimed at acquisition of complex skills and their transfer to the classroom.

3 *Practice in the workshop setting or under simulated conditions.* Practice involves trying out a new skill or strategy. Simulated conditions are usually achieved by practicing either with peers or with small groups of children under circumstances which do not require management of an entire class or larger group of children at the same time.

Level of impact. It is difficult to imagine practice without prior awareness and knowledge; that is, we have to know what it is we are to practice. However, when awareness and knowledge have been achieved, practice is a very efficient way of acquiring skills and strategies whether related to the fine-tuning of style or the mastery of new approaches. Once a relatively high level of skill has been achieved, a sizeable percentage of teachers will begin to transfer the skill into their instructional situations, but this will not be true of all people. It is probable that the more complex and unfamiliar the skill or strategy, the lower will be the level of transfer into the classroom.

4 *Structured feedback.* Structured feedback involves learning a system for observing teaching behavior and providing an opportunity to reflect on those observations. Feedback can be self-administered or provided by the trainer. It can be regular or occasional. It can be combined with other components which are organized toward the acquisition

of specific skills and strategies. That is, it can be directly combined with practice, and a practice–feedback–practice sequence can be developed.

Level of impact. Taken alone, feedback can result in considerable awareness of one's teaching behavior and knowledge about alternatives. With respect to the fine-tuning of styles, it has reasonable power for acquisition of skills and their transfer to the classroom. For example, if feedback is given about patterns of rewarding and reprimanding students, many teachers will begin to modify the ways they provide reward and reprimands. Similarly, if feedback is provided about the kinds of questions asked in the classroom, many teachers will become more aware of their use of questions and set goals for changes. In general these changes persist as long as support continues and then gradually things slide back toward the original pattern of behavior. In other words, feedback alone does not appear to provide reliable changes in classroom practice.

5 *Coaching for classroom application.* When the other training components are used in combination, the levels of impact are considerable for most teachers up through the skill levels, whether the object is the fine-tuning of style or the mastery of new approaches to teaching. For example, demonstration of unfamiliar models of teaching or curriculum approaches, combined with discussions of theory and followed by practice with expert feedback, reaches the skill-acquisition level of impact with nearly all (probably nine out of ten) teachers at the in-service or pre-service levels. However, for reliable use of new strategies to be sustained, direct coaching on how to apply the new skills and models appears to be necessary. Coaching can be provided by colleagues, supervisors, professors, curriculum consultants, or others thoroughly familiar with the new approaches. Coaching involves helping teachers analyze the curriculum content to be taught and the approach to be taken, and making very specific plans to help the students adapt to the new teaching approach. For maximum effectiveness in designing staff development to implement new curriculum standards or expand instructional repertoire schoolwide, it appears wisest to include several, and perhaps all, of the five training components.

Designers of training can be optimistic about achieving their objectives provided they are willing to create programs that bring together sufficient resources and training components. Where knowledge is lacking, guidelines for training should be based on a conservative interpretation of the available evidence. To show how this works, let us imagine that a staff development provider is attempting to build a sequence of training workshops that will ensure that 75 percent or more of the participants will transfer a complex new teaching strategy such as the inductive model of teaching (Joyce and Calhoun 1998) into their permanent teaching repertoire. This model is theoretically grounded (backed up by research indicating that it can achieve certain effects with students); is appropriate to the teaching of all academic school subjects; and can be comfortably implemented within the confines of the school day and with class-size groups of children. What will our staff development provider need to do if she or he wishes to use the training components?

1 Our provider should include a knowledge-oriented component designed to acquaint participants with the inductive model of teaching and its rationale. This component can include well-designed lectures, printed material, audiovisual presentations, and discussions.

   The prognosis for transmitting knowledge about the inductive model of teaching should be very good. However, were the training to end at this point, perhaps as few as 10 percent of the teachers would be able to use the inductive model of teaching in their classrooms.

2 Our provider should include a demonstration component in which the inductive model of teaching is modeled. This modeling may be live, through videotapes, or (a far weaker treatment) a written description of the model in action.

   The information acquired from the knowledge component should enhance the trainees' ability to identify the essential features of the teaching model. In turn, the demonstration should facilitate the acquisition and retention of the information targeted in the knowledge component. However, relatively few teacher candidates or inservice teachers will be able to use the inductive model of teaching skillfully in their classroom. It would surprise us if more than 10 percent of participants achieved that level of mastery.

3 Our provider should then include activities in which the participants practice the inductive model and receive feedback from instructors.

   The addition of the practice and feedback component should have a beneficial effect on information acquisition and retention, and should increase the ability of participants to identify the phases of the inductive model of teaching. The outcomes of the knowledge and demonstration components will also have a strong effect on the quality of the practice, and will facilitate the acquisition of the skill of using the inductive model. Assuming that these three components are carried out expertly, we would expect that nearly all of the participants would be able to demonstrate skill using the new teaching strategy. However, few participants will be able to walk from the training sessions into the classroom with the inductive model of teaching completely ready for use. We would be surprised if as many as 20 percent of them were able to do so. In Showers' (1982) study of transfer of training, no teachers transferred models of teaching without coaching.

4 Our provider should therefore include coaching at the point where the participants attempt to implement the inductive model of teaching in the classroom. Coaches may be peers, supervisors, principals, college or university professors, or others who are competent or becoming competent in the inductive model.

   Using the skill in its context requires a clear understanding of the students, subject matter, objectives, and classroom management variables in order to use the skill appropriately and forcefully. In addition, all of us are less skillful with a new model of teaching than we are with existing ones. Successful transfer of a new teaching strategy into permanent available repertoire requires a period wherein the skill is practiced in its context until it is as finely tuned as elements of the existing repertoire.

Sometimes, however, sets of teaching behaviors which support the existing repertoire may actually be dysfunctional to new models of teaching. We can see this when a teacher who is accustomed to running brisk and pointed drill-and-practice sessions begins to learn how to work inductively with students. The swift pace of the drill-and-practice, the directive feedback to the students, and the ability to control the content and movement of the lesson are at first somewhat dysfunctional as the teacher becomes less directive, relies more on initiative from the students, probes their understanding, and helps them learn to give one another feedback. The new teaching strategy seems awkward. Its pace seems slow. The teaching moves which served so well before now appear to retard the new kind of lesson. After a while, practice in context smoothes off rough edges and the new strategy gradually comes to feel as comfortable and under control as the old one.

Developing executive control has not been a common concept in training. Essentially it involves understanding an approach to teaching, why it works, how it works, what it is good for, what its major elements are, how to adapt it to varying kinds of content and students. It involves developing a set of principles that enables one to think about the approach and to modulate and transform it during the course of its use. All of these principles form part of executive control of a teaching strategy and thus form part of training content.

Both staff development providers and participants need to understand that they cannot simply walk away after a training session and have no difficulty. It is not uncommon for teachers who have attended relatively weak training sessions and then tried to apply the product in their own teaching to report, "Well, that doesn't work." Even with the strongest training there will be a period of discomfort when using any complex new skill. Even very experienced and capable teachers should be aware throughout the training process that they must prepare themselves for a second stage of learning that will come after skill has been developed.

Most pre-service and inservice teacher programs have offered weak training. When we think of a teaching model of average difficulty, we should assume that to study the theory will take as many as 20 or 30 hours (more for complex models). At least 15 or 20 demonstrations of the model being used should be observed with various kinds of learners and in several content areas. Demonstrations also need to be included when teachers are trying the model for the first time, when they are introducing students to the model, and when they are trying to adjust to using it.

Attaining competence with a complex new model of teaching also requires a number of practice sessions. Each teacher needs to try the model with peers and small groups of students from ten to 15 times before a high level of skill can be attained. If the transfer process has been realistically forecast, it makes good sense for teachers to want to build the highest level of skill they can before using the model in the more complex context of the classroom.

In summary, the Responsible Parties and the staff development provider must think about the five components of training, and design workplace support to ensure that every participant can reach a high level of skill in using the new curriculum or instructional strategy during training; develop executive control of this content and/or strategy; and use the strategy fully and appropriately once tangible support and staff development are withdrawn.

THOUGHTS ABOUT THE DESIGN OF STAFF DEVELOPMENT

Staff development that supports continuous study of teaching and learning at the school site must be embedded into the work-week and work-year of the school. For staff development of this nature to occur, the Responsible Parties must allocate time for all members of the school staff to meet weekly; in fact, regular meeting times are a prerequisite for sustained, in-depth, collective inquiry.

Once the structural provisions for regular meeting times have been established, the Responsible Parties can think about designing staff development to support student achievement. Let's see if we can think from the perspective of the Responsible Parties as they try to design quality staff development into their school improvement plans.

Student learning is the goal

Let's consider just the dimension of staff development where the objective is to improve student learning considerably, either by changing what students learn or by providing them with the tools to learn more effectively. The operative word is *considerably*. There may be other reasons for staff development; however, here we address the design of programs that have a high probability of improving student achievement.

So, what do we think about when we do that? First, we need to study student learning as described in Chapter 5. Then we have to solve two problems. One is to select content that will pay off in student learning and make sense to those who participate in the training; the second is to design the training so that implementation will occur.

There's nothing radical about this, is there? Nearly all school improvement teams and staff development providers would like to solve these problems. Yet we know that the bulk of staff development consists of brief workshops over content that seems reasonable but generally has little if any payoff in terms of student achievement; is selected through either brief or elaborate needs assessments; and leaves implementation within classrooms and across classrooms to the energy of individual participants. So what considerations will help us move beyond the status quo of the most common staff development offerings?

Expanding curriculum and instructional repertoire

First, we know that changes in student learning are brought about by changes in curriculum and instruction. We are not talking about changing schedules or methods of summative assessment of learning, or integrating subject matters, or involving parents more, or changing disciplinary practices or classroom management. *If we intend to increase student learning schoolwide, we have to change what and how we teach. A rule of thumb is that changing a curriculum area to produce effects on student learning requires changing one-third to one-half or more of the content and teaching/ learning strategies employed in that area.*

Using research from the professional knowledge base

We build our expanding repertoire around research-based models of curriculum and instruction wherever we can (Joyce and Weil 1996). We search for innovations that facilitate and document student learning (for example, Slavin 1983, in beginning reading; Fielding and Pearson 1994, in reading comprehension; Hillocks 1987, in writing).

Selecting a focus – why literacy tops the list in most settings

There are many possibilities for collective study and school improvement initiatives. Yet we know a staff can only inquire in depth into one area at a time. Therefore reading and writing are most promising because they pay off in all academic areas, while teaching all subjects as literacy makes good sense. A second possibility would be to select high-energy teaching/learning strategies, applicable across the curriculum.

Involving everybody

When the entire staff or the entire district make an initiative, the effects are far greater than when just a few people are involved or when various groups select different aspects of an initiative to pursue. Large-scale projects involving entire faculties and, in some cases, school districts, have demonstrated that "whole-school" and "whole-district" staff development programs often achieve higher rates of change in classroom practice than do staff development programs where teachers participate as individuals or as small groups of volunteers from several schools (Joyce and Calhoun 1996).

Designing the workplace

The built-in weekly time, preferably two hours or more, is used for the collective study of student learning as described in Chapters 4 and 5, for training as described below, and for peer coaching groups to meet.

Organizing everybody on the staff into peer coaching teams who study the curriculum and innovational innovations together, strive for good implementation, and study student learning in a formative way energizes the professional community, leads to much higher implementation in the classroom, and is much more likely to pay off in student learning. (In the following section, we address the research and formation of peer coaching teams to support implementation of curricular and instructional innovations.)

Now let's look at the factors the Responsible Parties need to consider as they design education to expand their own teaching practices.

Designing the training: workshops plus continuous support

Designing the training includes the design of workshops to ensure a high level of implementation of the curricular and instructional strategies being acquired; selection and design of content and instruction for these workshops; and the design of sustained support for implementation. All but the most mild classroom changes require training with the new content and processes. Here, the messages of research on curriculum implementation are unequivocal: very little implementation will take place, even in highly energetic school environments staffed with highly motivated people, unless training and follow-up in content and process are provided (Fullan and Pomfret 1977; Hall and Loucks 1977; Joyce *et al.* 1981; Calhoun and Allen 1996).

Thinking about the design of the series of workshops. The purpose of workshops is to enable people to develop the knowledge and skill that permits them to practice in the classroom and work their way toward executive control of the program components. Three dimensions or components appear to be necessary to achieve the level of control that permits practice (Joyce and Showers 1995):

- The first involves the study of the rationale and configuration of the program components through reading, study of research, and the analysis of demonstrations.
- The second is the analysis of student learning in response to the specific interactive teaching strategies that are embedded in the program components.
- The third is practice in planning instructional units and lessons.

These dimensions of training are probably best when mixed, with time for reading and discussing the professional literature, time for analyzing demonstrations, time for analyzing student learning, and time for planning lessons and units being cycled together over and over again. Optimally, workshop sessions need to be distributed throughout the year, probably at about three-week intervals, with content related to the continuous study of implementation by the workshop providers.

Designing the workshops to ensure skillful implementation. For the most effective implementation to occur, teachers need to reach a level of skill approaching that of "executive control," where they have complete understanding of each component, the complete range of skills necessary to make that component come to life in the classroom, including teaching the students "how to learn" within the program, and can study student learning formatively and adjust their behavior so that the students are fully reached.

Training research in all fields utilizes the concepts of "horizontal" and "vertical" transfer and the related concepts of "present" and "new" repertoire. (For reviews that utilize these concepts in educational applications, see Joyce and Showers 1995.)

Essentially, "horizontal transfer" is a way of describing a goal when the content of training is within or closely adjacent to the existing repertoire of the trainee. In that case, the trainee can easily carry the content of the training into the workplace – a horizontal transfer. An example in education is when the trainee is accustomed to regular use of a variety of simple and complex forms of cooperative learning and the content of the training is another simple form of cooperative learning. The process of the training explains the new procedure, its objectives and rationale, including relevant research; it is demonstrated several times, and practice in planning lessons is provided during the workshops. Given those training conditions, the teacher develops the knowledge and skill that will sustain practice in the new procedure. Accustomed to several modes of cooperative learning, the teacher can easily build during the workshops the skills that will enable him or her to use the content of the training in the classroom without further assistance. Then, the teacher can use the content of the training in the classroom without further elaboration.

Similarly, a practice that doesn't involve complex skills can be learned quickly and transferred to the classroom directly from a training session that recommends the practice and demonstrates it. Examples of such practices are ways of arranging bulletin boards, organizing a library table, and setting up computers.

"Vertical transfer" refers to a process whereby the implementation of the content of training requires new learning in the workplace *following* training through which initial skill in the content was achieved. There are two issues involved in whether the content of training requires vertical transfer for implementation.

The concept of repertoire. An issue in designing workshops and follow-up support is the extent to which the content of the training represents new repertoire for participants. In the example above, the teacher had great familiarity with the use of a broad variety of cooperative learning strategies. The new strategy had a close fit with that teacher's existing repertoire and s/he possessed many skills that could be reassembled into the new technique. But what about a teacher of equal ability who has never used any form of cooperative learning? The content that fit the repertoire of the first teacher is foreign territory to the second. Therefore, when implementing the new strategy, the second teacher has to learn a great deal *in the process of practicing the strategy in the workplace.* The term "vertical" refers to the slope of the learning in the workplace as contrasted to the workshop; learning that has to take place in the course of practice.

The complexity of the content of the training. Another issue in designing work-shops and designing the amount of technical assistance needed in the workplace to adequately support classroom implementation is the complexity of the content of the training. Executive control over complex curricular and instructional strategies, such as the inductive model of teaching, or Group Investigation – and the ability to use them powerfully and appropriately – is achieved only through repeated practice during which understanding of the strategy, and the ability to interact effectively with the students, is elevated.

In sum, for the design of staff development, there are two important implications of the concepts of horizontal and vertical transfer. One is that when staff development is designed to ensure the implementation of a curricular and instructional change, the degree to which that change requires vertical rather than horizontal transfer tells us a great deal about how we need to design the workshops or courses to develop a level of skill that will support transfer, and about the extent of follow-up training, including arrangements in the workplace for peer coaching and other forms of support.

When the content of training is within repertoire and only moderately complex, and transfer is horizontal, about one-third of the trainees will be able to implement the training without extensive follow-up, if the initial training is well designed, but two-thirds will require support in the workplace and periodic "booster" training until routine use has been achieved. If the content of training represents new repertoire and is complex, extensive follow-up training and regular coaching are necessary as the trainees practice and accomplish the new learning that is needed if executive control is to be achieved. If the initial training is very good, but follow-up training and coaching are not arranged for, fewer than 5 percent of the trainees will be able to manage the vertical transfer process (Joyce and Showers 1995).

Organizing resources, funding, and time

Time needs be built into the workplace of both staff and staff develop-ment providers. Providers, whether they are school-based or district/state/university-based, need to practice new curricular and instructional strategies with students and need to prepare videotaped demonstrations for use with staff development participants. Funding and other resources need to be concentrated on a few high-payoff staff development options rather than spread among a number of lightly funded, popular work-shops whose content is not extensive enough to make a real difference, or whose content is so extensive that even with optimal support few schools could implement it with fidelity.

The will of the professional community

No school improvement plans, however technically good they are, will succeed unless there is a solid, caring, even, to use Slavin's term, a *relentless* community whose members are determined to make education better wherever they work.

THOUGHTS ABOUT THE USE OF PEER COACHING TO SUPPORT STAFF AND STUDENT LEARNING

Let's think now about designing the social system of the workplace to support the study of student learning and the implementation of curriculum or instructional innovations selected to support student learning. Here, the school staff or Responsible Parties organize all staff members into peer coaching teams who study the innovation together, strive for a good implementation, and continuously study student learning.

In order to use "peer coaching" to support student achievement and staff learning, let's review its origins and its later refinements.

Peer coaching, as originally formulated and named by Joyce and Showers (1980), was developed to increase the implementation of staff development content. Through a combination of research syntheses and research studies conducted by Joyce and Showers, the following six characteristics evolved to form the practice of "peer coaching" to support teachers in implementing new teaching strategies (see Joyce and Showers 1995, and Showers *et al.* 1998, for extended explanations and illustrations):

- *Peer coaching applies when curriculum and instruction are the content of staff development.* Peer coaching is intended to affect curricular and instructional practices directly; thus the focus is on expanding knowledge and skill about curriculum or instruction. For example, knowledge and skill in the use of the computer as an instructional tool can be an appropriate peer coaching objective because the focus is on expanding curricular or instructional repertoire. Knowledge and skill in the use of the computer for recordkeeping does not fall into the same category. The application of a model of teaching in the teaching of writing qualifies. Knowledge of the nature of a new test on competence in writing would not.
- *The staff development content represents new practice for the clientele.* There are good reasons to continue to study aspects of curriculum and instruction in which one is already very competent, but as implementation has already been achieved, peer coaching should not be necessary. Peer coaching applies when the content is something that the clientele has not done before or has done only partially. In schools, the content should help teachers and administrators expand their teaching repertoire and the learning repertoire of their students.
- *Staff development workshops are designed to develop understanding and skill.* (Actually they are more accurately called a series of workshops, each session building on the last as well as on the practice in between workshop sessions.) The design of training must ensure that enough skill and knowledge are developed so that practice in the workplace can take place. The theory–demonstration–practice paradigm is the

classic one for ensuring skill. If adequate skill and knowledge are not developed, then practice will either not occur or may be awkward and ineffective. Peer coaching is useful only when adequate knowledge and skill – sufficient to sustain practice in the classroom – are developed as part of the workshops.

- *Peer coaching focusses on content where vertical transfer is necessary for classroom implementation.* In sports such as tennis, many skills can be learned in workshop settings, as well as the principles for using these skills; however, these skills are not fully developed except in match play. The learner has to reconfigure them and integrate the new skills and knowledge in real games. Just like sporting skills, teaching skills can be taught to a reasonable level in workshop settings and training situations; however, these new skills are not fully developed until the teacher can execute them at will and skillfully to enhance instruction and student learning. Thus, just as in sports, learning occurs during the workshop practice, but new learning takes place as the cognitions and skills are applied during actual classroom instruction.

Think back to the explanations of horizontal and vertical transfer in the section above. Horizontal transfer of workshop content is a condition where knowledge or skill can be transferred into the workplace without new learning having to take place. For example, a teacher may change instruction to provide more time for some aspect of curriculum or more practice time for students; however, the teacher does not have to learn a new skill to make this change, she need only be aware that this change may improve student learning.

Vertical transfer requires the application of new knowledge and the acquisition of new skills. Adding a new teaching strategy to one's classroom repertoire requires learning and applying this learning in the course of teaching, in other words, *expanding one's instructional repertoire beyond current practice*. Peer coaching is designed primarily to support vertical transfer.

- *"Follow-up" by experts supports vertical transfer.* Both by reviewing the literature and by conducting controlled experiments, Joyce and Showers discovered that even when workshops have been properly designed and the new knowledge and skill are developing nicely, very few people (fewer than 10 percent) navigate the *vertical* transfer demands when they operate by themselves. Research on military and athletic training, the preparation of therapists, and industrial training found the same result. In military, industrial, and athletic settings, training conducted by experts and supported in the workplace by experts greatly increased transfer and became the standard practice in those settings. Therefore it was reasonable to try the same solution in staff development for teachers; and in experiments it worked, increasing the number of people who could navigate the vertical transfer course from 10 percent or so to 75 percent or more (90 percent or more in the later studies). It turned out that the teachers' familiar cry for "follow-up" was right!
- *School-based personnel support each other to attain vertical transfer: they form peer*

coaching groups. How much can people (who are all learning the new practices) help each other attain vertical transfer?

In education, human resources and technical assistance to support teacher development are scarce, and investment in staff development is low in relation to the size and complexity of the teaching profession. In most settings, the investment in training needed to support changes in the classroom seemed too great to provide the expert training follow-up that appears to be needed. So, Joyce and Showers conducted a series of studies to explore whether teachers could work together to support one another through the vertical transfer process and achieve implementation and the expected effects on student learning.

Teachers were organized into small groups. Training was distributed so that the staff development provider could conduct workshops with the teachers every three or four weeks following initial training. The teachers were asked to share plans, discuss effects, and visit one another periodically to get ideas from one another (the one doing the teaching is the coach). And the teachers filled out weekly logs, studying their implementation and alerting the staff development provider to problems so that training could be modified accordingly.

The results were excellent. Transfer was accomplished by most of the teachers.

Time passes and more is learned

Gradually, refinements were made in the use of peer coaching to support student learning:

- peer coaching teams of two or three were much more effective than larger groups;
- the groups were more effective when the entire faculty was engaged in study;
- peer coaching worked better when building administrators participated in training and practice;
- peer coaching worked better when teachers avoided giving advice to one another, especially comments about teaching following observation; and
- the effects were greater when formative study of student learning was embedded in the process.

Today, peer coaching can be organized so as to virtually assure transfer for everyone.

MAKING CONNECTIONS TO OTHER LINES OF INVESTIGATION IN INSTRUCTION AND CURRICULUM

Peer coaching is – in the Joyce and Showers (1995) framework and research – nested within the training model. This model is designed to support people in making changes in knowledge and skill and to transfer these changes into classroom practice. The components of the model are familiar to many educators: information/theory, demonstration, practice, coaching.

How well does the research on staff development fit with research on curriculum and instruction for children? Think back to Gagne's (1975) early advice about the conditions of learning and designing instruction to build cognitive strategies and changes in performance: the need to provide information, demonstrations and "learning guidance," practice and spaced retrieval opportunities, feedback and the building of vertical and horizontal transfer.

Let's make another connection, this time to the research on literacy. Think about the research on reading comprehension (for example Palinscar and Brown 1984; Pearson and Dole 1987; Fielding and Pearson 1994) and the sequence of "explicit instruction": explanation of the process; demonstrations of the process; much supported practice of applying the process across different content; gradual fading of teacher support; application and articulation of the process in use; taking skillful control of the process so it can be used at will, eventually almost automatically.

Joyce and Showers, Gagne, and researchers working on reading comprehension such as Palinscar and Brown, Pearson, Dole, and Fielding, all studying and thinking about how to support changes in cognitions and performance, have come up with some very similar findings. These similarities can be used to integrate school improvement efforts and design better "instruction" in classrooms, in workshops, and in staff development intended to expand instructional repertoire.

EMBEDDING PEER COACHING INTO THE STAFF DEVELOPMENT AND SCHOOL IMPROVEMENT PLAN

Peer coaching groups are adult learning "support groups" who share plans and results, and during implementation work closely with the workshop provider/trainer (providing themselves with ample technical assistance). Recent developments in electronic technology greatly facilitate the relationship between faculties and the provider, even from long distances. Fax and e-mail are useful for communicating information and getting advice. Videotapes made by the trainer enable "demonstrations" to be made available for viewing by entire faculties, by peer coaching groups, and by individuals.

THE NATURE OF STAFF DEVELOPMENT NECESSARY TO ENSURE IMPLEMENTATION

Staff development programs must be as carefully designed as educational programs for students, and the implications of not doing so are serious. If a design is based on the concepts we have been discussing, there is a high probability of a successful implementation. If the workplace is not redesigned, the odds drop terribly – fewer than 10 percent of the teachers will be able to manage the vertical transfer. If the workshops lack adequate study of rationales or include too few demonstrations, or if the opportunity to plan is missed, then a failure to implement promising new curriculum or instructional strategies is virtually certain.

The staff development required to support changes in instructional practice and student achievement is substantial. In the San Diego project (Showers *et al.* 1998), the technical assistant spent more than 30 days helping the teachers learn to implement the new repertoire. In the University City project (Joyce and Calhoun 1996), covering nine schools, regular staff development was provided for and the technical assistant spent more than 50 days on site during a single year. In the River City project (Joyce *et al.* 1996) which covered 16 schools, the technical assistants were on-site more than 100 days per year.

The amounts of assistance required reflected the proportion of curricular/instructional changes that were being experienced by the teachers and the corresponding amounts of staff development/technical assistance that were needed to ensure an implementation. Also, in these and other successful programs, formative evaluation of implementation and effects on students were embedded, so that the teachers and administrators were brought into the study of their own behavior and that of the students on a systematic basis. In other words, action research was built into the staff development.

Part III Refining, renovating, and redesigning: taking steps large and small

When we move toward an evolutionary state we try to build a shared lens for looking constantly at the educational environment and the progress of the students within it. We develop a common cognitive model in which our students are moving about within the curricular and instructional village that we have created for them. Our lens scans the interaction of students and learning tasks, their interaction with one another and with us, and we find ourselves wondering what aspects of the environment can be made a little bit better, which ones should be considered for substantial renovation, and whether some aspects should be radically redesigned. In Chapter 8 we discuss the refinement complex and examine an interesting school in Nottingham, England, at some length. Chapter 9 discusses renovation and deals particularly with an English school that brings technology into all its curriculum areas in a major way. Finally, Chapter 10 is built around a lengthy scenario where many dimensions of the school are redesigned, along with quite a number of refinements and a considerable upgrading of the curricular structures.

8 Refining: thinking through sets of changes

Throughout the book, we maintain that it is in curriculum and instruction that changes make a difference in student learning; we see the social atmosphere of the school as an integrated part of the curricular/instructional complex. Refinement is the process of fine-tuning aspects of the learning environment. Renovation refers to the overhaul of a curriculum area, processes of instruction, or the interface between the students and the learning environment. Redesign is a more radical rearrangement of the components of the school and of how the students and faculty inquire together.

It's easy to underplay the potential effects of a collection of adroit refinements. Many small improvements can fine-tune a learning environment considerably and provide the opportunity to get a school on the road toward the evolutionary state.

The Just Read program that we described in Chapter 2 is an example. Although introducing action research to schools *via* Just Read means redesigning the way faculty members and parents work together – a considerable change for many of the schools we have worked with – the innovation itself merely alters the social climate of the schools to encourage reading, and enlists the parents and community members to make a collaborative effort, which in itself is not a radical change. Yet the impact on the amounts of reading done by the students is very great and results in increased skill in both reading and writing.

If we just consider how much one-on-one tutoring can help students (see Bloom 1984), and if we prepare parent volunteers to provide that service in critical areas, we can see the difference in student learning.

Refinements make a difference when they affect student behavior in a curriculum area. For example, those that increase practice in reading and writing can make a big difference. Those that increase study time in any curriculum area can make a big difference. Some refinements that accomplish this require uncommon, but not difficult, arrangements.

Keeping the library open for student inquiry and study after school hours, evenings, and weekends can be worthwhile in neighborhoods where students do not have good places to study once the school is closed. We are attracted to the arrangement in Pembroke School (Chapter 10) where the branch libraries of the town were joined with the high school libraries and staffed to be open the maximum possible hours.

The practice of having sets of laptop computers that students can check out to take home is also appealing. Technology is so important today that it is worth considerable effort to ensure that all students have access at home as well as in school.

The opportunities for refinements that will make a difference are myriad. Recently we watched an elementary school of 400 students make a simple refinement in the use of computers that made a substantial difference in achievement in quality of writing. The faculty had read a study that indicated that student access to word processing would improve quality of writing only if the students had access for at least three hours per week and preferably more. Their lab was booked for computer instruction and couldn't provide the needed access. However, they scouted around and found about 50 computers that local businesses were trading in for new ones. Using the halls of the school, they set up a student-use laboratory and provided access to the grade 4 and 5 students. Soon those students were writing on computers four or five times a week. Fluency in writing increased first. Then other dimensions of quality began to improve. Again, the curriculum in language arts had not changed, but the practice with word processors made the difference.

All these changes require concerted action. Without progress toward a Responsible Parties organization, even minor schoolwide changes cannot be effectively carried out. Together, they increase the exercise of collective decisionmaking and communal effort.

Let's visit a school that has made a virtual art form of refinements, with a total effect that is striking.

HEMPSHILL HALL PRIMARY SCHOOL

The school serves about 350 children from 250 families in the working-class community of Bulwell, Nottingham. About 60 percent of the children live in the catchment area, a post-World-War-II development that comprises the immediate neighborhood. Within the catchment, most families are two-parent households. The majority of the fathers have marketable skills in a variety of trades, and their employment provides a comfortable living. Most of the mothers left school early, married young, and have few skills that are easily marketable in today's workplaces, although they will be quite young when their children reach the age where intensive parenting consumes less and less time.

About 40 percent of the students who attend Hempshill Hall commute from a public housing project outside the neighborhood. The majority of these children come from households where the mother raises the children alone. Few of these mothers have marketable skills.

About 30 percent of the children in the school, most of them from the homes outside the catchment area, receive free (government-subsidized) lunches.

School "staff"

The school has a head teacher and ten full-time teaching staff. There are four paid teaching assistants. In addition, there are five assistants-in-training under a program developed by the head teacher, who capital-ized on the need of many of the mothers to begin to develop marketable skills.

Over the years, the head and staff have recruited additional assistance for their students. For example, arrangements with several teacher-education programs provide long-term experience for student teachers. There are usually a half-dozen student teachers working in some cap-acity in the school. Some of their major tasks include studying how stu-dents learn to read, studying how their cooperating teacher teaches reading, and tutoring an individual student into greater literacy. With the full support of the head, the university is using Hempshill Hall as a center for its students to inquire into teaching and learning and a center for the application of best practices in curriculum and pedagogy.

On average, 60 parent volunteers provide service each week for about a half-day to two days each. In this area, the school has capitalized on the nature of the community, drawing into the school those parents who have the willingness and time to be a major part of the school commu-nity. Parents are involved in tutoring; in reading with children; in a number of demonstrations and curriculum-relevant examples (for ex-ample sharing folktales or historical events they lived through; bringing in artifacts of different regions, cultures, or time periods). Some parents prefer clerical tasks; others prefer simply to help teachers with art work. The "formal" Hempshill staff work with the volunteers to ensure satisfy-ing matches between the areas where the parents feel confident and the needs of the classrooms and the school as a whole. For these volunteers, their work has become part of the fabric of the larger community and has come to be seen in the neighborhood as a way to prepare for future employment.

The volunteer program is one way the school lives its policy, reiter-ated again and again and prominently displayed in the school handbook: "You must be totally inclusive. Lots of people can help out if you will only provide the avenues and make them welcome."

The school as a social system: collaboration, inquiry, responsibility

The staff and parents have generated a thoroughgoing process for build-ing a collaborative, energetic social system in which school staff, parents, and students share responsibility for excellence in the academic, social, and personal development of the children. From the orientation letter to parents: "We are all equal partners at Hempshill Hall. We welcome parents who want to be fully involved in school life."

This social system has many dimensions. Here are a few:

Orientation of the parents and children to the school

Meetings between parents, children, and school begin before the children have reached school age. In the fall of each year, there are a series of meetings designed to build the student–parent–school partnership.

The Thursday Club

Neighborhood parents of children not yet in school are invited to bring their children to the school on Thursdays so that both parents and children can become accustomed to the school. Importantly, the Thursday club inaugurates for families the process whereby the school will undertake to orient them and provide them with opportunities to "talk" to the school. Parents and children can attend every Thursday for as long as they wish.

Parents as teaching assistants

Welcome becomes real and mutually rewarding – for students, parents, and teachers. The staff has organized its actions to ensure that parents are welcomed into the school. Parents are likely to be involved in whatever activity is going on and are invited to help their children. Perhaps the most compelling evidence that parents do feel like an integral part of the school community comes from the fact that approximately one person from every six families is successfully recruited to work as an assistant to the teacher. Many others visit frequently and can be found helping a child carry on an activity.

Holistic communication: school assemblies

Two or three times a week, the entire student body gathers as an assembly, led by Stuart Harrison who is both full-time Level 6 teacher and the deputy head. Often, a play is presented by a group of students. Many of the plays involve a considerable amount of improvisation and have emergent story lines.

These assemblies bring together the students as a whole school community; provide an opportunity to develop them into a civil, polite audience; and, incidentally, mean that each year they are participants or audience with respect to about 60 plays. The Ofsted* report comments, "Spiritual development is encouraged in the broadest sense and permeates the life of the school in a pervasive yet unobtrusive manner.

---

* The Ofsted report is a product of the government inspection team that is responsible for assessing the quality of the school. In 1994 the six-member team spent a week in the school; examined its documents pertaining to curriculum, instruction, management, and assessments; observed 121 lessons or parts of lessons; watched assemblies; held discussions with teachers; interviewed the governors (school lay council); attended a meeting of 65 parents; examined the responses by 114 parents to a questionnaire; held planned discussions with students from Year 6; and listened to a range of pupils read.

Opportunities are taken to bring out spiritual issues during lessons, as they occur. Regular, well-prepared school and class assemblies take place, often using stories that illustrate values or have a moral content. The assemblies contribute effectively to the school's overall ethos and values."

Communication and the home/school connection: the reading wallet
Every child in the school is provided with a vinyl briefcase, called a "reading wallet." Students carry their reading wallets home every day. The wallet contains "real" books and student work. Parents are encouraged to provide time for their child to read the books at home and are helped to learn how to support their child's reading.

The comment book
An important communication document in each reading wallet is a "comment book," a notebook in which teachers and parents write back and forth to each other on a weekly basis. If either makes a comment, the other responds. The comments discuss aspects of the students' academic and social progress and ways of helping them move forward.

To get the flavor of the interaction, let's look at the comments between the parents and teacher of a 5-year-old student.

September 4 (first day of school)
Teacher: ". . . Jessica has chosen some books to share with you, *The Greatest Show on Earth*, *Brown Bear*, and *Not Now, Bernard*. She could just concentrate on one or read them all equally. She can keep these as long as she wants – I will probably next share them with her next Monday." (This "sharing" refers to the twice-weekly conference with individual students about books they are reading. Every student in the school participates in at least two adult/student conferences a week; one of these conferences is with the teacher, and the other may be with a parent volunteer or paid teaching assistant.)

September 4
Father: "I read *The Greatest Show* with Jessica and her brothers, Jeroen and Dylan. We discussed the story and tried to find out what was happening from the pictures. Jessica enjoyed the story and understood all the pictures."

September 5
Mother: "Jessica read Dylan and me the *Brown Bear* book without much help. She also read Jeroen's book *The Red Fox*."

September 6
Teacher: "Thank you. Jessica now has her poetry folder and a poem to share with you."

September 9
Mother: "Jessica and her younger brother, Dylan, read the poem and she showed us how to shout 'all join in.' They both enjoyed it, so we read it a few times. She also read us the *Brown Bear* again."

Teacher: "I am pleased Jessica and Dylan enjoyed the poem. Also, it is interesting to learn what other books she is sharing with you. Jessica read *Brown Bear* with me together and she had remembered it really well. On the few occasions she had forgotten what came next, I just needed to jog her memory by beginning the next word, and she remembered and carried on. She is bringing home two new books to share."

September 14
Father: "Jessica, her brothers and I read *Bill and Pete* . . . Jessica and I read the story and Dylan told us what was happening in the pictures."

Mother: "Jessica, Dylan, and Jeroen read *Would You Rather* and enjoyed it."

September 17
Teacher: "Jessica shared *Would You Rather* with me today and she remembered quite a lot of it, using the pictures efficiently to help."

September 18
Mother: "Jessica played a matching game with Jeroen with words such as *the, they*; *is, in*; *come, comes*. After that, she read his book, *The Book Shop*."

Comment books like Jessica's go home with every student at Hempshill Hall all year long, as parents and teachers communicate about their common objective – helping the child become a successful reader. The teachers feel that the interchanges help extend the influence of the school into reading/writing activities in the home. The parents feel that the process keeps them in close touch with the student–teacher–parent triad that makes education work.

To make the nature of this connection more vivid, here are some excerpts from an interview with the mother:

> The comments make a real difference. They are one of the best things about having my daughter in Hempshill Hall. It really keeps you in touch and also keeps pressure on you as a parent. You feel that you have to read with the children every day because the teacher comments so regularly. It also is interesting to see how Jessica is learning to read. Yesterday, when I asked her about reading her newest book, she said that she could read it "because all the words were in my head." What we do now with Jessica adds about three hours a week to her concentration on learning to read.

Finally, communication is conducted through conventional reports – or are they just conventional? Let's look at an excerpt from a report on Dylan, Jessica's brother.

> Dylan is a friendly, confident, and sensible child, well liked by his peers. He always tries to do his best. He concentrates well and listens hard, asking questions whenever he is unsure. He has enjoyed helping new children fit into our class and routines – a great helper . . . Dylan is able to read independently with good concentration for long periods of time. He thinks carefully about what he wants to write . . . Dylan has

an inquiring mind. He recognizes number patterns readily and is able to relate his number concepts to new concepts. He is quick at solving mental maths problems. Dylan enjoys working on the class computer and particularly the inquiry problems on the Apple Mac.

There is much more; the report is extensive, but the attempt to capture and express the personality of the child is manifest. The faculty takes communication with parents *very* seriously and writes carefully and personally.

The curriculum framework
The curriculum is academically rich and integrative. Everything is taught as the achievement of literacy. Reading is taught through real (trade) books, both fiction and nonfiction. School subjects are divided into units that are approached as experiential and reading/writing inquiries. The curriculum is naturally, rather than artificially, integrated; i.e. it is organized around related concepts, not around topics. Teachers work together to think about the curriculum and develop units of work that build on previous experiences. The curriculum is, as articulated in the letter to parents, "based on the programmes of study in the National Curriculum Core Subjects of Mathematics, Science, English, and Technology." Working together, this staff has figured out how to integrate the curriculum conceptually and how to teach higher-order and lower-order curriculum objectives simultaneously.

Teaching, learning, and working together
A general inquiry model dominates teaching and learning. All teachers and all students follow a scheme where material to be mastered and problems to be solved are presented, and students, organized into groups, delve into the material and problems. Thus collaborative inquiry is the hallmark of the teaching/learning process, but individual students have responsibility for many strands of learning, and individual differences in achievement are closely monitored.

The school as a whole is the educative unit. In this, the school is very different from the typical setting, where schools assign students to classes in which teachers, working as individuals in miniature schools, progress through the curriculum. At Hempshill, everybody is responsible for all the students, working toward common goals and using common strategies.

Every effort is made to help the students feel that they are capable and that each is responsible for the learning of all. From the letter to parents: "We provide a warm, caring, 'family style' environment where your child can feel valued, living in harmony with friends – a real extended family unit." Within the context of the curriculum units, the students and teachers work together to plan specific activities. In a real sense, learning to cooperate, learning to live democratically, and learning to collaborate as inquirers – as scholars – fit together in a comfortable whole.

The mode of collaborative inquiry pervasive at Hempshill Hall also greatly diminishes the disciplinary problems typical of the chalk-and-talk, drill-and-recite school. "Discipline" is a matter of bringing the children into the social norms of cooperation, inquiry, and mutual respect. Thus the mode is socialization, rather than the enforcement of a code only tangentially relevant to the teaching/learning process. From the letter to parents: "*H*empshill *H*all *S*chool has a Mission – that all our children shall be *H*appy, live in *H*armony, and achieve *S*uccess."

The operation of the school is relevant to contemporary discussions about "whole-class" and "cooperative group" activity. *In a very real sense, the entirety of Hempshill Hall Primary is a "class" whose members cooperate as a whole and within which cooperative groups work within a common framework to pursue excellence.* Personal, social, and academic growth are perceived to be part of a whole.

Individual classrooms are not isolated educational settings. The classes operate as units where several teachers work together to plan and carry out their project plans and day-to-day inquiries. The familiar image of "chalk-and-talk" and "drill" is absent. Students can discuss their goals, and the whole class is driving at common substantive objectives. On a day-to-day basis, the students work from three-quarters to nine-tenths of the time in collaborative groups and as individuals to master those goals and develop their capacity as learners.

Reading and writing are taught using experience records and real books throughout the curriculum. This practice contrasts sharply with that of most schools, where language arts are taught as a subject of which the product is to be applied in the other curriculum areas. Reading and writing are pervasive activities at Hempshill Hall.

Similarly, technology is a tool to support learning, not an activity in itself. Like language skills, the use of the computer is integrated into learning in all subjects. Parents are urged to purchase small electronic word processors for their children and they are extensively used, as are about 40 computers in the school.

Staff planning

The staff works in teams to develop schemes of work that reflect the national curriculum. However, each scheme is developed as a bit of research for the students, and first-hand experiences such as field trips and secondary experiences such as videotapes and films are combined with extensive reading. Products of student research are expressed in writing, multimedia presentations, and enactments. Also, as part of demonstrating their understanding and application of science and humanities content, Year 5 and Year 6 students develop multimedia packages for student and class use at earlier levels.

Individual learning and responsibility

In all schools, even the ones with the most cooperative climates, individual students do the learning. As fits with the social climate at Hempshill Hall, individual responsibility and excellence are expected and supported. In this case, individual projects are included in the curricular units as offshoots of a class or school collaborative inquiry. The school does not make the mistake that some collaborative schools do of generating "group products" that are not an amalgam of individual inquiries. In addition, individual students develop their own inquiries, doing personal research and developing and testing their own hypotheses.

The tending of individual needs at all levels is a fluid part of the conduct of teaching. Every week, each student has two personal, one-on-one conferences with an adult over his or her individual reading and receives help in setting personal goals and in resolving problems.

Informal assessments, as described above, and formal assessments occur regularly. In cases where students are not making good progress in literacy or numeracy, staff members work together to modify a student's program and provide additional learning opportunities. Each spring, students in Year 1 who have not progressed above Level 1 in reading are identified and receive intensive assistance. In the spring of 1996, 52 students were so identified, and by the end of the school year 48 had reached Level 2, the stage where students can read simple books independently.

The Ofsted inspection report

What do external education authorities think of Hempshill Hall?

Whenever a school deviates from the chalk-and-talk, drill-and-recitation mode of pedagogy, people in both the United Kingdom and the United States ask, skeptically, whether the "basics" are being neglected. Largely, this skepticism is a product of the culturally normative image of teaching in which the teacher is the authoritarian controller of what will be learned and how it will be learned. And most people have had more experience with the chalk-and-talk, recitation model of teaching – the provision of information, oral or written, followed by queries to which one makes oral or written responses – than any other model. Thus, regardless of its inefficiency in producing student learning, its familiarity makes it "trustworthy."

Many members of the public believe, erroneously, that most teachers have moved away from the recitation model that worked so well for them as students. Thus, despite the long-recorded and current dominance of the recitation model of teaching in English-language countries, there are continuous calls to reassert recitation-and-drill as the major method of primary education and to eliminate inquiry and collaborative work as distractors from the major purpose of schooling.

Consequently, the opinion of external examiners and examinations becomes very important whenever a school strives for excellence through collaborative-inquiry models, even when it asserts, as Hempshill Hall does in its letter to parents, that "Although our [academic] aims are traditional, our methods are not always so, and you may find that your children will be taught very differently to the way you were taught at their age. We respect individual differences, and do not normally 'drill' whole classes together, regardless of ability."

With this cultural context in mind, here are some of the products of external examination of Hempshill Hall Primary School, from the Ofsted inspection report in December, 1994:

> Standards in reading, writing and speaking and listening, and in number and information technology, are good and sometimes out-standing . . . Pupils use text effectively for learning. They read widely and value reading as a source of information. They read accurately, expressively, and with understanding. Pupils enjoy books and speak warmly of the pleasures of reading . . . Pupils write with the coherence, fluency, and accuracy which is appropriate for their age and ability and often beyond. As they move through the school, they tackle successfully an increasing range of written work and plan, develop, and re-write their own text where appropriate. They are able to nar-rate, explain, describe, hypothesize, analyse, assert, compare, ques-tion, and deduce. They listen well to others and respond appropriately and sensitively . . .
>
> Pupils handle number well across the curriculum, mentally and in writing. They use measurement effectively in a range of different con-texts, particularly in science, technology, and history. They have well-developed calculator skills and interpret statistical data effectively in their work in humanities . . .
>
> Standards in information technology are good and sometimes out-standing. Pupils create, modify, and present information in English, art, history, and mathematics. They use databases to enhance the quality of their work in history. By Year 6, pupils build and study com-puter models confidently and control movement and other physical effects in technology.

While the Hempshill staff focusses mostly on its own internal collection of data, using it to plan next experiences and next units, it does look at how the students compare to others throughout the country. At the Key Stage 2 assessment for 1994–5, conducted when pupils were leaving Year 4 and were 10 to 11 years old, the percentage of pupils achieving Levels 4 and 5 in English was 70, compared with a national average of 48. In maths, the percentage reaching Levels 4 and 5 was 82, compared with a national average of 44.

A summary note on Hempshill Hall Primary

We learn in human *settings* – assemblages of children and adults brought together for the purpose of learning. The fact of assembly is more important than the *place* we usually call *school*, as is so apparent today when people can effectively relate to one another electronically. Essen-tially, because we can communicate so effectively through media, we can "assemble" without being in close physical proximity.

However, the familiar schoolhouse has great importance, for within it, and in cooperation with our surrounding community, staff and student bodies generate social climates that shape education and the substance and process of that education. Some schools are not only more *effective* than others in drawing students together to learn, but they pull the students toward specific kinds of inquiry. The social climate of great schools energizes all their students in particular ways.

In the best situation, a whole school is a center of learning for teachers, parents, and students. One such place is Hempshill Hall, where an overarching collaborative inquiry model has been used to design the educational environment for students and adults.

Making a school like this is simultaneously demanding and rewarding, as Marcia Puckey, the head at Hempshill Hall, knows so well. Yet, curiously, Hempshill Hall is created on the straightforward application of fundamental principles rather than arcane school-improvement strategies. The parents are brought into the partnership at the beginning, and easy communication and participation systems keep them in it. The faculty cooperates as a unit so that the atmosphere of school, classroom, groups, and individual work is cooperatively integrated. Literacy, inquiry, and cooperation are part of the curriculum as well, and the fundamental goals of literacy are not watered down by fragmented curricular efforts. Inclusiveness, perseverance, affirmative problem-solving, and a rigorous focus on student learning make up the school-renewal approach that makes this school one to emulate.

COMMENTARY

When we compare Hempshill Hall to an average school in the United States or the United Kingdom, what stands out is the great number of seemingly "little" practices that add up to the feeling of an extraordinarily warm and supportive environment within which students from both an unprepossessing neighborhood and an impoverished one flourish academically and personally. Many schools encourage reading at home and communication between parents and teachers. At Hempshill, the "reading wallet" and "comment book" are living components of communication. Many schools bring the student body together occasionally. Few have created a daily situation where improvisational role-playing engages students from 5 to 10 years old in the same room at the same time in the study of personal and social values. Many schools recruit parents to assist. In few do parents from one-fourth of the families come in and work nearly every day for several hours and involve them in a "home-to-work" educational program.

Just about anyone who has visited Hempshill Hall in the last five years will proclaim to you that the school "just feels wonderful." Parents – from one-fourth of the families – are everywhere, being taught how to help out. That alone will make a big difference *without making a change in the curriculum*. The "reading wallets" encourage "at-home" reading and encourage parents to read to their students.

In spring of 1998 Hempshill added the Just Read program and the results presented in the head's notes to parents tells the story of how many books the 350 students are reading:

Hempshill Hall Primary School
Head teacher Mrs H. M. Puckey

8 May 1998

Dear Parents

JUST READ

You won't believe how many books your children have read since we started Just Read – six weeks ago.

11,798

What an amazing total.

I have told the children that if we reach 20,000 by July 4 – 1998 that is! then we will all celebrate by having an American BBQ.

So, thank you for your help and support so far – please keep the interest and momentum up and we will all celebrate your success on July 4.

Best wishes

Marcia Puckey
Head teacher

Hempshill Hall Primary School
Head teacher Mrs H. M. Puckey

24 June 1998

Dear Parents

JUST READ

Last Friday we reached the grand total of 21,490 books that the children have read since we started 'Just Read' – well past our 20,000 goal – an amazing amount of books.

So on July 3 in the afternoon we plan to hold a BBQ on the school field – we are being supported in this by McDonald's and Domino Pizzas who are providing some of the drinks and some food. We could do all the cooking in the school kitchen but it would be much more fun if some could be cooked on real BBQs – for a more authentic taste.

If you can bring a portable BBQ and charcoal on the afternoon of Friday July 3 – and are willing to help with a little of the cooking – please will you let me know.

To add to the atmosphere all the children who wish can come to school on that day in bright summer clothes.

We hope to be holding the BBQ between 1.30–3.30 p.m. so that your child will not need to pay for a school meal on that date – we will be giving them a drink and biscuits at lunch time to push them on until the real food in the afternoon.

If it rains we will have to eat inside.

Best wishes

Marcia Puckey
Head teacher

Because most vocabulary development and the consolidation of skills in reading (Nagy and Anderson 1987; Nagy *et al.* 1987), the impact of increasing at-home reading by as much as one book each week will be felt in student gains. The "comment books" smooth out and consolidate the social system by encouraging a regular and gentle mode of continuous communication between parents and teachers. The impact of all these little changes adds up to a very nice total.

Hempshill refines aspects of its operation on a continuing basis. How? By doing it. The head has convinced the teachers and parents that school improvement is a part of teaching and parenting and has created a climate that matches the vision. A healthy climate for adults becomes a healthy place for children. The mode of continual search for improvement rubs off on the children.

The inquiry continues . . .

9 Renovating: changing a dimension of the learning environment

Now let's revisit the renovation of a curriculum area or a way of working with students that affects the entire curriculum. To make such a large change, we need to be operating with most of the hypotheses; a good bit of the new structure of school improvement has to be in place at least partially. The problems of creating time, inclusive governance, embedded staff development, and the action-research way of doing business need to be established. Connections to the knowledge base will be critical in the decisionmaking process. The school has established a broad governance group – perhaps not the full Responsible Parties operation as we envision it, but the whole staff and a goodly number of community members are meeting regularly (every two or three weeks), and the decisions of that group and affirmation by the school faculty and parents will be important as a curriculum area is selected.

In Chapter 3 the Southwood School had the proper conditions as it chose to renovate the writing dimension of its language-arts curriculum. The decisionmaking group, and all the teachers, strongly supported by district staff, studied the literature on the teaching of writing and the quality of the writing of their students, decided to emphasize expository writing, and selected several innovations to implement and study. These included providing better ways of stimulating regular writing, ways of helping the students study expert writers and experiment with their strategies and devices, and ways that teachers could model skills of various sorts.

The Morse School had created enough conditions to carry out the design and implementation of the Second Chance Program and carry it out as an action-research project.

Let's look at another school as it tackles the problem of infusing computer technology into the operation of the school and its effects on the entire learning environment.

BLENHEIM'S FORAY INTO TECHNOLOGY

Blenheim Hall's Upper School and Community College is a self-govern-ing mixed comprehensive school providing education for over 1400 stu-dents between the ages of 13 and 19. It has a large sixth form of nearly 500 students. Blenheim's students are drawn from a comprehensive range of backgrounds representing the diversity of a rural area in the Midlands that contains 32 villages of differing sizes.

Staff and students at Blenheim would be the first to admit that they are fortunate to work in such a well-equipped school. Opened in 1975, the extensive campus is located on a picturesque site at the edge of a pleas-ant village surrounded by woodland and overlooking a river valley. The rural nature of this site is further emphasized by the school's farm unit and a newly replanted two-and-a-half-acre copse which contains con-servation areas and nature trails.

Visitors to the school nearly always comment on the impressive level of facilities and how effectively these are being used and maintained by students. Each department has a suite of rooms and most have a resource area which is geared to individual or small-group learning.

From its early days the school has always placed a high priority on good examination results and on student responsibility. To meet the expectations of parents and the general public in its large catchment area, the school developed along fairly traditional lines. Emphasis was placed on the development of a strong and successful academic curricu-lum supported by a commitment to the care of each individual.

Even allowing for its favorable intake the school has consistently been able to achieve above-average results across the curriculum. The stand-ards achieved by Blenheim's students have been well above the national averages at all levels. In the 1995 GCSE examinations (taken mainly by 16-year-olds), 63 percent of students gained A to C grades in five or more subjects and 47 percent achieved these grades in eight or more subjects. In A Level examinations (taken mainly by 18-year-olds), stu-dents taking two or more subjects achieved an average point score of 21.4, which compares favorably with many selective private schools and the average score for comprehensive schools of 13.2. The 40 faculty members received generally high ratings from everybody who observed them. Nearly all the students believed they were getting an above-average education, although a number felt that the atmosphere was somewhat stiff. Creativity was not highly prized, although the upper-form students wrote long papers each term on topics of their own choos-ing. Although individual differences were treated kindly, students entering the school with poor literacy skills generally graduated with poor literacy skills.

Two 'staging posts' are of great significance in the story of Blen-heim's movement from a fine traditional school to an evolutionary state with student achievement far above what was imagined in its early and traditionally successful years. The first was a large grant from a high-technology company (Techrow) in its region and the second was its con-

nection with technical assistance in school improvement through the
Cambridge Institute. These occurred close together in time.

The school faculty and trustees were initially in a quandary about
whether to accept the award from Techrow. The benefactors wished to
see Blenheim become an exemplary setting for the demonstration of the
benefits of computers in education. The head found herself betwixt and
between. First, Agnes felt that she knew a substantial amount about leading a faculty whose members were academically rigorous and independent – people who constructed and taught their courses and whose
primary needs were for support in instructional materials. Second, she
thought of herself as forward-looking, and she was curious about the
potential for computers in education. Third, she knew nothing about
them and was aware that most of the faculty were in the same fix. Only
two or three faculty members had the experience with computers to envision much instructional use beyond word-processing applications. The
technology company envisioned a school where computers would be
used in a wide variety of ways and all students would develop a high
degree of computer literacy.

The quandary led to the beginning of what would become the
Blenheim Responsible Parties. Discussions with faculty, trustees, parents,
and representatives of the technology company led to several large group
meetings in which the decision was analyzed intensively. Representatives
of the company presented plans for a network linking several hundred
computers with extensive access to software. They envisioned augment-
ing the traditional instruction with data bases, spreadsheets, communication through the World Wide Web and directly to information sources
throughout the country and with many other countries. They imagined
instructional stations where teachers could use multimedia resources as
they taught: art history with access to electronic galleries and video lectures and discussions, science with simulations of cutting-edge experiments, and so on.

Nearly everyone was intrigued but too anxious to proceed. The vision
of their good school suddenly inundated with a mass of equipment no
one knew how to use was somewhat horrifying. What everyone realized
was that, whatever they did, they were about to make the most important
decision since the school was founded and that no one should be left out
of the decision. Thus the Responsible Parties came into existence along
with an Executive Committee that was charged with leading the process
– two trustees, two teachers, two parents, two officials from Techrow, the
head of library services for the region, and a community relations officer
of the telephone company.

Enter the Cambridge Institute. While taking her masters degree
Agnes had attended several conferences at the university and become
acquainted with an organization that specializes in helping schools
develop self-renewing capacity. She contacted them and two relatively
young women appeared for a meeting with Agnes and the executive
committee. Nancy specialized in the facilitation of decisionmaking
and Florence in educational technology. A series of meetings occurred

over the next week, during which Florence and Nancy also visited the school and interviewed teachers, parents, and students and had endless conversations with Agnes. At the end of the week came a day-long meeting with the committee, a meeting that commenced with a forceful report by Florence, Nancy, and Agnes, a report that made the following points:

- Without extensive and continuous staff development there was no point in going forward. The staff would have to study not only the computer, software, and potential uses, but how to revise the ways it teaches its courses and organizes course material. The advisers estimated that as much as 50–75 percent of the teaching would have to change if the potential of the technology was to be realized. The best points of the current teaching modes – effective lectures, discussions, and reading/writing assignments – would be at the core of the new courses, but a much greater proportion of the instruction would have to be inductive, and groups of students would need to be organized to inquire into topics and problems that would take advantage of the new information sources and devices for organizing data and writing that are permitted by extensive use of the computer.

  Therefore time would have to be built into the staff schedule to permit teachers to "go to school" on not just the technology, but the modes of teaching that would incorporate it. One of the very few staff development consultants in the nation who is expert in both curriculum use and models of curriculum and instruction would have to be engaged to provide the necessary staff development services.
- Extensive study would be needed to determine how to deploy the computers so that they could be used in the course of instruction and would also be available for the large amounts of independent and group study that would be needed.
- A very careful action research program would have to be instituted to determine the effects of components of the changes. Not only student learning – of the computer as a tool and of academic substance – would need to be studied, but also the implementation of the curricular and instructional changes made by the faculty.
- Whereas the faculty had been accustomed to working as individuals and department groups, now all members would have to work together to master a great deal of new knowledge and skill: a school-wide staff organization would have to be developed. The faculty would have to work together to restructure courses, share them, and restructure the school day so that much greater amounts of independent student inquiry and small-group inquiry could occur.
- Florence, Agnes, and Nancy had discovered that only about half of the students had access to computers at home. Therefore they recommended that a resource of portable computers be developed and that parent education on their uses accompany the program.

Perhaps the most dramatic effect of the report was on the Techrow members. They realized that they had been operating on the assumption that one could simply make technology available and it would be absorbed productively by the school. Now they realized the amounts of learning that were necessary. *Just as important, they realized that neither they nor anyone else knew just how much – or even whether – a massive infusion of technology would affect student learning, and that a very careful action research program was necessary if one were to find out whether and to what extent student learning would be affected.* Clearly, the students would leave the school much more computer literate than most of their contemporaries, but what would be the increments in academic learning or literacy? Would there be any?

Nancy and Florence counseled that the Responsible Parties take their time about making a decision and that Techrow consider a much larger grant, one that would incorporate the costs of the additional staff development and the technical assistance to develop the action-research program. Techrow had already been prepared to provide the consultants on computers and to install the networks and arrange the purpose of the computers. Now the company understood what else had to be provided. They realized that before most of the computers and software could be ordered the entire faculty had to learn to use them and to be acquainted with the options for curriculum and instruction and also for various types of hardware and software.

One of the Techrow representatives, following a conversation with Florence, came up with an idea to get things started without committing everyone to the entire breadth of the initiative. The idea was to provide all the teachers with laptop computers that they could use in both home and school, and to provide staff time to study and the resources to free the two most computer-literate staff members to provide assistance to the teachers as individuals. The Responsible Parties decided that all the staff had to agree with the exploration before that should be put in place.

After what seemed like endless deliberation, all the staff agreed and the first step could be taken.

Not long afterwards, Agnes, Nancy, and Florence wondered whether even that seemingly innocuous step had been a mistake. After the first three sessions, the staff appeared to be divided into three groups. About ten were thrilled. About 20 were anxiously proceeding, step by step. About ten were convinced that early retirement was preferable to the struggle to learn. Florence and another computer-wise consultant began to visit the school weekly, along with several members of the Techrow staff, all providing all the help they could to the staff.

The first action research study focussed on the progress of the staff after five months of study. The results were encouraging. About 15 members appeared ready to begin to study broad computer applications to the curriculum – study that would be the basis of the design of the order for the computers, the design of the network, and the deployment of the computers and the organization of space for them. About 15 more were ready for the general study of applications but were some distance away from envisioning how courses could be redesigned to take advantage of them. The other ten were progressing slowly, but less resentfully.

However, all of them were convinced that word processing would be a boon for student writing, and that literacy initiatives should have high priority should the program go forward.

This last finding resulted in the last debates about whether to accept the full Techrow offer and Nancy's and Florence's (with Agnes's) recommendations. The Responsible Parties decided that a positive decision would require affirmation by 80 percent of the trustees, parents, and staff with an understanding that dissenters would abide by the decision.

The vote took place and all the provisions for staff development, action research, and technical assistance were phased in over the next academic year.

The study of implementation continued to be central. Student learning was studied immediately in two areas: The literacy program for poor readers and writers was implemented (see Second Chance in Chapter 3 for a similar effort with substantial success). All students learned word processing rapidly, and a "writing across the curriculum" effort pleased everybody and resulted in modest increases in student quality of writing and great increases in fluency in writing.

Over the next months the major need of the staff turned out to be the reorganization of courses and the learning of new instructional models. The faculty had believed it could make those changes easily, but much more extensive staff development was needed than it initially thought. Essentially, the staff believed that it had a much wider repertoire than it actually had. Staff members were surprised to learn that Florence had a considerable repertoire of curricular/instructional models that were virtually unknown to them before the project began.

The curriculum gradually expanded. Cross-curricular courses appeared, and new and highly specialized modular courses in Information Technology were created. The latter had to be bolted onto the existing curriculum structure, with the inevitable strain on the timetable. New courses also brought about restrictions in time allocation for previously existing subjects. At the same time new teaching and learning methods required longer periods of time to operate effectively. The equilibrium of the old curriculum had been disturbed and new ways of creating coherence needed to be developed.

The students were respected as they learned their new technologies, and the inquiry modes that were introduced had an impact. As one student said, "The classes are quite relaxed, in the way that you are not treated like infants and told exactly what to do and the teachers treat you as adults."

In an interview one member of staff noted the importance of the language used by both staff and students in both expressing and reinforcing this student-centered culture. She also felt that it was interesting how there was a strong collective commitment to the values and culture of the school among its staff. Several of the staff interviewed commented on how the "staff pull together," "share the vision," and "have a shared philosophy about ways of working with students." The importance of "valuing the individual" was stressed and this identification with the fundamental principles of a comprehensive school came through in a great number of interview comments.

Staff members also recognize the significant role of the head teacher in developing the culture of change. New initiatives ("almost like mini-TVEIs" to quote one member of staff) have been continually introduced to keep the school moving. Several staff noted the importance of this "driven style of leadership."

The head teacher is also seen to have made a significant contribution through the way in which she has communicated the vision about Blenheim being "a school in which people matter most." The values which guide the school's work are given a high profile, particularly in assemblies, but also in all forms of communication with staff, students, and parents.

The school's television broadcast system has also been very significant in this context. In a large school it has helped to provide a way of continually expressing the values as well as sustaining a sense of community and collective identity. As this system has become increasingly "student-driven" it has had a profound effect, communicating the ethos and culture of the school. The way in which student's language reflects the culture of the school can be attributed in a large way to the success of this medium of communication.

The interviews conducted with staff as part of the Moving Schools Research Project revealed other interesting features of the school's culture. The way in which the school has developed has encouraged a "reflective" and "questioning" culture. Assumptions and ways of working have been examined and challenged through various staff development processes. This has helped to further develop an environment in which teachers feel able to experiment and take risks.

Several members of staff also talked about the culture of success that is self-perpetuating. The continual improvement of examination results is clearly a challenge, but it has certainly helped to maintain a culture of success. Feedback from parents suggests that they feel that the school provides their children with a "mandate for success." Staff feel that these successes have had a very positive impact on student attitudes.

The development of a student-centered culture has had other impacts, notably on student expectations and involvement. Students have an expectation that they will be listened to and that there will be good teacher–pupil relationships. They also have expectations about the quality of their learning experiences. In the last six years or so research and evaluation in the school has included student perspectives, and the involvement of students in preparing for and developing change is now becoming the norm.

The internal restructuring that began with the technology initiative has had many positive impacts on the professional development of staff. One of the main impacts has been the legitimization of role change. As a result, a significant number of staff have had opportunities for new responsibilities and challenges during their time at the school. The fluidity of structures that have evolved over the years has helped to renew the professional energies of the staff.

The Ofsted inspection report acknowledges the importance of the quality of leadership that has been provided by the head teacher: "The school is very ably led by a head who has clear vision and has created a stimulating educational environment in which both staff and pupils are motivated to produce work of the highest quality" (Ofsted 1996: 21).

All of the staff interviewed during this research commented on the significance of this leadership, and in particular upon how the style of leadership has influenced the way in which the school has developed. The vision and the shared values upon which the ethos of the school is based have been clearly and consistently communicated to the whole community. The strength of the "community spirit" within the school has also been a significant factor.

The quality of the debate about a wide variety of issues in the school continues to improve. Inquiry is assuming increasing importance in the management of change.

What the school tries next will be interesting to observe.

COMMENTARY

A description of the renovative efforts in every curriculum area and in all aspects of the social climate of the school, or of all the possible instructional changes that could be made, would take a very large book indeed. The important message from successful projects is that they have been made possible by collective inquiry, centered on student learning, and imbued with continuous study. "Quick and dirty" curriculum changes are very short-lived and can be very unpleasant as well. Trying to force through changes with heavy administrative pressure from within the school or from district, state, or national levels generally results in no real change but in considerable resentment. Perhaps most difficult for many folks is the realization that curricular and instructional change requires that *they* change through study and inquiry. Learning new things is not really difficult, is generally very enjoyable, but to understand its necessity comes as a surprise to many educators.

The journey continues . . .

10 Redesigning Pembroke School: unfolding an evolutionary state

We are trying to combine research and experience in curriculum, instruction, and organizational change. Although examples are placed throughout the text, largely in the form of scenarios based on real cases, envisioning the entire change process is difficult. In this section we provide an extended narrative, first describing a dynamic and effective school in action and then tracking the process by which a calmly vibrant individual created a community, a fully functioning Responsible Parties group. The roles of faculty, parents, community members, community agencies, and business partners were mingled as they strove to build a school where personal, social, and academic growth were seamlessly and rigorously promoted. The major features of the process are described from the American context. Annotations translate some of the major items into the context of the United Kingdom.

Throughout this case we will see the continuous use of the evolutionary change mode: intensive, schoolwide, learning-centered staff development, school improvement initiatives, action research, and development of the school culture.

SECTION 1: PEMBROKE ELEMENTARY SCHOOL TODAY

Place Pembroke halfway between the town center and the suburbs of Camden, a 150-year-old industrial city of about 50,000 people somewhere in the heartland of America. Imagine the Midlands as a similar setting. Camden's 20 schools serve about 10,000 students. There are three high schools, three middle schools, and 14 elementary schools.

People
Pembroke Elementary has 600 students and a staff of 19 teachers, 18 full-time paid aides, and a principal. Three full-time secretaries and two part-

time clerical assistants attend to communication and clerical necessities. Three of the teachers are designated as "team leaders" and are paid at the rate assistant principals receive in the education authority.

For 120 students English is a second language, and state and federal programs subsidize their education. Sixty of those students are children of parents who migrated from Mexico. The parents of 60 are from South Korea. Forty percent of the Pembroke students qualify for subsidies for lunches under current guidelines. A state multicultural/bilingual initiative subsidizes the salaries of four teachers. Included on the staff are also two teachers who serve the "profoundly deaf" elementary students of the district.

In most of the Pembroke households both of the parents work. About 10 percent of the households operate small businesses in the neighborhood. In about 20 percent of the other homes one of the parents works in a highly skilled occupation. Twenty-five percent are single-natural-parent households and, in half of those, two adults are in residence.

Budget
State funds provide $4000 per student per year, local taxes amount to $500 per year per student, and federal and state funds for bilingual education add an average of $100,000 per year to the school budget. Pembroke has two grants. One, from a local foundation, is for $25,000 to support "women in science and mathematics," an interest of the patrons of the foundation. Pembroke also has a grant of $10,000 from the state Endowment for the Humanities to support an "artists in residence" experimental program for elementary-school children. In addition, "business partners" pay the salaries of ten of the paid aides.

State and district moneys provide for several summer programs and state funds support a number of offerings for adults. The local community college offers a variety of courses on the Pembroke campus.

The school building
The structure was built in the late 1920s, when it seems like all the school districts in the entire United States used the same architect. When constructed there were two storeys of 12 classrooms – each floor a virtual replica of the other. The original ground-floor plan is depicted in Figure 10.1 and illustrates the typical "egg-crate" structure with classrooms around a wide hall. However, extensive remodeling has taken place, resulting in the present floor plan as depicted in Figure 10.2.

The changes reflect the school's new educational plan. The space has been opened up to accommodate the need for a much larger library and the multimedia and learning resources centers. The pods for the older children and the creativity center are on the upper floor. The elimination of the huge hall has dramatically increased space for instruction and self-instruction. The moveable partitions enable much of the ground floor to be opened up for large meetings. Both the cafeteria and gymnasium are housed in a separate structure.

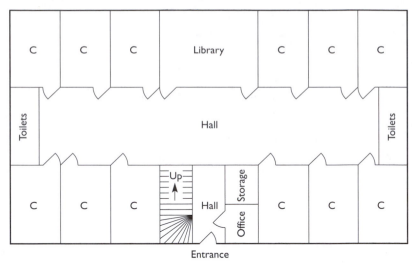

C = Classroom

Figure 10.1   Ground-floor plan for old Pembroke

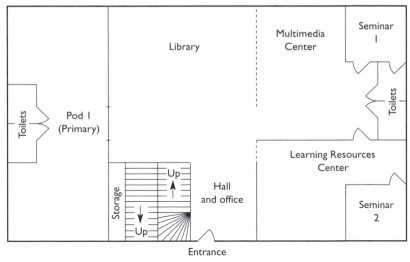

Emergency exits not depicted   - - - - - Moveable partition

Figure 10.2   Ground-floor plan for new Pembroke

THE WORKING SCHOOL

Let's visit the school in operation. We'll start by watching some teaching/learning episodes. Then we'll visit with the Responsible Parties, the governance group of the school. Finally, we'll follow a team of teachers through a day.

To begin, we'll watch some parts of the first day of school for 6-year-olds. Let's step inside Pod 1 and see what's going on this first day of school.

Scene 1: 6-year-olds start their inquiries

In one first grade class the children are gathered around a table on which is a candle and a jar. The teacher, Jackie Wiseman, lights the candle and, after it has burned brightly for a minute or two, places the jar carefully over the candle. It grows dim, flickers, and goes out. Then she produces another candle and a larger jar, and the exercise is repeated. The candle goes out, but more slowly. Jackie produces two more candles and jars of different sizes, and the children light the candles, place the jars over them, and the flames slowly go out. "Now we're going to develop some ideas about what has just happened," she says. "I want you to ask me questions about those candles and jars and what you just observed." The students begin. She gently helps them rephrase their questions or plan experiments. When one asks, "Would the candles burn longer with an even bigger jar?" Jackie responds, "How might we find out?" . . . Periodically, she will ask them to dictate to her what they know and questions they have and write what they say on newsprint paper. Their own words will be the content of their first study of reading.

Next door the children are seated in pairs. In front of each pair is a pile of small objects. Each pair of children also has a magnet. Their teacher, Jan Fisher, smiles at them and explains that the "U-shaped" object is called a magnet. "We're going to find out something about this thing we call a magnet. We'll begin by finding out what it does when it's held close to different things. So I want you to explore with your magnet. Find out what happens when you bring it close to or touch the things in front of you with it. And sort the other objects according to what happens." She, too, will take notes on the categories they form and use those to begin their study of written vocabulary.

Jackie is beginning her year with the model of teaching we call "inquiry training" (see Joyce *et al.* 1999). The model begins by having the students encounter what will be, to them, a puzzling situation. Then, by asking questions and conducting experiments, they build ideas and test them. Jackie will study their inquiry and plan the next series of activities to build a community that can work together to explore their world.

Jan has begun with the model we call "inductive thinking." That model (see Joyce and Calhoun 1997 for a complete treatment) begins by presenting the students with information or having them collect information and engage in classifying. As they develop categories (in this case objects according to how they respond to what they will eventually learn to call a magnetic field), they will build hypotheses to test. Jan will study how they think, what they see and don't see, and help them learn to attack other areas as a community of inductive thinkers.

Behind the scenes

Several aspects of the Pembroke approach to schooling underlie the ways Jackie and Jan are leading the students:

1 The overarching curricular and instructional approach will be disciplined cooperative inquiry. The students will be responsible for

working together to discover knowledge and skills and master them. The cooperative-inquiry mode of learning will be taught explicitly, as will the social climate of the teaching/learning relationship. We have watched these kids get their first lessons in learning how to learn.

2 Listening, speaking, reading, and writing will be taught together and tightly connected. From the beginning, the students will generate ideas that will be put down in words, and they will learn to summarize and synthesize findings, first in dictated form and later at their computers and on paper. As they learn to read, they will study how authors write and will use what they learn to enhance their own writing. This type of approach has been found, again and again, to generate greater student learning than "following the textbook" approaches to teaching the language arts and other subjects (Hillocks 1987; Joyce and Calhoun 1996; Calhoun 1997; Joyce *et al.* 1999).

3 The curriculum in science (and, as we will see, the other curriculum areas) is fully integrated with the teaching of reading and writing because the instructional models make it easy to integrate them. As the students construct inquiries in science, they engage in a great deal of reading and writing.

4 With their colleagues, Jan and Jackie have pursued the study of teaching intensively in the Pembroke staff development program. They have examined research on curriculum and teaching and studied effective models of teaching and learned to use them effectively. On this first day of school, the entire staff is making statements to the students in behavioral terms – the teachers are showing the children the kind of place this school is.

Scene 2: The Creativity Center

Let's come back after a week and walk upstairs and see what the upper grade kids are doing a week into the new term. We'll pause for a minute at the Creativity Center on the north end of the second floor. The place is crammed with materials, computers, desks for teachers, and a large work area where a local graphic artist and two aides, both students at the local college, are developing materials for an upper grade world-culture/global literacy unit. One of the aides is downloading e-mail messages from several schools around the world that the upper grade students have been writing to.

Scene 3: Inquiry in the social studies, reading, and writing

We make our way to Pod VI. Debbie Psychoyos' 5/6 grade has been studying demographic data on the 210 nations of the world, using the computer program PC Globe. Each of the nine groups of four have analyzed the data on about 20 nations and searched for correlations among the following variables: population, per capita GNP, birth rate, life expectancy, education, health care services, industrial base, agricultural production, transportation systems, foreign debt, balance of payments, women's rights, and natural resources. The kids are not novices at this kind of analysis – last year they conducted a similar inquiry into the United States.

The groups report, and what began as a purely academic exercise suddenly arouses the students.

"People born in some countries have a life expectancy 20 years less than folks in other countries."

"We didn't find a relationship between levels of education and per capita wealth!"

"Some rich countries spend more on military facilities and personnel than some large poor ones spend on health care!"

"Women's rights don't correlate with type of government! Some democracies are less liberal than some dictatorships!"

"Some little countries are relatively wealthy because of commerce and industry. Some others just have one mineral that is valuable."

"The United States owes other countries an awful lot of money."

The time is ripe for group investigation (for descriptions, see Sharan and Shachar 1988; Joyce *et al.* 1999). Debbie carefully leads the students to record their reactions to the data. They make a decision to bring together the data on all the countries and find out if the conclusions the groups are coming to will hold over the entire data set. They also decide that they need to find a way of getting in-depth information about selected countries to flesh out their statistical data. But which countries? Will they try to test hypotheses?

One student wonders aloud about world organizations and how they relate to the social situation of the world. They have heard of the United Nations and UNESCO but are vague about how they function. One has heard about the "Committee of Seven," but the others have not. Several have heard of NATO and SEATO but are not sure how they operate. Several wonder about the European Economic Community. Several wonder about India and China and how they fit into the picture.

Clearly, deciding priorities for the inquiry will not be easy. However, the conditions for Group Investigation are present. The students are puzzled. They react differently to the various questions. They need information and information sources are available. Debbie smiles at her brood of young furrowed brows.

"Let's get organized. There is information we all need, and let's start with that. Then let's prioritize our questions and divide the labor to get information that will help us."

Watching Debbie and the students, we can see the same elements of curriculum, teaching, and social climate that we observed last week in Jan and Jackie's classrooms:

1 Again, disciplined inquiry by a community of learners is featured.
2 Reading and writing are prominent.
3 The curriculum is integrated fully and naturally, again because the approach to teaching learning centers on cooperative inquiry and the

natural blending of information from various sources. Learning in mathematics is prominent, given the nature of the data to be managed. Science is important as the environment is studied in relation to the nations of the world.

4 Debbie, with Jan and Jackie and their colleagues, is studying curriculum and teaching and how to build the social climate of a school. Their staff development program lives in how they study and teach.

Now, let's continue our inquiry by trying to find out how this school came to be and how it governs itself.

INTRODUCING THE RESPONSIBLE PARTIES

Let's pay the school another visit on the following Thursday evening and sit in on a meeting of the Executive Committee of the Responsible Parties, essentially the governing board of Pembroke.

On the way down the hall to Seminar Room 1 we will notice that there is a class on English for adults in one of the multimedia classrooms. About 40 of the Korean parents are present. All have laptop computers equipped with translation programs like *Easy Language* (IMSI 1995) that enable them to write in their native language and get rough translations. They are learning to use those programs. In addition, we notice that they have a Berlitz program and manual on the learning of English. Glancing through one, we note that it provides them with tasks, such as shopping for various things, and the attendant words and phrases with which to accomplish those tasks. We will find out later that oral language use and reading and writing are taught simultaneously and by methods remarkably similar to those that are being used with the children (for a thorough discussion, see Calhoun 1997, 1999). We'll also learn that much of the substance these parents and other community members study is an introduction to American culture and society and how to live here successfully.

We also notice a large world map on one section of the hall, colored to portray cultural and linguistic patterns. A big chart on another section, labeled "Just Read: We are a culture of readers" depicts the number of books various groups of the children have read independently thus far in this term of the school year. We note that the section of the chart for kindergarten children's records includes books that parents or other caretakers have read to the children. The chart includes markers for goals. Apparently there is a celebration every 10,000 books. A headline on the chart indicates that the 600 children read 70,000 books the previous year.

Scene 4: The Executive Committee

Once inside Seminar I we are introduced to 14 people, about equally men and women and with roles as depicted in Figure 10.3. Four people are liaisons: one with the business partners association, one with the central office of the school district, one with city agencies, including recreation and libraries, and one with media and communications agencies, including the local commercial and public television stations, cable company, and telephone company. Four are parents. The neighborhood is divided into 12 sections and the community members in each section have elected two members of the Responsible Parties or 24 altogether. The 24 have elected the four we meet to be members of the Executive Committee. All 20 teachers in the school are members of the Responsible Parties, and they have elected four members of the Executive Committee. The other two are the principal, Christine Jurenka, and Harvey Thompson, one of the team leaders, elected by his peers. We learn that Chris and Harvey are not voting members. We will also learn that the Charter (see Glickman 1993) is such that final votes on important issues are made by the entire Responsible Parties group: the Executive Committee studies options and winnows them to ones the larger group votes on.

We also learn that Pembroke is operated in an ongoing action-research mode (see Calhoun 1994, 1996 and the discussion in Chapter 5), so that data are collected and research is studied before options are selected, and actions taken in important areas are studied as to their effects and reviewed in terms of their success. Decisions at Pembroke are taken in a data-rich environment. The voteless Christine chairs the meetings, and Harvey is the recorder. There are three items on the agenda as in Figure 10.4.

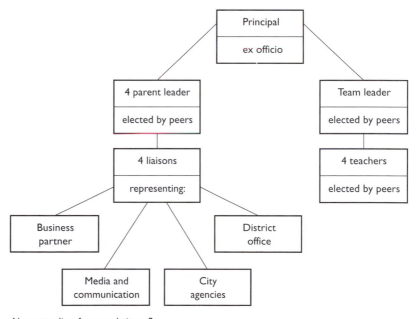

Also attending, for agenda item 2:
Cable system representative
Telephone company representative
Grocery chain representative

Figure 10.3 Executive Committee Responsible Parties

Agenda

1 Orientation of new parents and teachers and elections

As we all know, we have 83 new parents and two new teachers. We have to orient them. In addition, half the Responsible Parties have to be elected so the neighborhood clusters have to arrange their meetings and conduct the elections. You will remember that these are two-year terms without reelection, although retiring members can continue to serve on committees and are urged to do so.

2 Technology

The business partners and communications partners have an interesting idea to present for initial discussion.

3 Creation of agenda for a full Responsible Parties meeting next week and the community meeting the following week

Data on the summer term are partially analyzed and are a possibility. Just Read needs early attention, as does the bilingual program. The surveys will net some issues to discuss.

Figure 10.4   Agenda for the Pembroke School Executive Committee meeting

Christine reminds everyone that meetings are limited to 90 minutes. "That's so we don't get into the mess the school board is in, where most decisions are made after everyone has gotten exhausted and frustrated," she says in an aside to us.

Planning meetings and elections
She begins by having the agenda approved – a couple of announcement-type items are added to it – and begins with the orientation/election complex. A subcommittee proposes a series of meetings in the neighborhood "sections" to orient parents to the school, the governance charter, and the election procedures. With some minor changes, the plan is approved for presentation at next week's meeting, along with a plan for dividing the labor; two or three Responsible Parties members will conduct each meeting. The first newsletter of the term will advertise the meetings and include a copy of the Charter and a description of the election procedures.

They have a short break and Harvey suggests we have a look at the Learning Resources center at the north end of the ground floor because it will help us understand the proposal by the business and media partners. We learn that the school is open until 9 o'clock each weekday evening and for weekend hours as well. Parents and other community members use the computers in a variety of ways, and several small local businesses use them for accounting and other business purposes. Reciprocally, the businesses are "business partners" with the school and, among other things, sponsor courses in technology, tax preparation, and other relevant subjects. We remember that several businesses sponsor paid aides. The learning-resources personnel are also security personnel and work in shifts to cover the hours the school is open.

Inside the learning resources center we will find a collection of printed books, a library of computer programs including CD-ROM resources, and shelves of laptop computers. We will learn that the laptops are often moved into classrooms and are also available for student use at home. Parents can sign them out on evenings and weekends. The book collection is large for an elementary school and we find that the Learning Resource Center is also a branch of the city library. We have a lot of questions about the way so many innovations have occurred in one school, but Harvey hurries us back to the meeting. "We really try to keep meetings in bounds with respect to time. As it is, the teachers on the Executive Committee work somewhat non-standard hours so they can cover meetings without killing themselves. Chris was being funny with her crack about board of education meetings, but not completely. Board meetings are filled with political posturing and that is the only model some of the parents and teachers have, so we have had to learn how to run amicable, businesslike meetings. Christine took a lot of training on the subject and conducts a lot of little workshops for the Responsible Parties, the staff, and for parents. The business partners use her for their staffs, too."

Computers and technology
Chris introduces Don Duncanson, from the cable system, and Jacqueline Towers, from the telephone company, who will, with Nancy Targus, manager of the local outlet of a chain department store, make their proposal.

Nancy begins: "You all know that the business partners have worked with the school extensively in the area of technology. Many people thought it was very bold when the decision was made to put the bulk of the technology moneys into portable computers that could be easily moved from classroom to classroom and also taken home by kids and parents. We had to get special permission from the district office (a nod to the district liaison), and many school board members thought those computers would just walk away. But they let us do it, and it worked. All told, only six of the 200 computers have been damaged, amazing when you see them toted off in the backpacks of 6-year-olds.

"The classroom workstations have worked well and the learning-resources center is in good shape. We've added portable CD-ROMs and heaps of software. Classes can operate where all the kids have encyclopedias, data bases, and encyclopedias, and the language translators are a boon to the bilingual program."

Several hands go up and Christine speaks quickly. "Yes, the bilingual program will be a major topic this year, but let's stay with technology for the moment." Everybody laughs and the hands go down.

Nancy continues: "Thanks, Chris. By the way, concerned folks, technology may be a big help to us in that area. However, moving right along, here is our problem. Increasingly, the World Wide Web is becoming an important source of learning materials. Several curriculum areas, notably the social studies, are beginning to use the Web to augment instruction. But searching for information takes time, and the teachers believe that the home is the place for much of that work, despite the resources of the school.

"Now, our Charter makes equity a guiding principle of the school. Telephone and cable lines and modems are necessary for accessing the Net. We have surveyed the families and discovered that 85 percent have cable, all but 12 have telephones, and 15 percent have modems in the home. What we now need to face is whether the access to the Web will be added to the learning resources that are needed by all children. If the answer is affirmative, then is it important that all kids have access at home? If that answer is affirmative, then how do we assure that it is done in an equitable manner? We've asked the teachers to deal with the first question."

The teacher representatives report that the teachers have studied the usefulness of the Web as a learning resource and concluded that its usefulness is increasing in many areas, but that using it is more complex just because the sheer volume of material is so great and names for homepages and such are not standardized and can be very confusing. "We're not entirely sure, but it seems like about 20 percent of the kids' projects could conceivably be augmented by access to online information. The cross-USA and world connections could be invaluable in the social studies. There is a considerable increase in science programs and networks that the older children could access."

Considerable discussion follows. Several teachers have prepared Web pages that might be used to start children's inquiry on topics in the curriculum. Two children have developed astronomy projects with children in Perth. The e-mail from Debbie's unit seems very productive.

Chris indicates that five minutes remain. Nancy says: "Well, there is no need for urgent decisions. However, Don and Jackie have convinced their companies to make small grants that can ensure that all of our families have telephones and access to cable. Both companies will also provide $1000 each for modems, or enough for about 20 modems at prices I can arrange. Some other partners will probably chip in. However, if we were to make a decision to connect everyone, it would take most of this year's hardware budget. The current budget calls for additional workstations tailored to instructional needs, some more portable CD-ROM drivers, and 30 laptops. The cost of the modems for every family would take the laptop budget this year. However, in addition to learning resources, the benefits would be in communication . . ."

She turns toward Don and Jackie. From Don: "Newsletters, surveys, announcements could be made electronically and responses received that way."

From Nancy: "Aspects of conferencing between parents, teachers, and kids could be by e-mail. Kids and parents could report their Just Read records electronically."

From Don: "Kids could submit drafts of writing and get responses. If several kids had questions about an assignment, a teacher could clarify the assignment and put the clarification in the boxes of all the kids. And – this, I think, is compelling – the Korean and Mexican kids could communicate with people from Korea and Mexico in their original language and bring us lots of information."

From Nancy: "The modems would work with the computers in school as well as home. Together with the existing workstations, nearly 200 would be operable at one time if needed, accessing over cable or telephone lines."

Looking pleased, they subside. Chris leads the group to ask them to develop a detailed plan, including training for all concerned, and to repeat tonight's presentation to the larger group next week.

The district liaison, Clarice Jones, voices a concern. "Everyone knows that technology use in Pembroke is state-of-the-art – way above any other school in the region. But I keep getting asked why you don't use internal networks around servers. The other schools are doing that at a great rate."

Christine asks Nancy and Don to meet with Clarice to describe the rationale.

Harvey reminds everyone that there will be issues about the Web that will parallel ones already being raised by some people in the community over books – worry that the kids will get their hands on the wrong stuff. "At some point we've got to deal with this. We can't want the kind of divisiveness that has wracked many communities." There was general assent and Christine promised to put the issue to the next Executive Committee meeting.

Agendas
After another short break, the group considers the meeting of the larger Responsible Parties group, including the technology proposal and plans for orientation and elections. Business partner relationships will be on the Executive Committee agenda next week, along with a report by the older children, who are surveying the competence with computers of the entering kids and their parents. Supervised by Debbie, the students have been visiting homes, welcoming people, and interviewing them. The school community meeting will concentrate on Just Read, reorientation, revisitation of the Charter, and a reminder that the Charter is up for revision biennially, meaning this year.

We take a look at the Charter and are interested in the core ideas behind its provisions:

1 Community members (whether parents or not), community institutions, teachers, parents, and students will participate in a democratic process to make Pembroke a world-class school, socially and academically.

2 The process will be data-based. The study of curriculum, instruction, and student learning will be continuous and data will be related to

decisions. The best in the educational literature will be used as well, again in a public fashion.

3 The process will bring all parties together in the grand American experiment in common schooling.

4 "One for all and all for one" will be the principal of educational decisionmaking. Equity will be a mode of living.

5 All students can learn to an excellent degree. The program will be a relentless search for excellence for all.

6 The structure of the school will provide time for study and colleagueship for adults and students. The school will take responsibility for seeing that its staff has time and resources to continue life-long learning, so that staff members can become more and more effective as teachers and people and more and more capable of modeling educated democracy for the students.

For Pembroke, the trek toward this democratic process began five years ago, when Christine became principal and discovered that the parents and staff were upset because a district plan would send the neighborhood kids on buses all over the district to satisfy a court case alleging that segregation by neighborhood disadvantaged minority students. Christine brought together the business partners and began the collective process we have just observed in microcosm. The community, once organized, persuaded the district, the courts, and the state that they would create a fine school where they could capitalize on serving their polyglot neighborhood.

THE SCHOOL AS A CENTER FOR INQUIRY

Our next excursion is into the broad picture of curriculum, instruction, collaborative work among the faculty members, and the action-research mode that pervades Pembroke in ways large and small. We follow Harvey around for a few days and he introduces us to faculty, aides, and children, and allows us to watch his team in action.

The direct instruction team

We find that Harvey is co-team leader of a team responsible for guiding the education of about 170 children, aged 10–12. The team, depicted in Figure 10.5, includes three professional teachers besides Harvey: Marge is the co-leader and George and Debbie are the others. There are four paraprofessionals: Joan, Maureen, Tommy, and Mary.

Both Harvey and Marge are specialists in the teaching of reading and writing and he also in science and she in mathematics. Joan and Debbie have particular interest in the social studies and literature. George has become a computer addict and hopes one day soon to direct an operation such as the learning resources center. Joan and Maureen are college graduates, both working on their teaching credentials, and have the basic status of interns: over a two-year period their work with the direct

Team leaders

Harvey   Marge

Teachers

George   Debbie

Paraprofessionals

Joan   Maureen   Tommy   Mary

Figure 10.5   The direct instruction team

instruction team will be the field experience in their teacher preparation programs. Tommy is 19 years old, a high-school graduate, and "thinking about his future." He and many other youngsters like him are attached to direct instruction teams and instructional support centers throughout the school, where they work under close supervision. At the end of each year, Tommy and his peers discuss with Chris, Harvey, and the other team leaders their future roles and educational plans. As long as they remain attached to instruction teams, it is necessary for them to carry on programs to further their education. Mary is also a high-school graduate. She is married and the mother of two, and is a warm, supportive person who tends to gather around her the shy and lonely children. Among other things, she takes responsibility for the orientation of the new children who come under the guidance of the direct instruction team.

In one sense, about 25 parents are also members of the team. Several serve part-time as volunteer (unpaid) aides to the team, and Harvey and Marge operate a regular parent-tutoring series in which they explain the children's educational program and inform parents about ways of helping the children at home.

Harvey and Marge deploy the direct instruction team as required by their plans. While certain kinds of teaching are done only by the professionals within the team or the instructional support centers, all team members, including the paraprofessionals, function in teaching roles. The paraprofessionals, more often than the professionals, help the children move from place to place, setting up equipment and maintaining the environment as an attractive and efficient place. As they gain experience and confidence, the paraprofessionals are able to carry on more significant teaching.

SUPPORT CENTERS

Harvey's "staff" also includes professionals and paraprofessionals from three support centers: Resource, Creativity, and Assessment.

Learning resource center

Two teachers and four paraprofessionals staff this center. Physically, it includes the computer stations and carrels in the halls as well as the storage of the laptops, books and periodicals, files of documents, and cartons of materials that support curricular units. Altogether, nearly 200 children can be accommodated at any one time in the center.

Creativity center

The center supports the development of instructional materials and resource units. The professional staff and paraprofessionals help to research instructional materials and build them. They work with the staff of the direct instruction teams. As an example, a direct-instruction team might desire to create materials for a unit on one of the new nations of the world. They consult with the staff of the materials creation center to produce readable, new materials for all the children, including those with special needs. The center staff might contact embassies and consulates, help search the Net for information and materials, seek out films and videotapes, create overhead transparencies, and so forth. The materials creation center might develop projects on its own, but its primary purpose is to serve the needs of the direct-instruction teams. In so doing they free the school from dependence on commercial textbook publishers whose materials cannot be specifically keyed to local needs and interests.

The assessment center

One full-time professional and two paraprofessionals staff this center, whose assignment is to provide formative evaluation of student learning in reading, writing, and mathematics and to feed diagnostic information to the direct-instruction teams. For example, they use the NAMES Test to provide specific information about basic phonetic and structural analysis, so that the teachers know which phonetic skills the students possess and which they do not. They track levels of reading, following the students from where they can read simple picture-story books through juvenile fiction and non-fiction. The data are shared with parents and students as well as teachers so that they know the state of progress and the tasks necessary to reach the next levels of competence. Similarly, the center maps the progress of the students in arithmetic and in mathematical understanding. In writing, samples are collected periodically and scored for diagnostic use: that is, the scores give information not just about growth but about the learning needs of the students.

COMMENTARY

The reader has no doubt noted the unusual staffing pattern in the school, particularly the formation of the support centers and the unorthodox proportion of paraprofessionals to teachers. Figure 10.6 depicts the staffing of the school as a whole.

Let's see how this configuration functions as Harvey works his way through the day.

Principal (Chris)

Direct-instruction teams

Team 5–7	Team 8–10	Team 10–12
4 teachers	4 teachers	4 teachers
4 paras	4 paras	4 paras
175 students	175 students	175 students

Support centers

Resource	Creation	Assessment
2 teachers	2 teachers	1 teacher
2 paras	2 paras	2 paras

Kindergarten unit
Two teachers work as a team with students who attend for half-days as part of the 5–7 team.

Figure 10.6   Staffing pattern in Pembroke Elementary

A day with a teacher

The following week we spend as much time as we can following Harvey around and studying how the education of the children is arranged. Let's reconstruct our notes from Monday.

On Monday, at 7.45 a.m. Harvey convenes the meeting of his direct-instruction staff to discuss two aspects of the educational program. One project involves the learning resources center. The technicians have arranged to cooperate with a software development company who have developed a program by which the economic activities of a department store are simulated. The purpose of the simulation is to help students learn the economic principles that operate as a store purchases goods, sets prices, creates advertising programs, and organizes its personnel. The students are to learn these principles by making decisions in a game-type situation. As they make decisions about the price of a product, they will receive feedback on sales and will be able to adjust prices, advertising, and other factors to see if they can increase the product's profitability. While the program has been used successfully with older children, this is the first attempt to apply the technique with 10- to 12-year-old children. Harvey and Marge believe that given the success the children had with Sim City (the computer game) and several other simulations, they will have little difficulty with Sim Store. George is delegated to integrate the simulation with the unit on community economics and politics that is scheduled for November.

The other project that the direct-instruction team discusses is its fine arts program. Using artists in residence and personnel from the local art museum, and specialists from the creative arts and humanities staffs of the high school, they have developed a unit on contemporary America that meshes with a social studies unit. Some of the staff have reported a total lack of interest in art by a number of the students. They arrange for one of the museum specialists, who believes she is having great success with the children, to hold a demonstration later in the week so the staff can observe how she treats the content. Some of the team are dubious about the value of the unit in general, and Mary is assigned to discuss with the children their reactions to the program.

The meeting ends at 8.40 a.m. and Harvey prepares for a science discussion that he will lead at 9.00 a.m. Marge gathers Maureen, Tommy, and Joan about her and until 9 a.m. they discuss some of the problems they are having in the reading program. Specifically, three parents believe that the students should read only "classics" in the Just Read program. They have difficulty understanding the value of "ordinary" juvenile fiction. One had become quite angry with Maureen over the question. Marge decides to arrange a meeting with them as soon as possible to discuss balance in the reading diet.

9.00 a.m.: Harvey leads a discussion with ten children. This group has built a static-electricity generator and is conducting a set of experiments with it. Science is Harvey's own subject specialty, and he handles two project groups like this regularly, an advanced group (this one), and a group of rather difficult children whom he hopes to reach through their interest in science. Tommy observes Harvey during the discussion because he will be following up on what Harvey does during the rest of the week.

While Harvey's discussion goes on the rest of the team is deployed variously. Mary and Maureen lead a number of children to the resource center, where they help the children select books. Debbie continues her unit on world geography.

George spends a half-hour exploring Sim Store. Before the hour is over, Tommy leaves Harvey's discussion and sets up a large-group instruction room for a current events videotape which will be shown during the next hour to many of the children, part of a series located by the creativity center.

10.00 a.m: Harvey and George are in the resource center, helping their students operate Sim Earth. The operation goes well. The children are able to cope with the problems they are given and are excited about the work.

While he is there, Harvey also discusses with the center director some new individualized developmental spelling programs that the director says have just come on the market. Harvey's students have been doing very well with these programs, and the assessment center is preparing student/parent reports based on the assessment built into the program.

11.00 a.m.: Harvey spends most of the hour preparing a set of creative writing activities. Harvey designs the activities so that all the children will be grouped into teams studying collections of poems. They will analyze sets of poems containing three structures that they will attempt to master as they write their own poems (which they do as individuals). Members of the team will act as consultants for the various groups. The work of each student team will be shared with the other teams.

While Harvey prepares this unit, Marge and Maureen work with a small group of children making a videotape demonstrating three ways of performing division algorithms in base 8, 2, and 10. The tapes will be shown at parent meetings and entered in a state contest on mathematics. The rest of the children are working on independent research projects in the resource center.

12.00 noon: Harvey eats lunch with Mary and a small group of children. He and Marge have lunch with a different group of children each day so that every other week each child has an informal half-hour with one of the two team leaders. Mary accompanies Harvey because these children have recently transferred to the team from another school district. Her job is to make them comfortable and welcome, to get to know them, and to transmit any important personal information to Harvey and Marge. One of the girls was in a group that tutored some younger children that morning, and Harvey persuades her to describe to the others what she did and to tell them how she felt about it. This of course provides him with a child's-eye view of the tutoring activity.

1.00 p.m.: nearly all the children are still engaged in their research activities. Marge, Debbie, and George each have a small reading group gathered around them, working on comprehension skills. Harvey and Tommy take this morning's science group with them to the resource center, where the children are hunting for materials for their next set of experiments. When he is satisfied that Tommy can handle the situation, Harvey returns to the team suite and prepares the large-group instruction area for Debbie, who will make a general presentation on the global literacy unit.

3.30 p.m.: over coffee, Marge conducts a meeting with the entire staff about the reading program. She has some suggestions for individual conferences, and has a report from the self-instruction center about the student's progress with word-attack skills. The team's objective is to get the children to teach themselves everything possible, thus freeing the instructional time for things they have difficulty teaching themselves. Marge has set up the reading program so that much of it takes place in individual conferences during which the children discuss their progress in using self-instructional materials, and identify projects and readings for independent inquiry. Small groups are formed for units built around particular books and picture-word inductive units (see Calhoun 1999). Mary's role is with the children who have trouble keeping themselves at individual learning tasks. Her tactics are motherly and supportive, whereas Marge is rather brisk and direct, and they try to plan so that they work with the children for whom their styles are most effective.

4.00 p.m.: all the team members are working independently, preparing for the next day. Harvey prepares the agenda for the meeting next morning when he will explain the creative writing unit and the staff will discuss it. He also prepares a mathematics lesson for one group of the older children. Marge finishes up correspondence for the team (they share a secretary with another team) and George spends the hour with the computer support center planning the use of the simulated store the next day. Laura matches self-instructional reading units to student's needs during the next few days. Each day she does this for a certain number of children, so that each child's progress is checked by her or by

Marge at least once every two weeks. Joan, Maureen, and Tommy are in the independent inquiry center, developing resource units to be used with the next set of social studies units.

THE TEAM AND THE TEACHER

Harvey is a teacher with a large and complex staff of people who can do many things. He is a master at coordinating the work of other people and at developing curricular patterns that are tailored to the needs of the children he has, the community where they live, the requirements of the subject matter, and the large variety of instructional materials available. His staff includes the seven members of his direct-instruction team plus the specialists within the various support centers. Harvey's staff provides an individualized education which blends each child's interests, needs, and personal problems with the best the age can provide by way of educational technologies. The direct-instruction team members are the final decisionmakers in the educational process, so judgments about what each child will do and learn are made by the people who know him or her best.

Kinds of learning

Harvey and his team orchestrate an environment that uses three separate learning modes:

1 personal inquiry, where the students pursue interests of their own;
2 independent study, where they work with materials geared to their ability levels, and through the use of these materials learn to teach themselves; and
3 group inquiry, where they inquire into problems that are important to them and appear significant to their teachers.

The children, then, live balanced lives as learners. For personal inquiry they study things that they select, albeit with assistance from the teachers. In independent study they study things that they understand will help them to develop in skill and in intellect. In group inquiry they work with their peers, thrashing out what is significant and ways to learn it.

THE FEATURES OF PEMBROKE

Let's stand back from Pembroke for a few minutes and identify the complex of features that have been embedded in its organization and teaching/learning environment:

• *Governance.* Pembroke is developing an inclusive structure with many elements of democratic process. The Responsible Parties include community members as well as teachers, administrators, and a member of the central office. The team-leader structure provides broad governance and communication channels for the faculty. The Charter is a guiding document, a mini-constitution.

- *Business partners.* The strength of large and small businesses has been organized. Also, although they do not have specific membership in the Responsible Parties as an entity, they are free to attend meetings and speak up, and they are included in operating committees and task forces.
- *Adult education.* Most prominent at present are the offerings in technology and the reading and writing of English for foreign-born parents and other community members.
- *Community service.* In particular, computers and the library are available for community use. Computers are equipped for accounting and tax preparation. Cooperation with the city recreation department results in extensive offerings on the "shortened instructional day" as well as throughout the week, all through the year.
- *Business hours.* The school building opens at 6 a.m. and remains open until 10 p.m. Although instruction of children takes place largely during school hours, Wednesday from 1 to 4 p.m. is for faculty planning, peer coaching, sharing of data, and staff development.
- *Staff development.* All staff development takes place on those Wednesday afternoons except for attendance at conferences by teachers as individuals or in small groups. Four staff development days paid for by the school district are taken just before school opens in the fall and are devoted to a curriculum area that is under study. All told, the faculty has 32 half-days of staff development and four full days each year.
- *Differentiated staffing.* In the team and center structure, teachers and paraprofessionals are assigned to specific functions. The school has a much larger proportion of paraprofessionals than most schools and a larger number of staff devoted to instructional support.
- *Team teaching.* The team and center structure bring about many regular and many *ad hoc* co-teaching arrangements. The paraprofessionals are teaching members, not clerical assistants as in so many schools.
- *Home–school relationships.* Just Read, the computer program, the extensive inclusion of parents as aides, are obvious features of the development of a true sharing of responsibility for the education of the children. Parents receive instruction on at-home reading and writing projects, are kept apprised of student progress at regular and short intervals, and are offered instruction on tutoring as specific needs arise.
- *Nongrading and multiple-age grouping.* Students are with teams for two or three years and are mixed by age. The curriculum is organized so that all kids in the team study the same topics. For example, the global literacy unit will be studied by all the kids in Harvey's team.
- *Integrated-subject curriculum.* Literacy is the driving, pervasive theme. All curriculum areas are treated as literacy efforts. An inquiry mode dominates all subjects and unifies them.
- *Inquiry-oriented, cooperative instruction.* Basically, the students are taught to inquire into curricular substance and master it. There are no

separate "thinking-skills" programs. Thoughtful cooperation is basic.
- *Total "inclusion."* "Special" education is embedded in the curricular and instructional program.
- *Individual, small-group, and large-group instruction.* Appropriately, the teams arrange instructional modes as appropriate. Basically, students inquire both as individuals and in small groups. The entire team membership observes demonstrations, films, and tapes, and learns from lectures where appropriate.

Taken alone, any two or three of these would be regarded as a "full plate" for school improvement by many schools. However, they interact nicely, and many of them are easier to manage if one or more of the others are being developed. For example, the governance structure makes it much easier to communicate with the parents, and the school–parent initiatives make the partnership more solid, so the development and explanation of the other initiatives is much easier than it would be if communication had to be on an initiative-by-initiative basis.

Nongrading, multiple-age grouping, and differentiated staffing also fit together and work well in the team structure. Schools that attempt multiple-age grouping, but assign one teacher to each group and fail to change the curriculum, often end up with each teacher trying to manage the curriculums for several grade levels, which is very difficult. Nongrading requires continuous development plans for individual students and is also hard for individual teachers, working alone, to manage.

The appropriate use of large-group instruction is a very efficient use of staff. Instead of having four or eight teachers giving the same demonstration or talk to class-size groups, one or two teachers can have the same effect.

"Thinking-skills" programs that are not integrated in the basic instructional mode are both ineffective and essentially add another curriculum area to the program, crowding further an already packed schedule. An integrated curriculum that emphasizes literacy, inquiry, self-instruction, and cooperation builds the teaching of thinking into the school program.

Additionally, teams have a much easier time "managing" children than do teachers working alone. There are far fewer discipline problems and a greater range of teaching personalities to reach the children's range of personalities and learning styles.

SECTION 2: BUILDING A CULTURE OF INQUIRY

We return now to the content that is the body of this book: the process of building an evolutionary culture. We will tell the story of the transformation of Pembroke from a mediocre school to the inquiring culture that we met in Part I.

Many readers will be surprised to learn that we envisage a much shorter time to generate progress than do many practitioners of school renewal. During the first year of the journey to a self-renewing school, substantial increases in students' learning – and ability to learn – will occur. In that initial year, several important changes can occur: Community involvement can increase dramatically; the faculty can begin to engage in collective inquiry; staff development can be established as a regular and collective event; and there will be changes in curriculum and instruction that bring about increases in student learning.

Building a self-sustaining culture of inquiry takes about three years by our reckoning. We believe that if a longer time is set, say five or ten years, probably nothing will be accomplished. We also believe that making initiatives in curriculum and instruction, increasing community involvement, establishing staff development, and taking steps toward democracy all need to take place simultaneously. Moreover, the entire staff needs to be involved. Starting with just a few staff, with the thesis that others will gradually "buy in," has turned out to be unlikely to change a school. We begin with everyone.

Importantly, the work of building and sustaining self-renewal is never ended. Many aspects of the organization change: Personnel, composition of community, technology. Organizations can drift downward if they are not constantly rejuvenated through collective inquiry. The process is driven by the determination to help students learn how to learn, the recognition that changes in curriculum and instruction are the professional tool, and the willingness to develop an inquiring community of professionals who study student learning and how to improve it as a central dimension of teaching. Parents and community members and institutions are made an integral part of the school community and are themselves served in the process.

Let's beam ourselves back through time a bit and visit Pembroke as it was four years ago. Then we'll track its changes, reflect on them, and look at how they can be applied to any school.

Pembroke four years ago

In the old Pembroke we find George, the principal of ten years, an assistant principal who also works as a counselor, and 24 teachers who are assigned to classrooms where they are responsible for teaching most school subjects. There are several specialists: a full-time librarian, and art, music, and physical education teachers who are shared with other schools. George handles the scheduling of the specialists; he schedules the art, music, and physical education teachers into classrooms where they each provide about one hour of instruction to each class per week. There are two resource teachers in special education and four half-time aides who serve first and second grade classes. One full-time secretary works at Pembroke, and two building superintendents are responsible for the physical maintenance of the building.

Relation to the district office
The district has adopted a "site-based" management mode of operation which has had several effects on the schools. One is that discretionary funds for books, paper, staff development, field trips, and computers are

allotted to the schools and decisions on spending are made at that level. Each school is required to have a school site council, but the guidelines are vague and the style of principals determines the extent to which faculties are involved in various kinds of decisions.

To a limited extent, staffing decisions can be made at the school level. A case in point is that positions for aides and teachers can be interchanged somewhat, and schools can decide whether to have specialists in music or art or library science. George does not bring staffing issues to the faculty as a whole. He uses the specialists to free teachers from classroom duties and the faculty does not object.

An aspect of the movement toward site-based management is a shrinkage of central office staffs. Unfortunately, that shrinkage results in a shortage of district personnel who can support the schools in curriculum and instruction and arrange or deliver staff development to them. In the Pembroke of four years ago, George and much of his staff are content to be left alone to do their work. Let us see how they do it.

Curriculum development

Textbook adoption is the sole mode of curriculum development. Once each year George organizes the faculty for a day to look over textbooks and other instructional materials, particularly computer software and reference books for the library collection. They use a state-provided list of textbook series judged to be aligned with the state curriculum frameworks. The district requires that textbooks be changed in one curriculum area each year.

George and the secretary then complete the orders to publishers, making final decisions in the process. The librarian makes book orders from her budget, which has shrunk steadily over the last few years because George has merged the media and technology budgets and diverted part of them to duplicating services and paper, a move that is very popular with several teachers who use large quantities of drill-and-practice "worksheets."

Staff development

In addition to salaries for the teachers, the state government provides modest resources to each school for four staff development days each year. The school faculties are to organize the program for those days. When he makes the yearly schedule, George backs the four days against school holidays. He designates two of the days as teacher development, where the teachers arrange something for themselves as individuals – visits to other schools, mostly, but occasionally to conferences or workshops that might coincide with the scheduled days.

To select topics for the other two days, George canvasses the teachers for ideas and then scours the area for speakers on the most popular ones. The speakers are scheduled for the mornings, with the afternoons scheduled for developmental follow-up, that is, planning instructional activities that are intended to incorporate the "training."

Community relations

George also takes responsibility for the overall relationship with the public. However, twice a year each teacher consults with every parent about the progress of the children. With three or four exceptions, several of the teachers do not look forward to the conferences with parents, but they agree with George that not having them would be a public-relations mistake. George softens those teachers' feelings by having little parties for the staff late on the conference days. Twice a year, usually in the early fall and late spring, the school holds an open house for parents, and periodically during the year the classes present "parents' night" entertainments during which they display their work and sometimes put on a play, a dance recital, or a concert. Some of the upper grade children belong to a band and a chorus, both of which are directed by the music teacher, and these ensembles usually perform at the monthly PTA meetings.

Faculty meetings

George and the faculty agree that they hate meetings, but they have one every month, mostly to deal with logistics, book orders, organizing open houses, and such. George prefers one-to-one contact with people, chats with most faculty members at least once a week, and by the time a meeting rolls around, pretty well knows where most faculty stand on any issue to be faced.

Busing

Although the demography of the neighborhood is as we described it in Part I, about one-tenth of the neighborhood children get on buses every morning and are transported to other schools, and buses deposit about 60 children at Pembroke. The superintendent and the board have devised a complicated plan to ensure ethnic and racial integration in Camden's schools, and they needed Pembroke's Korean children to "balance" another school and replaced them with 60 black children. The Korean parents and kids are unhappy about this, but the former have been assured that the arrangement is a good one for their children.

Enter Christine

George has begun applying for superintendencies of nearby small school districts, which turns out to be relevant to our story. As part of his quest, he has connected with a leadership training program run by the county office of education and a branch of the state university. He has volunteered to supervise an administrative intern from their program on curriculum and administration, and on the "teacher planning day" that signals the beginning of the new year he meets Christine, who has been assigned to Pembroke. She and her husband have moved to Camden so that he can start a computer-service business. Christine has decided to cut down her work (the internship is half-time) for a year to finish her doctorate, help out in the business, and make the transition from curriculum director of a district, which she has been, to building administrator, which she intends to become on the way to a superintendency.

George's offer was the only one from Camden, so she took it with alacrity.

Christine's introduction

George is cordial. He is busy, but he gives her a quick tour of the school and introduces her to JoEllen, one of the second grade teachers. JoEllen is very experienced, has a forceful personality, and usually is assigned the two or three children who are thought to be most difficult to manage. JoEllen likes that because she sees herself as a strong disciplinarian. JoEllen and, eventually, George explain that Pembroke is a quiet school. That is, each teacher is expected to maintain an orderly and quiet classroom and keep the children working at their tasks. If a child is difficult the teacher is expected to inform George and he will arrange a conference with the parents to try to enlist their aid in controlling the child. If a child is very unruly he may be "sent to the principal's office." George likes to minimize this practice, but when a child is sent to him he chews him out thoroughly and threatens to call the parents and "get him in trouble" with them. According to both George and JoEllen the community likes a well-organized, calm school and most of the parents will assist with discipline when a problem is brought to their attention. Although busy getting organized for the school year, JoEllen is pleased to have an audience to whom she can explain what a fine job Pembroke is doing.

Christine and JoEllen see each other a number of times in the few days before school begins. The following interchanges are constructed from Christine's notes on discussions with JoEllen and others.

JoEllen is delighted to tell Christine what the school and community are like and to give her advice about how to fit in. "We're very friendly here and we're really open with the community. Most of the people in Pembroke's part of town are hard working. A lot of them have jobs in the town's big industry which makes small airplanes. They're skilled workers and most of the folks have lived here for several years. They want their kids to do well in school, but they leave education to us. It's not like the pushy parents in the suburbs always telling teachers how to teach. These people don't come to PTA meetings very often or visit the school. But most of them come down hard on their kids if we need backup."

"Do the teachers live in this area?"

"Oh, no, I don't really think any of us do. We live all over the city."

"Do you see the parents at social events or anything like that?"

"No, not usually. We have our open houses and our parent–teacher conferences, but we usually don't see them otherwise unless somebody comes in to visit the classroom or we ask for a special conference because we're having a problem of some sort."

"What is George's style as a principal?"

"Oh, George works real hard at his job. He gets us supplies and handles severe discipline problems, and mostly just leaves us alone. The district hires pretty good teachers. Most of us have been here for 10 or 15 years and we pretty well know what we're doing."

"Are people warm and close here, or what?"

"Oh, we all get along very well. We commute here, we get our jobs done, and we go home."

"Do you have a curriculum?" asked Christine. "That is, how do I figure out what is taught in each subject area?"

"Well, we spend most of our time on the basic skills. Most of us follow the textbooks in reading and arithmetic. We don't teach very much science here and everybody pretty well does what they think they ought to do in the social studies."

"Do you have curriculum committees?"

"Oh dear," says JoEllen, "you've probably been told in your graduate education program the theory that schools have committees that look at their curriculums and make plans about what ought to be taught, and so on. Well, that just doesn't really happen in very many places, and certainly not at Pembroke. Each one of us does our own job. We take care of ourselves and George takes care of the office. All you have to worry about is to teach reading and arithmetic really well and nobody will bother you. By the way, I can't imagine what you'll do here. The office runs like a clock, discipline is great, the teachers are great. I guess they sent you here so you'll know what a good school looks like."

"How do most people teach reading and arithmetic?"

"About five years ago the district adopted a comprehensive textbook series. It includes tests and everything. We all use it. This year the district offered some options, but we were unanimous not to change. The trouble is keeping the kids together. When they fall behind and we can't promote them they get the same books again. Some of these kids are just hopeless."

"How about audiovisual equipment?"

"Well," said JoEllen, "we have a lot of stuff. We have a videotape recorder and projectors and tape recorders and almost everything you could need. To be truthful, most of us don't use those very much. We pretty well teach by the book here."

"How about computers?"

"We all have three in our classrooms. A couple of people use them a lot. The kids go to the computer lab once a week for keyboarding."

Christine thanks JoEllen and makes her notes. JoEllen waves as they part, but stands looking after her for a few seconds, frowning just a bit.

Maryanne

Christine finds herself drawn to a first-year teacher, Maryanne, who was assigned to the school late in August to fill an opening caused because one of the teachers moved to another city suddenly when her husband was transferred by his company. George is good at working the system. The district personnel director told him that Maryanne was a "very good prospect" and George persuaded him to assign her to a Pembroke second grade rather than the sixth grade she had already been assigned to in another school. The director manipulated the other principal and found him someone else. Maryanne had no say in the decision.

Maryanne is not bent out of shape by the change. She is dominated by her excitement to get to work. The first day of school she gives each of the students a short diagnostic test in reading and a general diagnostic test in arithmetic. Christine walks into her classroom when she is giving the arithmetic test. Maryanne asks her if she has any ideas about diagnosis in reading and Christine says she might try the NAMES Test (Duffelmeyer *et al.* 1994), which concentrates on phonics. Christine says she'll help her give it and they could interpret it together and work on other diagnostics as well. The two women go with the children to recess and then meet JoEllen in the teachers' room for a moment. JoEllen greets Maryanne pleasantly.

"How's it going, love?"

"Oh fine. I'm just as nervous and excited as I can be."

"You'll get used to it," says JoEllen.

Christine and Maryanne meet again in the hall just before lunch. Maryanne tells Christine she has taken the children to the library and each has selected two books. The librarian was a little annoyed that she wanted them to be able to take more than one but had given in. George meets them as they reached the door of Maryanne's classroom and smiles reassuringly at her.

"How's it going, buddy?" asks George.

"Frankly, I'm scared stiff," she says, 'But I'm excited too."

"I think you're going to like teaching," said George. "Just hang in for a few weeks and get your sea legs."

She laughs.

"God," she says, "I wish I could teach as well as I can sail."

He laughs too.

"Listen," he says, "if you have any problems in the next few days just let me know. Especially, don't let them get out of hand. Christine might help you, too. I'm told she's an expert in the language arts. But with any discipline problems, come to me."

As George walks away, Maryanne whispers to Christine,

"Don't worry about it, just don't let anybody get out of hand."

Nobody does, in fact.

George, Theo (the assistant principal), and the physical education teacher mind the kids at lunch, giving the teachers a break. As the "new kids on the block," Christine and Maryanne are largely observers and then visit the faculty room.

The faculty room

The other teachers talk about clothes, shopping, some of the textbooks that haven't arrived, and exchange opinions about the "fastest" and "slowest" kids. As she confides later, Maryanne is amazed at how calm everybody is and how little they say about their teaching.

After a while, she asks "Does anybody know Carlos?", referring to a very shy little boy with very thick glasses.

"Oh yes, I had him last year," says Louise, one of the first grade teachers. "He's okay. He's lazy as hell, though, you have to really kick his butt." Everybody laughs.

"His whole damn family is like that," said one of the others.

JoEllen laughs.

"They sure are. Every other year I get one. Carlos is the first member of the family I haven't had."

"But he's kind of sweet," says Louise. "You'll see what I mean. But don't let him con you," she says to Maryanne.

Public and private teaching

Christine, who has decided to visit all the teachers for at least a couple of hours in the next few days, walks into Terry's fifth grade room simply because it was the first one she comes to. Terry is teaching arithmetic. She is drilling the children on the number facts, calling on one at a time. "Seven times six is . . ."

"Forty-two."

"Nine times seven is . . ."

"Sixty-two."

"What?" says Terry.

"Sixty-two," says the child, firmly. Some of the other children laugh.

"Sixty-three, dopey," says one.

Terry notices Christine, who has walked along the wall and sat down next to a bookcase in the back. She stops teaching.

"Do you want something, dear?" she asks.

"Ah, why no. . . . ," says Christine.

"If you're looking for George, he's probably in his office," says Terry, and waits without saying anything else. The children all look at Christine. The world of the classroom has stopped turning.

"Ah, well – okay," says Christine, realizing that this is no time for a confrontation, and she makes her way to the door.

"I'll see you around, dear," says Terry, and turns back to her class.

On the way to George's office Christine is both angry and confused. She finds George changing a lightbulb in an overhead projector. "These damn things are always breaking down," he says.

"I just stopped in one of the teacher's rooms and she didn't seem too pleased," says Christine. "Don't they expect us to visit them?"

George looks at her and smiles.

"Well," he says, "I guess the answer to that is both 'yes' and 'no.' Listen, I've got a call to make after I finish this. Come on by after school. Two or three of us are going to have a beer before we go home and there are a couple of people I'd like you to meet. Bring Maryanne along."

As the school day ends, Christine goes by Maryanne's room to pick her up and spends a few minutes helping her arrange magnets and other objects on the children's desks. Unlike many American elementary school teachers, Maryanne is very comfortable with the physical and biological sciences and has decided to lead from her strength. She still can't tell how much arithmetic the children know and stuffs the test she has given them into her book bag. Looking at the test will help somewhat, but she decides that she will begin at the beginning the next day and review counting and addition. Just where their skills reach and where they do not is the mystery she has to solve.

Before they leave, the door opens and they see two big, friendly men they have not seen before. They enter wielding brushes and mops and she realizes that they are the building superintendents.

"You must be Maryanne," says one, and sticks out his hand. "We're the janitors. They call us something else, but we kind of like being called janitors." He looks around the room. "Hey, kid," he says to her, "ask the children to put their chairs on their desks tomorrow, would you? It makes it a lot easier to clean the place up. Lots of janitors want the chairs kept in rows, but we don't really care about that. But it saves us about ten minutes for every classroom if they'll just lift up those chairs."

"Why, sure," she says. His companion is looking at one of the blackboards.

"Hey," he says, "let me show you how to clean this thing right. I think the manufacturers are trying to drive us crazy." He makes them wait while he expertly wipes the board clean. He grins at her. "Making your class run smoothly," he says, "is really a matter of a lot of little tiny things."

Kiki

George takes Christine and Maryanne to a smoky bar which is part of the local pizza parlor and introduces her to four teachers who are sharing a pitcher of beer. Maryanne realizes from the conversation that they, too, are relieved after the day, although they are ten or more years older than she. "Are you always nervous on the first day?" she asks and they all laugh.

George and the teachers banter back and forth. Occasionally, one will bring up some matter that he may attend to and he makes a note in his Franklin Planner.

Gradually, Christine realizes that three of the teachers are, with JoEllen, George's informal leadership team, informing him about how well things are working and helping him find areas to improve. Kiki, the fourth, is a resource teacher.

Just before they all leave, George says he'd like their help, in a week or two, in designing the evaluation process for teachers – he has to prepare performance reports each year. They agree. One comments: "I really liked last year when you visited each one of us just once but for half a day instead of twice for an hour."

The others murmur similar comments.

Christine realizes she has part of her answer to the question about classroom visitations.

Christine, Maryanne, and Kiki stay after the others have left and Kiki moves over next to Maryanne. She is very friendly and casual, but wants to talk to her about little Carlos.

"His sight is actually okay," says Kiki. "Oh, he has those monstrous, thick glasses and everything, but you know he isn't really blind or anything. The problem is that for some reason nobody found out that he couldn't see very well until last year because he's so quiet and withdrawn. Everybody thought he was stupid and he certainly didn't learn anything, or that is, very much, so he's got a lot of catching up to do and the worst part of it is that I think his family treated him in such a way that he actually thinks he doesn't have any brains. I want to tutor him once or twice while you watch so we can share some ideas."

"Sure, I'd love it."

"I didn't find him until last May. He was doing really badly and his family said he was really dumb. And his teacher, Louise, agreed with them. George wanted me to find out whether he should be in the special day class, but the psychologist and I found that he is really very intelligent and quite delightful. He just had to hold his head about an inch away from a book in order to read it. Or that is, try to read it, since he hadn't learned to read yet. So we kind of stumbled on him in a roundabout way. That's not so unusual. If a kid has any kind of a handicap, most people think they're dumb. That's one of my big problems."

"What do you do most of the time?" asks Christine.

She laughs. "Mostly I cope with the other teachers' resentment because I'm not in one classroom all day with 25 kids.

"Seriously, I do three things here. One is that I arrange for kids who have speech defects and things like that to get some special help from the teachers who work in the county office. The second thing is that I try to identify the kids who need some special help. I test them or get them tested and we try to find out whether they qualify for special services. Anyway, I try to work out individual programs for those kids. I see my real job as helping teachers work with kids like Carlos, including kids who are very slow and hard to manage and so on. About half my time I tutor small groups and the rest of the time I try to work with the teachers. Actually, you can tell that I'm really on the job right now, trying to give Maryanne a fix on Carlos."

They walk out to their cars together and Kiki says, "Frankly my biggest problem is that this is such a well-ordered place that any kid who just doesn't sit in his seat and do what he's asked to do gets into trouble. I keep getting kids referred to me whose main problem is that they're not half dead." Maryanne looks at her in surprise. "Oh yes," says Kiki, "you'll find out that this is a hell of a school for any kid who isn't a real conformist. I'm the specialist for learning disabilities and support for the extremely handicapped. There's a special class for the *behaviorally disordered*." Sarcasm saturates the last two words. "Translated, that means 'got in trouble with the wrong teacher.'"

Christine makes another note.

Starting where you can

George and Christine meet the next day to discuss her duties. He says that part of the time he wants her to just "shadow" him, learning how he does his job and discussing parts of it. "Then, look the place over and see if you can find anything that needs fixing. I think it's just about right, but you may be able to think of something. Then, we need an area that's *yours.* I want you to have something of your own. I'd like to see how you do it. Is there something that appeals to you right off?"

"Well, three things, actually. I'd like to support Maryanne and I notice there are three second-year teachers in the upper grades. I can get to know them and work out a little scheme to support them."

"That's great. I'm sure they can use the help, although everyone in this business needs to take responsibility for their own classrooms. Team-teaching, you know, was tried and just doesn't work. By the way, I think JoEllen will take Maryanne under her wing, but that doesn't mean you can't support her, too. Henrietta, the fifth grade teacher, can use a good bit of help. You'll figure it out pretty fast. By the way, because the second grade teachers don't have tenure, you can visit them whenever you want. Just let them know ahead of time. It's a custom here to visit tenured people only for the evaluation observations, except for the morning rounds, when I pop my head in to see if anybody needs anything. Now, what's the other area?"

"Community involvement. I'd just love to get to know the community and look for ways of involving more parents in the education of their kids."

George ponders that for a minute. "Well, except for the PTA, I think that's a great idea. You can work with me in relation to the PTA. But we all know that better parent help means better education."

"I mean the larger community, too."

"Like?"

"Oh, like searching for business partners."

"That's a good idea, too, but I don't think it will work in this neighborhood. Maybe you can raise us a little money, though, for copy paper and software. A lot of the teachers would use the computer more if they had some more skill-building programs."

"Well, I'd like to try."

"You've got it." George appears relieved that finding her areas was so easy.

"While we're talking about it, there's something else I'd like to study and think about with you."

George looks at his watch, but nods for her to go on.

"I'd like to look at computer use. I've noticed that we have 60 computers in classrooms and 30 in a lab, and I'm not sure how they're all used."

"Boy, that needs attention some day. I think it's great for you to look into computer use, but go easy, will you? Most of the teachers are not red hot for technology. The lab does a great job. Charley's a bit protective, though. But look at it and we'll talk."

"Thanks. One last question." George smiles.

"What does Theo do?"

"That's one of the things you'll learn from me – how to play the angles. Ordinarily elementary schools this size don't have assistant principals. Theo is in line to be the next principal in the district when there is an opening. There was one last year, but the incumbent decided to stay on for a couple more years, so I persuaded the folks downtown to let us have him."

"What does he do?"

"Darned near everything. Buses, cafeteria, playground, and safety. He also runs the teacher suspension program, which is the key to why this is such an orderly school. Listen, I've got to run, but I'll fill you in on that in a day or so. By the way, you can have your desk where you want it."

This last refers to Christine's idea that she move her small table to the lobby of the school where she can watch people come and go and get a sense of the interface between the school and the public.

The business district

Christine and her husband, Bill, have dinner in the little downtown street of the neighborhood the next evening. They have their choice of five little restaurants, all advertising ethnic cuisines: Mexican, Italian, Korean, Chinese, and "The All-American Bar and Grill," essentially a pub with a few tables and a roast-beef buffet. On the street they find two cleaners, a newspaper and magazine store, a tiny but pleasant wine shop, a hardware store, two small boutiques, and various other small stores.

They decide on pasta, but have it in the Grill. Discussing the neighborhood, Christine decides to do a door-to-door trip in the business section and recruit business partners. Bill suggests that she also contact the telephone company, the power-and-light company, the city library foundation, and the Coalition of Social Service Agencies.

The transformation of Pembroke begins that night, as Christine and Bill count potential resources.

ANALYSIS: THE PEMBROKE SCHOOL AS A SOCIAL SYSTEM

The organization of the Pembroke of four years ago seems familiar enough, but how did it come to be? Only 150 years ago a relatively small proportion of the population were in school and most of those attended one-room schoolhouses (two rooms at most), set in the immediate neighborhood or, in rural areas, located centrally amidst the farms, or on the edge of small towns. By the middle of the century some schools had increased in population and it seemed convenient to assign different teachers to children of different ages. The school might have developed as a series of one-room schoolhouses, but instead some teachers were assigned to work with the younger children and some with the older ones, and the school began to be organized into something called "grades."

In his fascinating study, Lortie (1975) points out that one of the reasons for the graded organization was convenience with respect to the hiring of staff. If a teacher left, another was simply hired to take his or her place. If the number of children increased or decreased a teacher could be added, deleted or reassigned to another school. New teachers could take up their duties with minimum interaction with other staff members. *Individual teachers* were responsible for all (or a large part of) the instruction of the children in their classes and did not have the complexity of adjusting to a group of fellow professionals, as would have been the case had a different organizational form been used. Lortie calls the organization that resulted a "cellular" structure. That is, each classroom can be regarded as a cell within which the given teacher is responsible for organizing the children, managing discipline, and teaching the several subjects which came to be common in the curriculum. Teachers became accustomed to working alone. They could make decisions about when and how to teach each subject, more or less independently of the other teachers. As the school grew, the role of "principal teacher" emerged, and when the school became large enough to accumulate administrative responsibilities which could occupy someone full time, the nonteaching "principalship" developed, an official management position with responsibility for the other personnel, public relations, and logistics.

Over the years, principals developed a variety of approaches to the role, especially in terms of their conceptions of the duties that it entails, and two poles stand out as important: one emphasizing teaching, the other focussing on management. For some principals, curriculum and instruction became the main part of their work and they configured the job as that of a lead teacher, actively guiding the teachers and working alongside them. For a larger number, the management of the school building, logistics, relationships with parents, and "discipline" filled most of the role. Either way it became customary for principals to relate to the teachers on a dyadic basis, that is in a one-to-one relationship, rather than organizing the faculty to take collective responsibility for the management of the curriculum and program. The principal "supervised" the work of the cells. In some schools with the principals who chose the "management" conception of the role, there was so little contact between principal and classroom that the "cells" never had more than cursory attention. Hard as it is to imagine, many teachers were visited in their classrooms by a principal or other official only about once a year. In a very real sense, teachers in those circumstances were operating their own miniature school districts, tenuously coupled to an organization that was a vague presence – an almost mythological "downtown."

In most districts, principals were as loosely connected with the district offices as the teachers were with them.

Since the teachers were assigned primarily to instruct the students, very little time was provided for them to interact with one another. They could see one another occasionally at lunch time or when recess was scheduled with other classes, and some of them would chat after school. But most of the teachers' day was occupied with instruction, leaving relatively little time for cooperative planning with their peers.

Thus the cellular organization served to isolate teachers from one another, and they became independent operators, mostly making their own decisions and taking responsibility for their children. Collective action was not the norm.

Human groups in workplaces develop not only routine ways of getting their jobs done, but also norms which affect many aspects of behavior. Gradually, normative patterns of behavior developed in schools

organized like Pembroke (and most other schools). An important example was the rise of norms governing the "privatism" of teaching.
Teachers regarded their classrooms as private domains. Their duties isolated them from each other during working hours: they rarely visited each
other to observe one another's techniques. Not only was teaching in isolation normal, but violating privacy when teaching became a taboo. A
teacher entering another person's classroom was expected to be there on
business. "Can I borrow some chalk?" "Do you have that story book?"
"Have you seen the science kit anywhere?" "Can you ask Gwen to take
a message home to her sick brother? I'd like to let him know what his
homework is." For a teacher to simply come in and sit down in the back
of the classroom and watch a fellow teacher became unusual, so unusual
that the staff became uncomfortable when it happened. (Teachers were
supposed to tend to their own knitting and not bother one another!) It
was all right, of course, for principals to come by, but gradually the
teachers came to wonder out loud what even the principal was doing
there, and in many schools principals felt that they had to ask permission
to come in and observe. It was not written down that teachers and
administrators were not supposed to observe one another, but the pro-
hibition was nonetheless powerful. Other norms developed also to regulate intrusions on the private classroom. Staff development was not to
intrude. Curriculum changes were to be optional. Technologies, such as
film, videotape, and computers, were to be incorporated only if the
teacher "believed in them."

> Many people would think that the old Pembroke is a really good school.
> We obviously do not. Can you list the features that many people would
> find attractive and the ones we find wanting?

SECTION 3: PROSPECTS FOR CHANGE

The Pembroke School described in Section 2 will be a difficult one to
improve unless it changes substantially as a socioprofessional system.
Most members of the faculty work in isolation from one another. They
are not close to the community and are somewhat disdainful of it.
George is concerned with the maintenance of order. He is friendly to
them, but he permits them to work separately and has not organized
them for collective action. He lets Kiki solve her own problems in giving
service to children with special needs.

Unless changes are made the Pembroke staff will "teach" Maryanne
that its way of life is the normal and proper professional one. Unless
changes are made, she will fumble her way to a reasonable level of teaching competence but will not be informed by the practice of others or by
expert supervision. However, Christine has entered the picture, and the
business partners will not be far behind her. Nor will other changes.

Christine gets going

Although she is in the temporary position of administrative intern, Christine has an intuitive sense of leadership and wants to exercise it. She has asked for areas of responsibility where she senses that much can be done quickly and easily, and she makes her first moves in those areas. Knowing how important indigenous leadership is to school improvement, she will be watching the faculty closely and soliciting its views.

Computers and technology: an opening wedge

Christine makes a survey of the number of computers in the school and how they are deployed. She hops in and out of the classrooms, saying hello to the teachers, counting the computers, cheerfully ignoring the dirty looks she gets from several of them. Their earlier estimate was almost right: There were three computers in 18 of the classrooms. Six in two of the fifth grade classrooms, where, as Harriet (one of the fifth grade teachers) puts it, "Sandy [her next door neighbor] will never use them and we just moved them in here!" Harriet is glad to chat with her and they and Carlene, the other teacher who has "borrowed" *her* neighbor's computers, eat together at lunch several times. Christine's notes indicate that there are 60 computers in the classrooms. On first count, she found 30 in the lab. Ninety computers had appeared – almost one for every five students.

As George predicted, Charley is protective. Christine pops in and out, asking him questions and getting short, but civil, answers. She learns that he has accumulated heaps of software. He has arranged the schedule so that all the classes have a 40-minute period with him each week and he has 40 minutes between each class to set up for the next one. He doesn't believe it was productive to teach primary children word processing. They use drill-and-practice programs on math facts and phonics skills for the most part. The last month of the year he shows them "Kids and Pics" and lets them explore it. "Not much worthwhile happens, but they love to try to create things, and it's the last month of school."

The fourth, fifth, and sixth grade kids are occupied with typing programs he calls "keyboarding," and with a simple word processor on which he makes them copy things already written. "Typing is the basic skill here. It will help them all their lives."

One day Christine comes by and finds Charley in the storeroom behind the lab. Looking ahead, he is accumulating some external CD-ROM drives and software, but what strikes her is about 20 old computers, clean and in plastic covers, arrayed on the shelves. A couple of days later, she asks him what is in store for them. "They're obsolete. I cleaned them up and stored them, but I don't know what the district will do with them eventually."

"Will they take a word processor that is compatible with those on the later models?"

"Yes. But they're kind of slow. I don't know who would want to use them."

"Would they be OK, say, for a typist working at 50 or 60 words per minute?"

"Oh, yes. But they wouldn't do graphics very well."

Now Christine has located 110 computers plus five in the library, three equipped with CD-ROM drivers and two dedicated to the library catalog. In a closet behind the office, she finds four more "obsolete" machines. The total has risen to 119, or one for every five children. The school budget from the district includes a budget line sufficient to purchase 15 more, plus a variety of peripherals.

She brings Harriet, Sandy, Carlene, Kiki, Charley, and Maryanne together for a meeting and tells them what she has found so far, and that she wants to organize a committee to study the state of the students' skills and develop a school plan to use technology to increase student learning, both with respect to the computer itself and with respect to academic learning.

"I'd like to have at least one teacher from each grade."

Sandy offers, "I'll do it for the first grade, and I think Nancy would be interested. She says she doesn't know much about computers, but she has lots of interests and I wouldn't be surprised if she and her husband have one at home and probably surf the Web in areas of their interest." They make suggestions for the other grades and offer to approach the teachers.

"Talk it up a bit," says Christine, "but I think I'd like to approach them myself so I can get to know them a little better."

By the end of the meeting Charley has agreed to survey the kids' skills during the next two weeks, with Christine helping. They also agree to survey the parents of their classes and learn how many computers are in the homes and what they are used for. They also agree to keep records of how they use the computer for instruction and to share the results. The next meeting is set for two weeks hence.

Christine sits down with George and tells him about the meeting and what she has in mind for the short run. She also asks him if one of the staff development days can be devoted to computer use. "I think the topic should be how to make the best use of the three computers that are in the classroom. A good consultant can show the folks how to use an LCD panel with their overhead projectors for editing writing, using encyclopedias and data bases, and a bunch of other things."

"We'll bring it up at the meeting next month," says George. "I like to have the teachers make these decisions, you know."

"You bet," says Christine.

Over the next few weeks a number of changes occur.

The "committee" learns that half the households in the neighborhood have computers with word processing software and printers. The upper grade teachers begin to ask the students to use the computer for written work. So do Nancy, Maryanne, the other second grade teachers, and Sally, a recruit of Nancy's.

Christine works with the committee members to develop lessons where the projection of the computer image features prominently. They concentrate on writing and on content where the encyclopedias and data bases are useful. They invite the other teachers in to observe, and at one faculty meeting share what they are doing.

The "obsolete" computers appear on tables in the halls and become available so that classes can have access: teachers can now conduct lessons where all the kids can be using a computer at the same time. Students as individuals can use them also.

Charley's survey indicates that only 20 percent of the primary students and 50 percent of the upper grade students can use a word processor. He is appalled, because he thought that the "keyboarding" programs would bring word processors within the reach of all the children, but realizes that he may have been too restrictive in his offerings. He concentrates on word processing for a couple of months. Most of the teachers who use computers are very pleased and the others have no objection. He agrees with Christine that he will then proceed to teach the students to use graphics, and the upper grade students to use spreadsheets.

Charley also tells Christine that George is about to spend the computer budget on 15 desktops that will be distributed evenly among the classrooms. Bill finds a supplier who is selling out his inventory of laptops and works out a price that would provide 30 laptops for the price of the 15 desktops. Christine organizes a meeting with Charley and George and they take the proposition to the "committee." Chris's idea is that they be stored in the library where any class can sign them out, so that the members of entire classes can each have one for periods of time. In addition, individual students can sign them out for evenings and weekends.

George is afraid that the computers will be stolen if they leave the school, but Christine shows him several studies on "take-home" programs showing that there is very little chance of loss (see for example Joyce *et al.* 1996). Finally he takes the idea to a faculty meeting on a day when Christine is attending an out-of-town conference; to his surprise, not only the "committee," but several other teachers support the idea and the "low computer users" don't object, although they can't yet envision how to use them.

For the first time, George wonders whether Christine might be more of a "people person" than he first thought.

Christine is very pleased that the idea passed without her presence, and she revises her time-line. By the end of the year she expects all the children to be using word processors regularly, to be able to use graphics, to have the upper grade students using spreadsheets in units based in the classroom or the lab, and to have at least half of the teachers integrating the computer into their curriculum units. Somehow telephone lines and modems will appear in the spring and everyone will be "online" by the time the school opens in the fall, with Web pages starting the children on inquiries related to the curriculum. Her little committee is meeting regularly and studying how the computer can enhance the language-arts curriculum. Charley is pleased that his lab is intact and can be used for more advanced instruction than he had thought was possible, and is impressed with the increased use of the computer and the possibilities that are opening up. At district meetings of the school computer coordinators he finds that he suddenly has a lot to say and is looked to by many of the other computer teachers.

As Chris organizes the business community and the parents, Charley will start offering courses to parents and personnel from the businesses under the district adult education program.

The bilingual teachers have begun to use Spanish Assistant with their Spanish-language students and are searching for a program in Korean. They eventually find *Easy Language*.

Giving business an opportunity to serve – and be served: a second wedge

The computer initiative has begun the process of involving businesses in a serious way. Eventually the "technology partners" will use the school as a setting for studies to learn more about how to use computers in educational applications and the kind of training that teachers, parents, and students need to do to get real effects.

Christine now interviews the heads of all the small businesses and community agencies in the neighborhood and discusses school and schooling with them. They have a series of meetings in which they discuss a variety of ideas for working together. Out of those meetings comes the idea for the courses that Charley begins to offer. In addition, several are upgrading the computers in their businesses and decide that their older models can either be used by another business or agency or be given to the school.

The head of the branch library indicates that there is pressure from the city to close some of the branches and that the lease for the Pembroke neighborhood branch expires next summer. Everyone gets agitated. (You can see where this is leading – the branch will move to the school next summer!)

No big ideas emerge at this point. However, when Chris approaches the manager of the local telephone company, Jacqueline Towers, she comes to visit the school, sits in on a meeting of the "committee," and says that she might be able to obtain a small grant from the telephone company foundation to put in telephone lines throughout the school, purchase a number of modems, and pay for Web access for a year or so.

"If I can wangle this," she says, "we'd want to arrange some publicity – and publicity for the school as well."

Chris has found a powerful partner, one having links to television stations, cable networks, and access to innovations from all over the world.

Gradually the members of the business community become closer and closer to each other and to the school. They rejuvenate their neighborhood business association, include community service agencies, and relate to the school as a group. When the Responsible Parties are formed, they will be included, as will the officials of the Camden branch library and the directors of the Camden library system.

Parents and other community members

Chris enjoys having her desk in the hall inside the main entrance to the school. She can watch the traffic of teachers and students and visitors. When she is at the desk visitors often come directly to her desk and she introduces herself and learns their business. If they are headed toward a classroom she often accompanies them, chatting about their children. She learns that many of the parents visit only if they have received a call that their child is "in trouble," and she often takes a few minutes to introduce them to the teacher who has called them and observe the beginning of a conference.

Except for the open house at the beginning of the year, few parents come to the PTA meetings unless their children are participants in a performance. However, virtually all of them proclaim great interest in the progress of the children, and the PTA officers want to find ways of involving themselves and the other parents more in the school, but has not been able to think of anything of significance. George is friendly to them, but takes a "you discipline the children and leave education to us" stance that discourages participation.

In mid-November Chris approaches George with three ideas.

One comes from Kiki's observations that many of the parents have a great deal of interest in learning to use a computer and that many of them would help their children with word processing if they knew how. The idea is that Charley offer workshops for parents as described above. George agrees, but doesn't think that people would actually come, and has many questions about having the school open in the late afternoon, evenings, and weekends and "where will the money come from?" Fortunately, Chris has anticipated those questions and has worked out solutions with the adult education division of the district office.

The second is to train parents in the administration of individualized reading tests to help the teachers with the diagnosis of student needs. George is hesitant and wants to take his time thinking about the idea. He doubts if the parents have the ability to learn to give the tests.

The third is to begin the at-home independent-reading Just Read program. Chris wants to suggest Just Read to the faculty and then, if they approve, to the PTA and the business partnership she has cooking.

George puts her off on that one. "I like the relationship we have now with the parents. I don't think I want a bunch of parents running around here and bothering the teachers."

Chris expected that George would not be initially pleased and does not press the issue, but she gives him some articles to read (O'Masta and Wolf 1991; Joyce and Wolf 1996; Wolf 1998) and indicates that she will be back to him.

At the end of the meeting George tells Chris that Theo, the assistant principal, will be leaving at Thanksgiving. A principal has retired suddenly for personal reasons, creating an opening that Theo will fill.

"That means, Chris, that I'll want you to take on some of his duties, which will leave less time for these 'make work' projects you've put together. It will help you learn more about the 'real work' of running a school."

"That's great. Is there anything in particular that I should get right on?" She realizes that she actually has little idea about Theo's duties beyond those mentioned when she arrived at the school. She and Theo are cordial to one another and have lunch occasionally, but he has never described any of his duties. He bustles around and she has seen him talking to students and parents, but . . . odd.

"Talk to Theo, will you, and see what's the highest priority for now."

"Sure."

A blip – or is it?

The staff development day on computer use is backed up against the Thanksgiving holiday. Chris has organized the day. All the committee members and Margaret Jacobs, the curriculum coordinator of the district, work with her. The focus is on the teaching of writing. The committee has contacted the other teachers and found out how they do and don't use the computer, what kinds of writing assignments they give their students, and what they know about word processing. The workshop is conducted in Charley's lab, and he has set up several computers with projection panels and large monitors.

The committee members and Margaret all demonstrate how just one or two computers, with projection panels or large monitors, can be used to help whole classes generate and edit writing. Then they demonstrate how to use the "hall lab" and Charley's lab with the students working as individuals.

Most of the teachers who are not on the committee are amazed at how much the others are making use of computers and see how the current emphasis on word processing might pay off for their students. They are amazed at how much the curriculum coordinator and Chris know about the teaching of reading and writing.

Several teachers suggest that they should stick with computers as a topic for the rest of the year's staff development days. Chris suggested that the issue be brought up at the December faculty meeting.

The only sour note is that Terry and two of the other upper grade teachers have called in sick. At the end of the day, Chris and Margaret stop by George's office (George did not attend the workshop, except for lunch) and chat for a few minutes. George appears busy with paperwork and is cordial but distracted. Chris mentions that Terry and two others have called in sick. George says that is fairly normal.

"A lot of the folks don't like staff development. Or they don't like the topic for one of the days. So they find a way out. And who says they're not sick?"

"Do you mind if I schedule another day for them and teach the workshop myself?"

"You mean release them with substitutes?"

"Well, that's one way."

"Who would pay for the substitutes?"

"My office can take care of that," says Margaret, smiling.

As they leave the school, Margaret remarks to Chris that she believes this is an important moment. "I think they'll resist and they will go to George. Then we'll learn more about lots of things."

She continues, "You know that Harry V— [the superintendent] wanted you over here in the hope you could wake the place up a little?"

"Not really. He said there was plenty of work to do here and he thought I'd find it interesting."

"The plot was thicker than that. If you don't mind, I'd like us to have a meeting with him to talk about what you are doing here at Pembroke. If there's a fuss, I'd like him to have a context."

Literacy

Chris got to know Margaret in her quest to study achievement in reading and writing. By the middle of October her committee has expanded to include two first grade, all four second grade, two third grade, one fourth grade, and three fifth grade teachers, along with Charley, Kiki, and the other special education teacher, Kathleen, whom Kiki has recruited. Counting herself, 16 persons out of a full-time staff of 26 are active and the four kindergarten teachers are beginning to attend meetings – difficult for them because their work schedules are not congruent with those of the rest of the faculty.

Chris involves the committee in the study of achievement in reading. The district administers the Iowa Tests of Basic Skills in the spring of each year in grades 2 through 10. Chris begins by presenting an analysis of the scores in reading. She seeks out Margaret, whose specialty is the teaching of reading, and rehearses her presentation with her. Margaret is intrigued and shows up at the meeting where Chris makes her first presentation to the committee. She stops by the office and brings George along.

She begins the meeting by projecting an overhead transparency and commenting on the data.

"Grades 2 to 5 have average scores on the reading battery between the 45th and 48th percentiles, so the average doesn't change much. Not only that, but if we go back three years and pick up this year's fifth graders, who were tested in the spring of the second and third grade, and correlate their second grade, third grade, and fourth grade scores, we find that the correlation is about $r = 0.80$, which is about as high as a correlation can get, given the error variance of the tests. In other words nearly all the kids with the lowest and highest test scores in second grade were the lowest and highest at the end of grades 3 and 4."

> Of the 25 poorest readers in grade 2, 22 were among the lowest in grade 3 and 21 were among the lowest in grade 4.
>
> Of the 25 best readers in grade 3, 24 were among the best in grade 3 and 23 in grade 4.

Transfixed, everyone stares at the overhead, and Chris answers a couple of questions about correlations and error variance. George comments that the overall scores look pretty good for a school in a neighborhood like theirs.

Chris moves on and discusses gender.

Average male and female scores

	Grade 4	Grade 5
Male average	37th percentile	38th percentile
Female average	54th percentile	57th percentile

"Notice that at each grade the female average is about the 55th percentile and the male average is between the 35th and 40th percentile, although just as many males as females have scores above the 75th percentile.

"If we just make a distribution of our scores, forgetting national percentile ranks, the distribution of male and female scores looks like this."

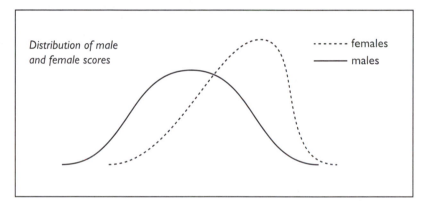

Distribution of male and female scores

------- females
——— males

Everyone gasps. Chris continues, "Our average male score is about at the 35th percentile of the female distribution. However, that's typical – that's the picture that emerges from the national assessment of educational progress in both reading and writing.

"Now, here's the next to last bit of data for this session. The fifth grade is important, because at its end we graduate the students into the middle school. So it's important to learn whether the kids can handle the material typically used in sixth grade and above. That's where grade-level equivalent scores (GLEs) are useful. Here's the distribution of last spring's reading scores for our fifth grade students."

Grade-level equivalent scores

5.8 or above	50 percent
3.0–5.8	30 percent
3.0 or below	20 percent

"You'll notice that the average and median scores convert to a GLE of 5.8. Half our students are above that level and should be able to handle middle-school textbooks and references. But look at the other end. Twenty percent of our kids are leaving fifth grade reading about at the level of the average second grade student. Any student who leaves fifth grade with a score of 5.0 or lower is liable to have serious difficulty with middle-school material."

A heated discussion follows. Explanations fly around. Chris and Margaret know that initial reactions by teachers and administrators to data like these are generally self-centered (Hall and Loucks 1977, 1978). And they are. Most of the comments defend the competence of the school and explain the problem in terms of the kids, parents, and neighborhood. George is incensed. After the hubbub has subsided, he bursts out "What are you trying to do, destroy us?"

"No," interjects Margaret, smiling but serious. "She's trying to save these children."

An argument ensues, primarily over the dangers of letting data like these become public. When it subsides, Chris says, "And now for the good news." She puts up another overhead.

Tutoring of students having special needs	
Average gain (untutored students)	7 percentile points
Average gain (tutored students)	20 percentile points

"Kiki and Kathleen work with children under a number of conditions. One is one-to-one tutoring. Here are the grades 3 and 4 reading scores for the children they tutored and the ones they worked with in groups of six. Notice that the students they worked with in groups of six gained an average of 7 percentile points in the year interval between testing. The students they tutored gained an average of 20 percentile points."

Everyone is fascinated. Then Chris displays her last overhead, which shows the achievement gains of students in a number of innovative programs that have been developed in various parts of the United States and studied intensively. "Margaret and I have had a number of discussions recently, and believe that we should explore some of the curricular and instructional approaches that have great success with low-achieving students – actually they benefit *all* students – and tutoring arrangements as well, because what we found with the kids Kiki and Kathleen tutored fits with other studies of tutoring (Bloom 1984; Slavin and Madden 1995). Also, better use of the computer can help.

"What I'd like to do is bring in a top consultant to work with us in the literacy area. Margaret is acquainted with several of the very best. I can certainly work with you up to a point, but I think our kids deserve the very best."

Moving on

Thus begins the trek toward the powerful programs we found in the Pembroke of today: the at-home reading program (Just Read); the diagnostic system with tutorial help; the multidimensional approach to beginning reading; the intensive "second-chance" program; and the effective involvement of parents, community members, businesses, the library and other social agencies, all add together to make an environment where failure is virtually unknown but outstanding achievement is a regular event.

COMMENTARY

Time passes.

Chris uses personal diplomacy to build toward a democratic decision-making community where the faculty and parents think through the school as a learning organization and build the charter that will serve as their constitution.

When George leaves to return to the town where he grew up as principal of its small high school, Chris becomes principal and begins the organization of teams: she and the team leaders divide the bureaucratic leadership tasks with the leaders of the centers and bring important decisions to the faculty–parent community.

Data collection and analysis fuel their continuous action-research process.

Margaret and the consultants provide continuous technical support with both process and curricular/instructional substance, and weekly time for collegial decisionmaking and staff development is established.

The business partners become more and more active and the school is open 16 hours on weekdays and eight hours each weekend day so that the library service and the computers are available for students and community and a range of courses, including multimedia "distance" courses, is available for parents and children.

Greater use is made of paid and volunteer aides and they receive substantial training, especially in literacy development.

The state university at Camden collaborates with Pembroke to create a professional development school. Many of the pre-service practicum courses are taught by the team leaders and other lead teachers.

Christine has used sensible curricular/instructional and community involvement initiatives to get things going, and continues to tend the action-research process where fresh initiatives are begun and studied and the older ones are tended and rejuvenated.

The bilingual program is designed for parents and students studying English together and at the same time continuing to explore their ethnic heritages.

The school becomes a "training ground" for district leaders.

Within a few years Kiki and Harriet are principals, have connected their schools to Margaret and the external consultants for support, and have begun the trek toward a self-renewing organization. Charley is the district coordinator for technology and is connecting the district schools to distance-learning opportunities as well as expanding and consolidating the role of the computer in the lives of the district's children.

Christine is the district coordinator for school renewal as well as principal. Her major vehicle is staff development for principals and the building of leadership teams. Where does that "training" take place? In Pembroke. And in their own schools, as they conduct their action research on the development of collegial self-renewing organizations devoted to excellence in education.

Note that Christine tended her people well and treated the hypotheses that form the structure of school improvement as dimensions of the school-improvement process to be tested continually. She involved people as much as she could, looked at the state of involvement, and then added ways of improvement, making a decisionmaking group of her Responsible Parties rather than dictating to them. She obtained both technical assistance and administrative support from the district office and brought in persons who could connect the school to the knowledge base and provide adequate staff development for them. Inquiry, inquiry, inquiry combined with inclusion and a broad-based approach.

Part IV Policymaking for school renewal: making the context through national, state, and local education authority policy

Schools are not independent entities. They exist in a society to serve that society – not just the portion that they serve directly.

They also exist in a context created by local education authorities, state and provincial governments, and national governments.

In Part IV we discuss the contexts created at all three levels. Although we will analyze past and current policies we will emphasize the development of policy to help schools achieve an evolutionary state. Such policies will neither be "hands off" nor be invasive. The important issue is whether national, state, and local policymakers can adopt the same type of collaborative inquiry that we believe is the essence of a self-renewing school.

11 Supporting evolution: working at a distance from the school

We begin our discussion of policies to support the evolving school with a memorandum we wrote a couple of years ago to Jeanie Weathersby, then an official of a US state department of education. The memo followed a discussion of how that state could make more effective initiatives – it had already made many – to improve education. Dr. Weathersby has been a strong voice for creating initiatives from an action-research framework and after careful reviews of the knowledge base and the collection of information about the targeted area. As a part of her work she has recently studied staff development in her state, examining schools that have had significantly higher and lower than average achievement for three consecutive years, correcting for socioeconomic differences in student populations. Her study indicated that the difference in staff development was in collegial, concerted effort: the higher-achieving schools were more evolutionary than the lower-achieving schools (Weathersby and Harkreader 1998).

Our memorandum is similar to ones we have written to school districts, state agencies, and units in the national government. Their problem as they decide what to do to further the education of their students is that they work at a distance from the school environments, which is where learning happens. *Notice that we believe that district offices operate "from a distance" in much the same ways as do national, state, and intermediate agencies.*

Plainly, no one will disagree that school improvement as it affects students happens in schools, where changes in the educational environment affect students directly.

The most beautiful curriculum plan, developed in the offices of school districts or states, has no effect without implementation in schools. Charged with the creation of educational policy, but recognizing the reality that policies that do not affect school environments are exercises in futility, the "central" offices of school districts and state departments of education reach for policies that can really "make a difference." No policymaker wishes to preside over the construction of curriculum plans that are not implemented, and all recognize that the relationship between schools and policymaking entities has been frustrating. Policymakers feel impotent, and school personnel become alienated as they cope with what feels like a bombardment of initiatives and regulations they try to fit to their local situations, often with a sense that this year's initiatives will become next year's old news as the policymakers enter a new round of efforts.

We argue here that a reexamination of the realistic connections between policymaking entities and schools can lead us to a rather more comfortable and efficient way of working. We have not synthesized a complete "policy for policymakers," nor do we believe that we have cooked up a scheme that will immediately remove the feelings of alienation that we sense as we work with schools, on the one hand, and district, state, and federal officials on the other. However, we are greatly concerned about the losses of connection that currently exist, and offer our thoughts on the nature of the dilemmas that nearly everyone appears to be facing.

We draw on our recent experiences with intensive programs of school improvement; the large-scale studies of school renewal, which we have just reviewed; the findings from an extensive study of 46 initiatives in a large state; the national urban–rural program; a nationwide study of pre-service education; the study of the staff development/school renewal capability of a large state; and a very recent study of more than 100 schools engaged in action research to improve their programs. Although most of our clinical service spends its time spreading initiatives with a good track record in the United States, the United Kingdom, and a dozen other countries, the first part of this chapter deals with some problematical practices that we encounter in all countries.

THE STATE–CENTRAL AND OFFICE–SCHOOL SYMBIOSIS

What is obviously different about planning school improvement initiatives at a state, federal, or central-office level, compared with the school level, is that initiatives made anywhere but at the school have to be shaped to take account of the lack of direct administrative structures for organizing people and resources. Thus initiatives by state and federal agencies are generally shaped so that they rely on the structures in place in the local education agencies. District policymakers similarly rely on structures for implementation in the schools. To be effective, the important initiatives require curricular and instructional changes. Unfortunately, many local education agencies and schools are not very well positioned to make significant curricular, instructional, or technological changes. One cannot assume that initiatives requiring more than administrative action (adding special classes, buying technology) will fare well at whatever level they are initiated. Federal and state initiatives *have* added many categorical programs, changing the face of the schools in many ways. However, especially given the magnitude of investment, they have been notoriously ineffective with respect to student learning, because delivering high-quality education within those programs involves changes in curriculum and instruction that are very difficult for local agencies and schools to make under present circumstances. Recently, and partly because of local agency complaints, many states have been experimenting with more flexible guidelines for the administration of categorical initiatives so that they can be better integrated, but there has always been sufficient flexibility to bring initiatives together at the district level, given imaginative and integrated administration.

THE "SITE-BASED" ALTERNATIVE

Both states and large districts have recently embraced "site-based" approaches, providing resources to schools. Discouragement with their ability to make substantial differences has led to the currently fashionable attempt by states to bypass the central administrations of districts by providing money directly to schools and asking them to generate school-improvement plans tailored to their situations. A parallel attempt by large districts is similar, as decentralization plans by districts reduce the influence of the central office personnel and provide greater authority to schools. Although there are many persuasive arguments for this avenue (in several settings we attempt to help schools capitalize on the opportunity), several large-scale studies indicate that the "money-to-the-site" strategy is a very low-probability proposition. In Rosenholtz's terms, thinking about schools that are "moving" and schools that are "stuck," the recent studies indicate that only about 10 percent of schools are "moving enough" that they can effectively implement initiatives requiring changes in the curricular and instructional environment. The really massive California school improvement program, where 6400 schools have received nearly a million dollars each as discretionary money for school improvement, is the crushing example (Berman and Gjelten 1983). However, there are other well-heeled initiatives that have come up with the same dismal finding (David and Peterson 1984). From our point of view, a big disappointment is that so few schools are able to get themselves going that we have not been able to discover an easily influenceable variable that can help us direct site-based initiatives better. Leadership and the cohesiveness of the faculty as a problem-solving unit show up regularly as characteristics of "moving" schools, but those are not quickly affected by school improvement strategies. For now, suffice it to say that schools are currently doing the best they can, and money and the injunction to improve will not, by themselves, cause "stuck" schools to move forward.

STANDARDS, PRESSURE, AND ACCOUNTABILITY: THE POLITICO-PSYCHOMETRIC COMPLEX

Equally as popular as categorical programs and site-based renewal schemes are initiatives that attempt to get school districts and schools to move by announcing standards of performance, testing achievement, and publishing the results in such as way as to make the schools and districts accountable to their patrons for performance. This complex, sometimes called "high stakes" testing, has a poor track record so far. In at least one state the complex has increased retention and nongraduation without increasing student learning. There has been little research on the causes of the poor performance of this type of initiative, but we think a reasonable explanation relates to the problems with the other types of initiatives: the conditions that enable curricular and instructional change are simply not in place, so, although distressed by the pressure, most districts and schools do not know how to respond in ways that would fit the objective of the pressure. A technical problem is that most programs in this complex rely on year-end testing to determine achievement. The year is over by the time the results are in. Another is that there is a tendency to use off-the-shelf tests developed by commercial firms that may not capture what an initiative is about. For example, there are schools today who are creating truly computer-literate students, but the test battery does not capture that accomplishment. Six years after its initiative in the language arts, California was pilot-testing its tests on quality of writing (abandoned after this memorandum was written because of complaints by pressure groups and school personnel). Meantime, folks are terrified that their "test scores" will go down because the tests are out of whack with respect to the initiative. It matters little that the fear is groundless.

A frequent effect is that the "accountability" initiatives drive curriculum and instruction toward the narrowest of curricular goals, because most folks believe those are what the commonly used tests measure.

COMPOUNDING THE PROBLEM: TOO MANY, TOO WEAK INITIATIVES

Initiatives have proliferated amazingly, for there is no lack of proponents for all sorts of things (many sensible on their own merits), and state and federal organizations are organized around interest areas whose existence relies on getting some portion of the money to promote change. A long-term study of one state found 46 separate and uncoordinated initiatives operating simultaneously, of which 25 or 30 might touch any given school! (See Joyce *et al.* 1982; Joyce and Belitzky 1997.) The curriculum areas, technologies, the categoricals, SIP, various programs for students whose first language was not English, programs for the gifted and for special education categories, all found their way into legislation. The education resource pie was cut so thinly that only a few had substantial resources, and those were directed at complex changes requiring technical assistance that was too thin a subslice of those pies. The effect of diluting resources is not good. Possibly worse is that schools and districts feel bombarded. After a while, folks have a tendency to stop up their ears. We advise schools and districts alike to concentrate on one or two priorities at any given time, shaping them so that the initiatives to follow will find the setting more ready to receive them. ("But we have so many needs!" you can hear the cry.)

SO WHAT MIGHT WORK?

If the most common practices are low-probability shots, how can high-probability ones be found? One way is by studying successful innovative teams who mounted programs of some scale, albeit a scale much smaller than the state level, and trying to find out what they have in common. It looks to us like:

1 They concentrated on building colleagueship and leadership. The purposes of the programs were constantly before the group, as was the fine-tuning of the program.
2 They provided lots of training, on the substance of the innovation, on leadership, on collective-problem-solving, and leadership, to appropriate personnel.
3 They studied implementation and reoriented their practices on the basis of information. They knew if they were getting somewhere.
4 They made curricular, instructional, and technological changes. They went with content that had a good track record.
5 They studied effects on students formatively and continuously.

To do all this they had to build, *ad hoc*, staff development systems, leadership training programs, and formative evaluation systems for implementation and student learning, and find strong content, different enough from present practice that it could make a difference in student learning.

Essentially, the successful programs filled in the holes in the current system's implementation capability on both the organizational and technical levels. They probably have high levels of implementation because they build a more cohesive social system with better and broader-based leadership, develop good training with good follow-up, and study what they do, *including implementation*, right from the beginning.

As an aside, all the successful programs we have found have improved student learning in the first year of implementation!

Suppose that a state or district were to concentrate its resources on one substantive initiative for a substantial period of time, and were to conduct the initiative so that districts and schools received enough technical assistance to approximate the procedures of the successful projects, building the foundation for a functioning staff development and technical assistance system that could sustain future initiatives in curriculum and instruction and for site-based initiatives.

Could such a concentrated effort not only achieve many of its immediate goals, but also leave behind improved systems and cadres of technical assistants to help with the next effort?

A note on clientele

The system needs to ensure that teachers, administrators, and classroom aides are engaged as individuals in continual professional development; that schools develop collegial organizations that continuously strive for curricular and instructional improvement; and that needed state, federal, and district initiatives are implemented through effective staff development that generates common action.

This concept derives from the reality of the way education personnel relate to staff development offerings: as individuals, as members of faculties, and in relation to statewide initiatives where training is geared to all or to specific categories of personnel. Correspondingly, however, the concept fits the several types of motivational structures that operate in the education profession. Individuals can fit their perception of needs to offerings or individually generated activities, can work with colleagues in their organizational units, and can make common cause with the larger community to achieve common goals or solve common problems (see Joyce and Showers 1995 for an expanded rationale). Site-based school renewal requires decisionmaking, action, and the study of consequences by faculties working as a unit. District-wide initiatives require collaboration among a large number of entities.

Essentially, when initiatives are made, there needs to be clarity about whether they are directed at providing services to teachers as individuals, to schools as entities where the entire faculty needs to be involved, or to districts that have to provide support for district-wide initiatives. **We recommend that each initiative be planned with clarity about whether its intent can be satisfied through service to individuals, districts, or schools, and about how the mechanisms contained in the initiative will ensure that those services can be delivered**.

In short, when an initiative is made, it needs to be thought through completely to ensure that the mechanisms that are designed will reach the appropriate level of personnel: individuals, schools, districts, or state.

As to the things that would make good candidates for the content of focussed initiatives that would address several needs . . . well, that's a subject for a really long discussion sometime (see Chapter 5).

COMMENTARY

The essence of the memorandum is the emphasis on the simple fact that governmental agencies and school districts are not the schools themselves. What can they do? What should they do? In the next chapter let's take a look at the role of the school district in supporting evolving schools and generating district-wide initiatives that can make a difference.

12 Reforming reform: renewing the local education authority

Throughout the book we have emphasized the critical role of school districts both in supporting the schools and in making initiatives pertaining to the needs of the area they serve. Here we discuss the changing policies with respect to school districts and their vital role in supporting the schools.

We begin with excerpts from another memorandum, this time to the officials of another state and the district and school personnel of that state. The document is one of a series following a study of staff development/school renewal capacity in the state prepared to lay a base of information that can be used to unify and reorient the initiatives of that state. The memorandum was prompted by the realization that the role of the local education authorities was shifting because of a number of past changes in policy at federal, state, and district levels that had not been articulated clearly but had greatly affected the ability of districts to support their schools.

REFLECTIONS ON PLANNING

The most ambitious of the recommendations in the report of the Study of Staff Development and School Renewal is that the state shape its initiatives so as to create a comprehensive staff development/school renewal system. The major issue that emerges from the staff development evaluation study concerns the long-term discussion over whether to take steps to build a system that ensures that

- all educators are in the regular study of curriculum and teaching;
- the content of staff development is likely to improve student learning;
- the design of staff development includes the elements that ensure implementation; and
- all schools move into a self-renewing state.

> The goal is greatly to increase the effectiveness of initiatives by schools, districts, state, and federal government to improve student achievement. The central thesis is that this will require the development of a comprehensive system to replace or integrate the *ad hoc* arrangements that are seriously hampered in bringing about the implementation of intended changes.

BASIC CONCEPTS IN PLANNING A SYSTEM

Three concepts to guide general planning have emerged from the study and reflections on the research and the condition of initiatives in most state systems:

- the importance of the building of community among professional educators at the state, district, and school levels;
- the settlement of locus-of-control issues, particularly with respect to state, school, and district relationships;
- the embedding of action research as a management principle in state and local initiatives.

These topics overlap considerably when we consider what it will take to build a system. In this memo we will concentrate on the role of the school district and what we see as locus-of-control issues.

THE DEVELOPMENT OF COMMUNITY: STATE, DISTRICT, AND SCHOOL

Over the last 30 years the focus of attention in educational policy has shifted dramatically from maintaining the public school system to improving it while maintaining it. Two strands of social concern have led to the shift. One derives from the dramatic changes in society as literacy, including social and technological literacy, has become essential to the health of society as a whole and to the quality of life of individuals living within it. The other is that education is the only institution with the strength and technology to solve social problems caused by poverty and immigration by preventing those problems from occurring in future generations. In addition, of course, schools are charged with the general responsibility to generate a highly educated, creative, socially committed populace.

The bureaucratic procedures that were formerly employed to manage schooling are not adequate to generate school improvement on the scale that is necessary to meet the considerable challenges of the present world. Those procedures focussed on the development of compliance-oriented regulations as federal and state resources were directed at specific problems and resulted in the massive categorical programs (particularly Title I, Special Education, and ESOL) that were added to the curriculums of the schools. The notorious ineffectiveness of the categorical programs over the last 30 years has increased awareness that the strategies for managing those innovations were seriously lacking. The imperfections have become clearer and easier to correct, as is indicated by the growing list of highly successful small-scale programs.

The improvement of education is now recognized as dependent on changes in curriculum and instruction that require expansion of teaching repertoire that can only be accomplished through far greater and more intensive staff development than has existed on a large scale in the past (Joyce *et al.* 1993). Additionally, it is now believed that innovations in educational practice depend on shared ideas about how and what to teach: changes are not mechanical but are carried by understandings that have to pervade the community of implementers (Fullan 1982; Fullan and Stiegelbauer 1993) as changes are made, studied, and adjusted. People cannot just be told what to do. Nor can they simply be given resources and told to solve a problem. Everyone has to work together, bound by a shared understanding of the nature of the goal and how to achieve it. Communities of inquiring educators carry innovations.

RECONCILIATION OF LOCUS-OF-CONTROL ISSUES

Education is in a period of transition where a number of issues need to be resolved to enable the development of fully productive relationships between federal and state governmental agencies, school districts, and schools.

Until the late 1950s states legislated that communities must provide education to their children and local communities established school boards and districts that did so. Curriculums followed tradition. Textbooks reified tradition and were very important in carrying the curriculum: fewer than half of elementary schools had a school library before the mid-1960s, for libraries were not thought to be necessary for the education of young children. Even today, when the national assessment of reading progress indicates that only about one in five secondary students visits the school library once a week for *any* purpose, one wonders how far education has strayed from the textbook-only approach.

States had minimalist curriculum guides, developed hastily and published via the mimeograph machine. The chief sources were textbooks. Reciprocally, the textbooks followed the normative guides. The curriculum offices of the larger school districts combined with the national professional organizations in the curriculum areas to generate curriculum guides that provided the most thoughtful boundaries around educational practice. The textbook–guide–textbook syndrome was not conducive to change. In the 1950s about one-third of the students did not learn to read or write competently enough to profit from secondary education, and only about one-third of high-school graduates received any form of higher education.

Until the 1950s nearly all school funds were provided by the levying authority of the local school district. In the late 1950s the federal government and foundations began to provide R&D resources for curriculum development. Both of these interests were based on a recognition that the districts and states were not investing either in research or in development and most districts were too small to do so.

Gradually the federal government and, soon after but slowly, the larger states, began to address areas of national concern that districts, schools, and universities were not dealing with systematically. Thus were born the categorical programs, initiatives to stimulate curriculum development, and initiatives to improve teacher education and create staff development options.

Until that time state departments of education were relatively small and concerned themselves primarily with certification and education. As the federal government entered the education arena, portions of the resources were deliberately allocated to "strengthening state departments of education," and departments of education began to expand, particularly as units were created to administer the growing federal initiatives.

As departments of education became stronger, states became more active in influencing districts and schools, primarily by interfacing with them over the administration of the categorical initiatives, curriculum development programs, and dissemination projects. For the first time school districts and schools had access to monetary resources for program improvement and could adopt programs developed by others. A series of national curriculum development laboratories and centers were set up and a set of heavily funded federal initiatives in the early-childhood area, notably headstart and follow-through, appeared, accompanied by resources dedicated to development.

As the federal resources increased, state departments and school district cabinets increasingly reflected the federal initiatives, and the relationship between state government and districts changed dramatically as state officials and local officials had to cooperate over an increasing range of enterprises.

Test development and use speeded up during the 1960s in a way that would ultimately profoundly change the relationship between states and districts. While commercial testing companies and some nonprofit firms had developed "standardized" tests of ability and achievement for many years, the use of those tests accelerated greatly in the 1960s, and the practice of publishing the results in local newspapers and newsletters began during that period, partly because of the lobbying activities of real-estate sales organizations and developers.

Taxation and school finance

As local districts began to face increasing public opposition to taxation, especially rises in taxes, states took a more active role in raising money for schools and the traditional relationship between school districts, which had been viewed as local and independent, changed radically. "Cap" initiatives and legislation reduced the ability of districts to raise money – in many states preventing communities who were willing and able to invest in the highest quality education from doing so. There is a trend toward having property taxes moved to the state to be distributed equitably to the districts, removing from the districts one of the functions that gave them identity: decisions about funding local education and going to their electorates for approval. In many states districts became more and more dependent on federal and state funding.

As they lost the power to raise money through local property taxes, boards of education and superintendents became more and more preoccupied with budgetary matters, and cost-cutting became endemic. To reduce expenses, many slimmed down or eliminated central-office supervisory and curriculum development personnel and budgets for staff development. Schools and teachers who had depended on those personnel for support and stimulation were suddenly without them.

Summary of changes

In the space of two decades, some radical changes in relationship had occurred:

- The financial base of education had shifted from the local to the state and national.
- Heavily funded initiatives were generated by the federal government, directed at lower achieving students. Schooling had been lengthened substantially through the establishment of early childhood programs.
- District and state offices followed the pattern of federal initiatives and a large proportion of state–district transactions related to those initiatives.
- Districts made deep cuts in the categories of personnel in the best position to support schools and teachers.
- Curriculum development efforts sponsored by federal and state government were found to have little effect on practice.

If those changes didn't create enough confusion, some spinoffs were just as complicating.

SITE-BASED MANAGEMENT COMES TO TOWN

A very important change emanated from the fiscal crisis that plagued local school districts and the consequent downsizing of central offices. That was a move toward "site-based" management. Neighborhoods were clamoring for greater control of local schools. District "middle management" was disappearing. Teachers' organizations complained bitterly about regulation and interference. No one doubts that education takes place in individual schools and that high-quality faculties make high-quality schools. "Site-based" management, including the management of school improvement, seemed readymade to satisfy many complaints and constituencies.

> In the process of moving toward the individual school as the unit of
> education and the unit of change, little thought was given to what that
> movement would mean for the district or for school–district relations.
> What is a school district if it delegates the responsibility for the quality
> of education, or makes schools responsible for improving themselves
> without the capacity to support their efforts?

Increasingly, fiscal matters and infrastructure services have come to
dominate school-district policymakers as curricular and instructional
matters have become less prominent. Categorical programs have continued, but frequently are managed as "flow-through" programs to the
schools.

States increasingly make initiatives that are directed toward schools
rather than districts, with districts acting as the fiscal agent rather than
in a leadership capacity.

PRESSURE

Increasingly states and large school districts have concentrated on means
for focussing schools on higher standards, and on the development of
testing programs that stress accountability by schools. This change has
two interesting types of impact on the relationship between state, district,
and school:

• The first is that the states have emerged as the developer of standards
  of quality education and as institutions that require levels of accountability that schools and school districts have never faced before.
• The second is that districts and schools have increasingly looked to
  states for direction, even while proclaiming their independence (and
  even primacy) as the institutions responsible for educating the young
  people in the society. The portion of the study that examined governance in 29 schools in the state found that although the schools were
  free to pursue initiatives reflecting local concerns and imagination, *all
  the schools pursued directions that were either stimulated by federal/state priorities
  or promoted by national organizations.* Also, none of the districts used local
  funds for staff development/school renewal initiatives. While complaining about state and federal control, they generated no directions
  of their own but pursued areas promoted (and funded) by the entities
  they were complaining about.

NEEDED RECONCILIATION

The whole set of changes occurred in the absence of a concept to guide
the sets of initiatives that resulted in the changes. *Simply put, it is time to
develop such a concept.* Otherwise, the levels of the organization are not in
a position to work together to improve education. A clear example is
that if states provide funding to schools for school improvement efforts

without having a district support system in place to provide the really intensive and skillful support that will enable those schools to make and sustain school-generated initiatives, then another institutional arrangement needs to be developed to provide that support.

Another example is the critical issue of changing the workplace to provide *time* for school renewal efforts to be organized, including the staff development that is necessary to bring about changes that will make a difference to student achievement. To change the workplace, where should various control responsibilities reside? Does the state take responsibility for presenting a model of a changed workplace to the districts that then have the responsibility for deciding whether to use that model and if so, how? Or are the schools to be the decisionmakers, and if so, what kinds of support will they need?

Once decisions are made about the locus-of-control question, plans can be made either to strengthen the flow-through/regional network strategy or to strengthen the district support system for schools.

ACTION RESEARCH AS AN EMBEDDED MANAGEMENT MODE

Initiatives from the state, district, and school levels should be conducted within an action-research paradigm where the community of persons involved in generating the initiative study its implementation and effects on practice and student learning, and modify continually in an effort to make it more effective.

Unquestionably the massive categorical initiatives would not have experienced 30 years of failure should they have been studied carefully and their effects on practice and achievement been recorded carefully so that modifications could have been made.

> But so it is with all current initiatives: the study of what happens when an initiative is conceived needs to be built into the initiative itself: not a summative evaluation by an external agency but an ongoing collection of data and a periodic review of those data with an eye on how to improve the initiative.

The embedded study of implementation and effects needs to permeate the levels of the system. Thus, whether initiatives require state, district, or school action, the embedded study of effects needs to be a way of acting with the understanding that practice will be modified until satisfactory levels of effect are achieved.

The study examined more than 1000 staff development offerings in the state and *not one of them* contained provisions for studying their effects!

THE DISTRICT AND THE SCHOOL

The picture depicted in the study of this state's operation is typical of the picture throughout the United States. Essentially, districts have weakened themselves and many state and federal initiatives have bypassed the states. Districts have a crisis of identity at the very time when schools have been asked to renew themselves and desperately need support.

Worse, many large districts have adopted policies that distance them from the schools that are inextricably part of them. Several large districts in the United States have examined the standard test pictures of their schools and actually put schools on notice that they will close them if they do not improve themselves within a certain period of time (usually about three years)! Districts that do that sort of thing are making policy that repudiates the understandings the country has had for generations about the responsibility of districts to ensure that their schools are in the best shape possible.

The reconciliation of the locus-of-control problem requires a recognition that school district and school personnel are part of the same organization and have reciprocal responsibilities to each other. If schools as entities are to become evolutionary they will need consistent and compassionate support from district personnel who can bring to them the technical assistance they need.

The downsizing of curricular and instructional personnel in districts needs to be reversed. Rather, they need the personnel who can help schools through the tasks defined in Chapters 4–7 and illustrated in Chapters 3 and 8–10.

THE UNITED KINGDOM

As in the United States, the UK is grappling with the attempt to energize education from a centralized position and to help schools generate the energy to improve themselves. Here is a memorandum from David Hopkins to his colleagues in which he tries to put the national policies in perspective.

To: Colleagues
From: David Hopkins
Subject: The policy context in England

In reflecting on the history of educational change in England over the past three decades or so one is struck on the one hand by the radical shifts in policy, and on the other by the continuity of experience in schools. This is the main reason why in this book we have not reified policy or taken the policy context as being immutable, rather we view policy as a variable (irritant?) with which schools and their communities need to contend as they plan and execute their own improvement journeys.

To understand why we are where we are now, and in order to take some control over the policymaking process, it may be helpful to briefly review the evolution of policy in England over the past four decades or so. Change in English education since the mid-1960s has gone through a number of distinct phases – four are identified here. Each has had a significant influence on the character of schooling and the morale of teachers, and on the context (if not the achievement) of young people who live out their daily lives in that place called school.

From the mid-1960s to the mid-1970s we saw the disestablishing of the tripartite system of education (i.e. the division between grammar, technical and secondary modern schools); the abolition of the 11+ examination (that sorted children into those types of school and that in many cases, through failure at the examination, labeled and scarred them for life); and the move to a general system of comprehensive schooling. Although not every LEA implemented all of these reforms, the comprehensive school was a reality by the late 1960s. The Plowden Report of 1967, with its emphasis on child-centered and "progressive" educational methods had a great impact on the character of primary education at that time. The report was the product of a "blue riband" nonpartisan committee chaired by Lady Plowden that represented mainstream liberal thinking at the time. Similarly influential was the Schools Council, a national body dominated by educators rather than politicians, civil servants, or "the great and the good" that was the major force for curriculum developments during this period. It promoted designs for teaching that were influenced by developmental psychology and a desire to involve students more actively in their learning. Lawrence Stenhouse, one of the major curriculum developers of the time, argued strongly and persuasively that teacher-based research should be inextricably related to curriculum development, and in so doing helped reconceptualize the nature of teacher professionalism. All of these influences contributed to a liberal ethic in English education during this time. It is also fair to say that these influences conditioned the attitudes of many, but obviously not all, of those who are in senior educational positions today.

The period from the mid-1970s to the mid-1980s can be characterized as being the "battle for the control of the curriculum." The oil crisis of 1974 scuppered a number of the liberal proposals, such as the James Report, that advocated a unified approach to initial teacher education, induction, and inservice training – reforms which many of us are still arguing for today. The oil crisis also had another and more conservative effect by supporting and reinforcing the increasing demands for more accountability in education. The infamous "Black Papers," published at the time through a series of high-profile pamphlets, began the public debate on the quality criticism of teachers and teaching and of standards in schools, and the call for a return to "traditional values." Even the Labour Prime Minister James Callaghan, in his Ruskin College speech of 1976, attacked the "secret garden of the curriculum." The Schools Council, which was seen by many to be the guardians of the "secret garden," responded defensively and consequently its influence began to wane.

As a consequence, most LEAs introduced schemes for school evaluation and accountability, which began in some ways to lay the basis for the current inspection system. In a separate initiative, Her Majesty's Inspectors of Schools (HMI), who then had more independence and genuine influence than now, published a series of influential documents (the "Red Books") that began to lay the basis of a national "entitlement" curriculum. This was a reasonable, intelligent and liberal attempt to create a national curriculum based on the principle of entitlement that incorporated a broad and inclusive view of schooling. (In reality there had been a national curriculum for many years, in the form of the booklets of past questions issued annually from the various examination boards!)

The moves to accountability were of course strengthened by the advent of the Thatcher government and its pervasive approach to social reform based on market economics. It must be added parenthetically, however, that the major policy moves of the mid-1980s – the Technical and Vocational Education Initiative (TVEI) and the introduction of teacher appraisal, although initially unpopular with teachers, contained elements of a school-based approach to curriculum and teacher development which many LEAs and schools began to exploit in innovative ways. It is interesting to note that the subsequent popularity of both of these initiatives was a result of their being modified and adapted by educationalists, rather than as a consequence of fulfilling their original intentions.

The potential in these initiatives was soon marginalized by the education reform acts of the late 1980s and early 1990s, which is the third phase identified here. The public debate on educational standards, which began in the mid-1970s, became increasingly polarized, and resulted in a plethora of nationally inspired changes. The politicians had resoundingly won the "battle for the control of the curriculum." As a result, a variety of legislative efforts to improve and regulate schools occurred during the 1980s that culminated in a series of Education Reform Acts of which 1988's was the most important. The Education Acts of the early 1990s further consolidated these.

While the detail of this radical reform agenda is beyond our scope here, it is worth briefly summarizing the four fronts on which this attack on the traditional organization of the school system was carried forward. The first was prescription, of which the prime examples are the National Curriculum and the schemes for National Testing at age 7, 11, and 14. Second is decentralization, and here local management of schools (similar to site-based management), the increase in the power of school governors, and the demise of the local education authority were the main policy initiatives. Third is competition, which was encouraged by the expansion of grant-maintained status for schools, open enrollment which was supported by the publication of "league tables," and a general emphasis on the use of performance indicators. Finally, there was the privatization of those who provide services to schools. This ranges from cleaners to advisers, the creation of curriculum agencies and, more recently, school inspectors.

Although these reforms served the purpose of creating more efficiency in the education system, which was to be welcomed, many feel that their draconian implementation has had a deleterious effect. Their purpose seemed to be accountability and control, rather than professionalism and development. A good example of this is the current inspection system run by Ofsted, the Office for Standards in Education. While few would argue against the need for some system of accountability, many feel that the Ofsted approach is too intensive and too accountability-oriented to serve genuine improvement efforts, although we are currently seeing some (welcome) moves towards embracing some form of self-evaluation in the current round of inspections.

As we move through the 1990s the educational agenda is increasingly being dominated by a concern to implement and institutionalize this radical reform agenda. This quest for stability, however, is being sought against a background of continuing change, as well as increasing expectations for student achievement.

We have now entered a new phase with the advent of the "New Labour" government in 1997 and Prime Minister Tony Blair's commitment to "education, education, education." The publication of the 1997 White Paper (proposed law) "Excellence in Schools" provides an outline in policy terms for Labour's general approach to school improvement. Some of the White Paper themes that are directly related to school improvement are

- the drive to raise standards of achievement and learning;
- a particular emphasis on literacy and numeracy;
- the importance of the early years of education in providing the foundation for learning;
- refining teaching and learning strategies to impact on specific achievement goals;
- strengthening school management and professional development in the support of student achievement;
- the use of target setting as a key school-improvement strategy;
- developing innovative partnerships to support learning.

These themes (which are more fully developed in the White Paper) not only provide a policy framework, but also highlight some of the key ingredients for a successful contemporary and systematic approach to school improvement. The most obvious manifestation of this new style of educational governance is the emphasis on target setting, the continuing stress on accountability, and the introduction of mandatory national schemes for literacy and numeracy in primary schools. In this sense, and unsurprisingly, the educational agenda of the new government is little different from that of its predecessors. The explicit focus on school improvement, however encouraging, may be a mixed blessing.

As with any new initiative, much is expected of the new government's reform program, particularly from those desperately seeking simple and rapid solutions to complex problems. The historical contradictions in the English system remain, and may well be exacerbated in the near future. The traditional liberal ethic, which placed so much emphasis on teacher autonomy and professionalism, appears to be at odds with much of the recent legislation that emphasizes central control. Even the new laws contain inherent contradictions. For example, are assessment and inspection intended to encourage development or accountability? Can a system that emphasizes competition also promote equality of access and provision? Can a system that is so focussed on target setting promote a broader range of learning outcomes than just those measured by standardized tests? Can a nationally prescribed program for literacy and numeracy in the early years of education be suitable for all pupils and schools?

Of crucial importance is the key question: can a reform agenda that has school improvement as its core resolve such contradictions and promote an approach to educational change that is not just a "quick fix"?

Our approach to school improvement, which we outlined on previous pages, implies a clear and direct focus on what is required at the school level to enhance student achievement. To us, school improvement is a strategy for educational change that focuses on student achievement by modifying classroom practice and adapting the management arrangements within the school to support teaching and learning. In our experience, schools that are most successful at school improvement are those that have adapted or modified external change to suit and enhance their internal purposes. They have learned how to work within a centralized policy context, to take control of change rather than becoming victims of it. The conundrum of how schools can pursue such an agenda in a centralized-change context provides the challenge we have set ourselves in this chapter.

DESIGNING NATIONAL AND STATE POLICY: LEARNING TO BUILD LEARNING COMMUNITIES

The relative ineffectiveness of national and state initiatives with respect to curriculum change and student learning should not obscure some of the considerable logistical achievements of merely conceiving and managing such enormous enterprises. We have worked in urban districts in the United States where fully one-third of the adults in the schools were paid for by combinations of the categorical programs. In addition, food services to poor children combine with a variety of medical services to create a "health level" much higher than would otherwise be the case.

However, the initiatives that are intended to affect the learning environment of the students should be much more effective than they are, and can be made so. Acting on current knowledge will not build a perfect bridge between intent and practice, but there is adequate knowledge on which to shape much more effective initiatives.

The units that design and administer the initiatives can themselves become self-renewing and operate in an evolutionary state. In addition to reemphasizing the role of the school district in school improvement as well as in maintaining the educational system, states and districts need to operate from an action-research stance.

One priority is to generate research and development – essential to the health of the educational system. Each school cannot have a cadre of advanced scholars on board. Curriculum thought by advanced scholars is important and needs to be brought to the students, partly through improved instructional material and partly through the study of how to teach, so that advanced knowledge is incorporated in the daily life of the living curriculum. Continuous research and development is badly needed to provide schools with tested alternatives from which they can choose. In the United States, research and development resources, both to develop new curricular and instructional patterns and to learn more about helping schools move to evolutionary states and make *their own* initiatives, have been decimated, which was a serious mistake. States and school district authorities have never invested in research and development to any particular extent. In the United Kingdom research and development resources are virtually nonexistent. Despite this, there has been progress in certain areas of instruction (see Chapter 5) and in literacy (also see Chapter 5): much more is known than is being used. Also, in the United States the investment in higher education should be paying off more, in research as well as teacher preparation. There are about 40,000 education professors *part of whose job is to produce knowledge*, and the yield is not great considering those numbers, partly because the limited R&D moneys make it difficult for a professor to obtain even a few thousand dollars to defray the expenses of a modest study. Higher-education budgets have been cut so severely that even duplicating services are often barely available to them. One of us was sharply brought up against that reality a half-dozen years ago when he agreed to teach a course for a local university. Accustomed to running workshops with quantities of handouts, he took about 200 pages to the secretarial pool to be duplicated for the 100 students who had enrolled in the course. He got a bill for $1000 which he was expected to pay personally (The fee for teaching the course was $3000.) And he had prepared another 300 pages for duplication!

Second, as we discussed in Chapter 11, comes the direct route – creating initiatives designed to generate evolutionary schools. Knowing that nearly all other initiatives are bound to fail unless they fall on schools where Responsible Parties can pick them up, refashion them to fit their circumstances, and implement them as action-research enterprises, policymakers can try to support the development of settings where their initiatives can be effective. A bad alternative, one bound to fail, is to continue to make initiatives that *might* work in schools that are not self-renewing organizations. One reason for the use of pressure is to try to force schools to increase student learning. Well, *that* won't work. So, why not try to increase the schools' capacity to generate productive change by building a generic initiative around the hypotheses about what makes an evolutionary school?

There have been such initiatives with that intent in the past, notably California's massive School Improvement Program, and the more recent AB1274 program. Both failed miserably because they implicitly assumed that schools were already in an evolutionary state, and did not include the provisions to help them move along. Initiatives that are directed toward the schools need to take into account the developmental state of the schools. An initiative that will be a resounding success in a school that is already in an evolutionary state, like the current Pembroke School, would have been a resounding failure in the old Pembroke. A large-scale initiative to generate evolutionary schools will require massive technical support. There is a 20-year history of providing money to individual schools and saying, essentially, "You're on your own, good luck." Several of those efforts have added several hundred thousand dollars to the budgets of individual schools over a period of three or four years to help them become self-renewing, but have reported little effect (see, again, David and Peterson 1984; David 1991) *because* they have failed to change the structural conditions we have been talking about, and because technical support was not available to help them make those changes. As a rule of thumb, as much as 50 percent of the resources from any given initiative might be allocated to staff development and the other dimensions that increase implementation. Lest this seem like a lot, consider the costs of failure! As Elmore (1996) has pointed out repeatedly, national and state initiatives will continue to have limited effect at best if they are not accompanied by support.

The support needs to take human form, and we reiterate the importance of the school district. School districts and intermediate agencies are the only feasible setting for the support personnel to help schools move toward an evolutionary state, or simply to make successful initiatives in targeted curriculum areas. Policymakers at all levels have made the assumption that district "middle management" support personnel are not needed, and this is a mistake of a very serious sort. Districts need a full complement of curriculum personnel who can provide the most direct sort of support to teachers and school administrators. And principals and lead teachers need a great deal of help to build the knowledge and skills to create evolutionary schools – or carry out the development and implementation of efforts in curriculum areas.

OPERATING FROM AN ACTION-RESEARCH PERSPECTIVE

Organizations other than schools can operate according to the hypotheses we have presented here. Units in ministries and Departments of Education can build in time for study, gather around them the persons who can share conceptual responsibility for initiatives, build caring organizational structures, and build staff development into the workplace. Perhaps most critical, such units can operate from an action-research perspective.

Consider the current initiatives in education for the 1.4 million California students who are not native speakers of English. The people of the state have been the policymakers in this last year, passing Proposition 227 by a wide margin. The essence of the proposition is to discontinue "bilingual" programs for these students in favor of "English immersion" programs. Although there is a complex of social issues surrounding the passage of the proposition, the voters of the state are certainly correct with respect to one factual issue: the bilingual programs have not been very successful. In one district that we studied recently, 25 percent of the students were placed in bilingual programs, and of those who had been in the district for as much as ten years, only 4 percent (!) had made enough progress to exit the program competent in English. Now the national, state, and district policymakers should have recognized long ago that the bilingual programs were not successful, sought for reasons why, and taken steps to correct the situation and study the effects of the changes. However, they were inactive. Now the people have spoken. There is just one hitch. The teachers of all those students could have taught them English, *by either approach*, if they had known how to do so. The immersion alternative will surely fail unless there is a massive program to help teachers learn how to do the job. And the really sad thing is that there is a good enough research base that a basis could readily be developed for the staff development that would make either bilingual or immersion programs successful (see Chapters 5 and 6).

The other massive categorical programs have many of the same problems that attend the ones for second-language learners. Basically, as initiatives have operated for students having special needs, the exit rate of 4 percent appears to be common. Implementation of curricular initiatives is not good.

The real problem is not that the initiatives were not well intended. It is that data about the failures was ignored and the support necessary for effective implementation was not provided.

REALISM

Altogether, the remedy is to realize that effectiveness will be built through learning, rather than through the belief that we already know. Policymakers and their advisors are in a position where the public trust requires that initiatives, whether to create evolutionary schools, to build the capacity of school districts, or to make curriculum changes, be carried out as inquiries, rather than as if the policymaker had, as a result of position, the luminous insight that can ignore reality. The reality is that schools need help rather than admonition, and the complexity of making policy at a distance from the school should humble all of us.

Coda: history and current context

The improvement of the content and process of education is an ancient topic. What is new, a concern of only the last three decades, is a focus on *how* education can be improved, and that focus has led to a search for effective structures for school renewal. The search has been difficult.

This little book is part of the stream of work carried on to create effective structures (guides to action) by which schools can change themselves and also utilize developments in research and development external to them.

THE PERENNIAL INTEREST IN WHAT IS TAUGHT AND HOW IT SHOULD BE TAUGHT

Calls for educational reform have been made in some of the earliest written words that have been preserved for us as part of the archive of Western civilization. The Old and New Testaments contain precepts for education; the documents themselves became the substance of important aspects of secular as well as religious education. The Greek and Roman philosophers entwined thought about education with their reflections on the nature of society and science. (There are strong parallels in the other cultural strands of the world, as in the basis of the Islamic education in the Koran and the influence of Gautama Siddhartha in Asia.)

Even in the Middle Ages the Catholic writers not only gave considerable attention to education, but many, such as Aquinas, called for reforms.

The Reformation can be seen almost as much as a call for educational reform as a religious movement, and was concerned not only with changes in religious governance and doctrine, but also with how the young were to be introduced to the world.

The Renaissance not only changed ideas and generated the beginnings of contemporary science, it also laid the base for common schooling, although it was slow in coming. Then, virtually all the philosophers (such as Locke, Rousseau, and Kant) from the late 1600s until today, and from every European area, spoke of what the curriculum might or should be and how it should be taught. In America, Jefferson and Franklin in particular championed education and had specific ideas about its content – although, oddly, despite their influence (and that of other education-minded philosophers) on the United States Constitution, that document made no reference to education as a function of the national government but left education to the states.

Throughout the nineteenth and twentieth centuries philosophers (such as Whitehead and Russell in the United Kingdom and Dewey and James in the United States) continued to speak of the purposes, content, and process of education. Now they were speaking in the time of the common school (that is, provisions had been made to educate everyone) and were referring to the education of *all* men and women, whereas their predecessors lived in the time when few persons received formal education.

Throughout most of the twentieth century there have been a variety of reform movements intending to improve the curriculum of the common school. Conspicuous among these was a movement to update the content of curriculums, first in science and mathematics, and later in all subjects, particularly to bring content and process in line with contemporary scholarship. (That movement, which continues today, collides with the views of some religious and political groups who prefer the old curriculum and methods and regard the academic reforms with suspicion and even anger.) Also, as we have emphasized several times, initiatives targeting serious problems were made. The definition of "special needs" was broadened considerably and special education became a large part of the educational system, as did components devoted to supplementing the education of the poor.

Currently the public and governments have great concern with the quality of education and seek avenues to improve it in the ways we discussed in Part IV.

RECOGNITION OF AN IMPLEMENTATION PROBLEM

Beginning in the 1960s scholars began to realize that very few of the philosophers, movements, or government initiatives were affecting mainstream practice in the schools. Euclid was effective insofar as his treatise on geometry was used, virtually unchanged, as the basic course until very recently; modernizing the geometry course to reflect 2000 years of scholarship was controversial and difficult. We speculate that Euclid would have been proud of his accomplishments as a scholar and teacher but that he had no intention of freezing the course for two millennia.

The failure of reform efforts makes for depressing reading, but a few items are worth attention.

Science teaching today is rarely as modern as Aristotle would have preferred, and the humanities and social sciences fall short of Plato's educational ideals. The academic reform movement of the 1950s and 1960s, intended to bring the curriculum areas in line with advanced scholarship of the twentieth century, generated some wonderful and effective curriculums and teaching models, but could not be implemented on a large scale.

The movement to make the school a living laboratory for the education of democratic citizens fared no better: there was some brilliant development and little implementation.

The highly targeted initiatives for students having special needs and for the children of poverty have largely failed, and have even resulted in less powerful curriculums for those who most need rich ones.

Computers, television, and film are little used in schools, which from a technological point of view are seriously out of phase with the rest of society.

And the normative curriculum in the basic subjects – reading, writing, and mathematics – has not increased in effectiveness despite great advances in the storehouse of knowledge for teaching them.

A CHANGE OF EMPHASIS: IMPROVING THE SCHOOL AS AN ORGANIZATION

Beginning in the mid-1960s, scholars began to realize that school improvement depends not only on good ideas about goals, content, and models of teaching, but also on the development of structures for school improvement; structures that could generate the implementation of initiatives from within and without the school (see Miles 1992 for a retrospective on the problem). By the 1980s the study of school improvement as a sub-field of education was beginning to take shape (see Fullan 1982 and Joyce *et al.* 1983a for early formulations). Since then, considerable energy has been devoted to the study of school renewal and a variety of approaches have been developed and evaluated, approaches that we have called "doors to school improvement" (Joyce 1990, 1991). Some of the approaches are oriented toward changing the culture of the school so that it can generate initiatives in curriculum and instruction (Barth 1990; Bonstingl 1992; Glickman 1993), others around the action-research paradigm (such as Calhoun 1994), and others on the engineering of effective initiatives from without the school (as summarized by Joyce *et al.* 1993). Sometimes the various approaches have been pitted against one another by their advocates.

We are convinced that the study of success and failure has reached the point where schools can improve their performance dramatically and where initiatives generated through research and development can be incorporated in the programs of schools. We believe that arguments about the merits of "inside-out" and "outside-in" approaches are not of much use. Schools can improve themselves and they can also be improved by adopting research-based curriculums and models of teaching.

In both cases our theme is that school renewal depends, as we have said throughout, on the development of an inquiring workplace where both adults and students are in continuous study. We are also convinced that the nature of school renewal will not be by the adoption of formulas but by the change in structures that makes each assay an adventurous inquiry that generates knowledge and skill for the participants.

Bibliography

Achilles, C. M. and Nye, B. A. Reinventing education through school improvement research that has resulted in student gains. Paper presented at the annual meeting of the International Congress for School Effectiveness and Improvement, Memphis, Tennessee.

Adams, A. H., Johnson, M. S., and Connors, J. M. (1980) *Success in Kindergarten Reading and Writing*. Glenview, IL: Good Year Books.

Adams, M. J. (1990) *Beginning to Read: Thinking and Learning About Print*. Cambridge, MA: MIT Press.

Adey, P. and Shayer, M. (1990) Accelerating the development of formal thinking in middle and high school students, *Journal of Research in Science Teaching*, 27(3): 267–85.

Adler, M. J. (1982) *The Paidea Proposal: An Educational Manifesto*. New York: Macmillan.

Afflerbach, P. P. (1990) The influence of prior knowledge on expert readers' main idea construction strategies, *Reading Research Quarterly*, 25: 31–46.

Afflerbach, P. P. and Johnston, P. H. (1986) What do expert readers do when the main idea is not explicit? in J. E. Bauman (ed.) *Teaching Main Idea Comprehension* (pp. 49–72). Newark, DE: International Reading Association.

Ainscow, M., Hopkins, D., Southworth, G., and West, M. (1994) *Creating the Conditions for School Improvement*. London: David Fulton Publishers.

Allington, R. L. (1983) The reading instruction provided readers of differing reading ability, *Elementary School Journal*, 83: 548–59.

Allington, R. L. (1990) What have we done with the middle? in G. G. Duffy (ed.) *Reading in the Middle School* (pp. 32–40). Newark, DE: International Reading Association.

Allington, R. L. (1991) The legacy of "slow it down and make it more concrete" in J. Zutell and S. McCormick (eds.) *Learner Factors/Teacher Factors: Issues in Literacy Research and Instruction* (pp. 19–30). Chicago: National Reading Conference.

Allington, R. L. (1994) What's special about special programs for children who find learning to read difficult? *Journal of Reading Behaviour*, 26(1): 95–115.

Allington, R. L. and Cunningham, P. M. (1996) *Schools that Work: Where All Children Read and Write*. New York: HarperCollins.

Allington, R. L. and McGill-Franzen, A. (1989) Different programs, indifferent instruction, in D. Lipsky and A. Gartner (eds.) *Beyond Separate Education: Quality Education for All* (pp. 75–98). Baltimore, MD: Brookes.

Allington, R. L. and McGill-Franzen, A. (1992a) Does high-stakes testing improve school effectiveness? *ERS Spectrum*, 10(2): 3–12.

Allington, R. L. and McGill-Franzen, A. (1992b) Unintended effects of educational reform, *Educational Policy*, 6(4): 397–414.

Almy, M. (1970) *Logical Thinking in Second Grade.* New York: Teachers College Press.

Alvermann, D. E. and Muth, K. D. (1990) Affective goals in reading and writing, in G. G. Duffy (ed.) *Reading in the Middle School* (pp. 97–110). Newark, DE: International Reading Association.

Alvermann, D. E., O'Brien, D. G., and Dillon, D. R. (1990) What teachers do when they say they're having discussions of content area reading assignments: a qualitative analysis, *Reading Research Quarterly*, 25: 297–322.

Alvermann, D. E., Umpleby, R., and Olson, J. R. (1996) Getting involved and having fun: dilemmas in building a literate community in one lower-track English class, *Qualitative Studies in Education.*

Anders, P. L. and Levine, N. S. (1990) Accomplishing change in reading programs, in G. G. Duffy (ed.) *Reading in the Middle School* (pp. 157–70). Newark, DE: International Reading Association.

Anderson, R. C. (1993) The future of reading research, in A. P. Sweet and J. I. Anderson (eds.) *Reading Research into the Year 2000* (pp. 17–36). Hillsdale, NJ: Erlbaum.

Anderson, R. C. and Freebody, P. (1981) Vocabulary knowledge, in J. T. Guthrie (ed.) *Comprehension and Teaching: Research Reviews* (pp. 77–117). Newark, DE: International Reading Association.

Anderson, R. C. and Nagy, W. E. (1992) The vocabulary conundrum, *American Educator*, Winter: 14–18, 45–7 (ERIC ED354489).

Anderson, R. C., Hiebert, E. F., Scott, J. A., and Wilkinson, J. A. (1985) *Becoming a Nation of Readers: The Report of the Commission on Reading.* Washington, DC: The National Institute of Education.

Anderson, R. C., Wilson, P., and Fielding, L. (1988) Growth in reading and how children spend their time outside of school, *Reading Research Quarterly*, 23: 285–303.

Anderson, R. C., Raphael, T. E., Englert, C. S., and Stevens, D. D. (1991) Teaching writing with a new instructional model: variations in teachers' practices and students' performances. Paper presented at the annual meeting of the American Educational Research Association, Chicago.

Anderson, V. and Hidi, S. (1988/1989) Teaching students to summarize, *Educational Leadership*, 46(4): 26–8.

Anderson, V. and Roit, M. (1993) Planning and implementing collaborative strategy instruction for delayed readers in grades 6–10, *Elementary School Journal*, 94: 121–37.

Annie E. Casey Foundation (1995) *Kids Count Data Book: State Profiles of Child Well-being.* Baltimore, MD: Annie E. Casey Foundation.

Apple, M. and Neane, J. (eds.) (1995) *Democratic Schools.* Alexandria, VA: Association for Curriculum and Supervision Development.

Applebee, A. N. (1984) Writing and reasoning, *Review of Educational Research*, 54(4): 577–89.

Applebee, A. N., Langer, J. A., and Mullis, I. V. S. (1988) *Who Reads Best? Factors Related to Reading Achievement in Grades 3, 7, and 11.* Princeton, NJ: Educational Testing Service.

Applebee, A. N., Langer, J. A., Jenkins, L., Mullis, I. V. S., and Foertsch, M. (1990) *Learning to Write in Our Nation's Schools: Instruction and Achievement in 1988 at Grades 4, 8, and 12.* Princeton, NJ: Educational Testing Service (National Assessment of Educational Progress. ED 318 038).

Applebee, A. N., Langer, J. A., Mullis, I. V. S., Latham, A. S., and Gentile, C. A. (1994) *NAEP 1992 Writing Report Card.* Washington, DC: Prepared by Educational Testing Service under contract with the National Center for Education Statistics for the Office of Educational Research and Improvement, US Department of Education.

Armbruster, B. B. and Brown, A. L. (1984) Learning from reading: the role of metacognition, in R. C. Anderson, J. Osborn, and R. J. Tierney (eds.) *Learning to Read in American Schools: Basal Readers and Content Texts* (pp. 273–81). Hillsdale, NJ: Erlbaum.

Armbruster, B. B., Anderson, T. H., and Ostertag, J. (1987) Does text structure/summarization instruction facilitate learning from expository text? *Reading Research Quarterly*, 22: 331–46.

Aspy, D. N. and Roebuck, F. (1973) An investigation of the relationship between student/levels of cognitive functioning and the teacher's classroom behavior, *Journal of Educational Research*, 65(6): 365–8.

Aspy, D. N., Roebuck, F., Willson, M., and Adams, O. (1974) *Interpersonal Skills Training for Teachers.* (Interim report #2 for NIMH Grant #5PO 1MH 19871.) Monroe, LA: Northeast Louisiana University.

Atkinson, R. (1975) Mnemotechnics in second language learning, *American Psychologist*, 30: 821–8.

Ausubel, D. P. (1960) The use of advance organizers in the learning and retention of meaningful verbal material, *Journal of Educational Psychology*, 51: 267–72.

Ausubel, D. P. (1963) *The Psychology of Meaningful Verbal Learning.* New York: Grune and Stratton.

Ausubel, D. P. (1980) Schemata, cognitive structure, and advance organizers: a reply to Anderson, Spiro, and Anderson, *American Educational Research Journal*, 17(3): 400–4.

Ausubel, D. P. and Fitzgerald, J. (1962) Organizer, general background and antecedent learning variables in sequential verbal learning, *Journal of Educational Psychology*, 53: 243–9.

Ausubel, D. P., Stager, M., and Gaite, A. J. H. (1968) Retroactive facilitation of meaningful verbal learning, *Journal of Educational Psychology*, 59: 250–5.

Baker, E. T., Wang, M. C., and Walberg, H. J. (1994/1995) The effects of inclusion on learning, *Educational Leadership*, 52(4): 33–5.

Baker, R. (1995) "Implementation and impact of *Just Read* in the Holtville Unified School District." Master's thesis, San Diego: San Diego State University.

Baldridge, V. and Deal, T. (1975) *Managing Change in Educational Organizations.* Berkeley, CA: McCutchan.

Ball, S. and Bogatz, G. A. (1970) *The First Year of Sesame Street.* Princeton, NJ: Educational Testing Service.

Banks, J. A. (1997) *Educating Citizens in a Multicultural Society.* New York: Teachers College Press.

Barr, R. (1992) Teachers, materials, and group composition in literacy instruction, in M. J. Dreher and W. H. Slater (eds.) *Elementary School Literacy: Critical Issues* (pp. 27–50). Norwood, MA: Christopher-Gordon.

Barry, A. L. (1997) High school reading programs revisited, *Journal of Adolescent and Adult Literacy*, 40(7): 524–31.

Barth, R. S. (1990) *Improving Schools from Within.* San Francisco: Jossey-Bass.

Barth, R. S. (1991) Restructuring schools: some questions for teachers and principals, *Phi Delta Kappan*, October: 123–8.

Barton, P. E. and Coley, R. J. (1996) *Captive Students: Education and Training in America's Prisons*. Princeton, NJ: Educational Testing Service.

Baveja, B. (1988) "An exploratory study of the use of information-processing models of teaching in secondary school biology science classes." PhD thesis, Delhi, India: Delhi University.

Beach, R. (1987) Strategic teaching in literature, in B. Jones, A. S. Palinscar, D. S. Ogle, and E. G. Carr (eds.) *Strategic Teaching and Learning: Cognitive Instruction in the Content Areas* (pp. 135–59). Alexandria, VA: Association for Supervision and Curriculum Development.

Beck, I. L. (1984) Developing comprehension: the impact of the directed reading lesson, in R. C. Anderson, Jean Osborn, and R. J. Tierney (eds.) *Learning to Read in American Schools: Basal Readers and Content Texts* (pp. 3–20). Hillsdale, NJ: Erlbaum.

Beck, I. L. (1993) On reading: a survey of recent research and proposals for the future, in A. P. Sweet and J. I. Anderson (eds.) *Reading Research into the Year 2000* (pp. 65–87). Hillsdale, NJ: Erlbaum.

Beck, I. L. and Juel, C. (1992) The role of decoding in learning to read, in S. J. Samuels and A. E. Farstrup (eds.) *What Research Has to Say About Reading Instruction* (2nd edn). Newark, DE: International Reading Association.

Beck, I. L. and McKeown, M. G. (1990) Conditions of vocabulary acquisition, in R. Barr, M. L. Kamil, P. Mosenthal, and P. D. Pearson (eds.) *Handbook of Reading Research: Volume II* (pp. 789–814). New York: Longman.

Beck, I. L. and McKeown, M. G. (1992) Young students' social studies learning: going for depth, in M. J. Dreher and W. H. Slater (eds.) *Elementary School Literacy: Critical Issues* (pp. 133–56). Norwood, MA: Christopher-Gordon.

Beck, I. L., McKeown, M. G., and Omanson, R. C. (1987) The effects and uses of diverse vocabulary instructional techniques, in M. G. McKeown and M. E. Curtis (eds.) *The Nature of Vocabulary Acquisition*. Hillsdale, NJ: Erlbaum.

Beck, I. L., McKeown, M. G., and Gromoll, E. W. (1989) Learning from social studies texts, *Cognition and Instruction*, 6(2): 99–158.

Becker, W. (1977) Teaching reading and language to the disadvantaged – what have we learned from field research? *Harvard Educational Review*, 47: 518–43.

Becker, W. and Carnine, D. (1980) Direct instruction: an effective approach for educational intervention with the disadvantaged and low performers, in B. Lahey and A. Kazdin (eds.) *Advances in Child Clinical Psychology* (pp. 429–73). New York: Plenum.

Becker, W. and Gersten, R. (1982) A followup of follow through: the later effects of the direct instruction model on children in the fifth and sixth grades, *American Educational Research Journal*, 19(1): 75–92.

Becker, W., Englemann, S., Carnine, D., and Rhine, W. (1981) The effects of Distar in W. Rhine (ed.) *Making Schools More Effective*. New York: Academic Press.

Bellack, A. (1962) *The Language of the Classroom*. New York: Teachers College Press.

Bennis, W. G. (1989) *Why Leaders Can't Lead*. San Francisco: Jossey-Bass.

Bereiter, C. (1994a) Implications of postmodernism for science, or, science as progressive discourse, *Educational Psychologist*, 29(1): 3–12.

Bereiter, C. (1994b) Constructivism, socioculturalism, and Popper's World 3, *Educational Researcher*, 23(7): 21–3.

Bereiter, C. and Bird, M. (1985) Use of thinking aloud in identification and teaching of reading comprehension strategies, *Cognition and Instruction*, 2(2): 131–56.

Bereiter, C. and Scardamalia, M. (1987a) An attainable version of high literacy: approaches to teaching higher-order skills in reading and writing, *Curriculum Inquiry*, 17(1): 9–30.

Bereiter, C. and Scardamalia, M. (1987b) *The Psychology of Written Composition*. Hillsdale, NJ: Erlbaum.

Berman, P. and Gjelten, T. (1983) *Improving School Improvement*. Berkeley, CA: Berman, Weiler Associates.

Berman, P. and McLaughlin, M. (1975) *Federal Programs Supporting Educational Change, Volume IV: The Findings in Review*. Santa Monica, CA: The Rand Corporation.

Bintz, W. P. (1997) Exploring reading nightmares of middle and secondary school teachers, *Journal of Adolescent and Adult Literacy*, 41(1): 12–24.

Block, J. W. and Anderson, L. W. (1975) *Mastery Learning in Classrooms*. New York: Macmillan.

Bloom, B. S. (1971) Mastery learning, in J. H. Block (ed.) *Mastery Learning: Theory and Practice* (pp. 26–53). New York: Holt, Rinehart, and Winston.

Bloom, B. S. (1974) Time and learning, *American Psychologist*, 29: 682–8.

Bloom, B. S. (1981) The new direction in educational research and measurement: alterable variables. Paper presented at the annual meeting of the American Educational Research Association, Los Angeles, CA.

Bloom, B. S. (1984) The 2 sigma problem: the search for group instruction as effective as one-to-one tutoring, *Educational Researcher*, 13: 4–16.

Bloome, D. (ed.) (1987) *Literacy and Schooling*. Norwood, NJ: Ablex.

Bloome, D. (1989) Beyond access: an ethnographic study of reading and writing in the seventh grade, in D. Bloome (ed.) *Classrooms and Literacy* (pp. 53–107). Norwood, NJ: Ablex.

Bond, G. and Bond, E. (1961) *Developmental Reading in High School*. New York: Macmillan.

Bonsangue, M. (1993) Long term effects of the calculus workshop model, *Cooperative Learning*, 13(3): 19–20.

Bonstingl, J. (1992) *Schools of Quality: An Introduction to Total Quality Management in Education*. Alexandria, VA: Association for Supervision and Curriculum Development.

Bredderman, T. (1983) Effects of activity-based elementary science on student outcomes: a quantitative synthesis, *Review of Educational Research*, 53(4): 499–518.

Bridge, C. (1989) Beyond the basal in beginning reading, in P. Winograd, K. Wixson, and M. Lipson (eds.) *Improving Basal Reading Instruction* (pp. 177–209). New York: Teachers College Press.

Brookover, W., Schwitzer, J. H., Schneider, J. M., Beady, C. H., Flood, P. K., and Wisenbaker, J. M. (1978) Elementary school social climate and school achievement, *American Educational Research Journal*, 15(2): 301–18.

Brophy, J. E. (1992) Probing the subtleties of subject-matter teaching, *Educational Leadership*, 49(7): 4–8.

Brophy, J. E. and Good, T. L. (1986) Teacher behavior and student achievement, in M. E. Wittrock (ed.) *Handbook of Research on Teaching* (pp. 328–75). New York: Macmillan.

Brown, A. L. and Campione, J. (1986) Psychological theory and the study of learning disabilities, *American Psychologist*, 14: 1059–68.

Brown, A. L., Campione, J. C., and Day, J. D. (1981) Learning to learn: on training students to learn from texts, *Educational Researcher*, 10(2): 14–21.

Bruner, J. (1961) *The Process of Education*. Cambridge, MA: Harvard University Press.

Bruner, J., Goodnow, J. J., and Austin, G. A. (1967) *A Study of Thinking*. New York: Science Editions.

Butler-Kisber, L. (1993) Action research: incorporating the voices of children. Paper presented at the annual meeting of the American Educational Research Association, Atlanta.

Calderon, M., Hertz-Lazarowitz, R., and Tinajero, J. (1991) Adapting CIRC to multi-ethnic and bilingual classrooms, *Cooperative Learning*, 12: 17–20.

Caldwell, B. and Spinks, J. (1988) *The Self-managing School*. Lewes: Falmer Press.

Calfee, R. C. (1992) Authentic assessment of reading and writing in the elementary classroom, in M. J. Dreher and W. H. Slater (eds.) *Elementary School Literacy: Critical Issues* (pp. 211–26). Norwood, MA: Christopher-Gordon.

Calhoun, E. F. (1991) A wide-angle lens: how to increase the variety, collection, and use of data for school improvement. Paper presented at the annual meeting of the American Educational Research Association, Chicago.

Calhoun, E. F. (1992) A status report on action research in the League of Professional Schools. Paper presented at the annual meeting of the American Educational Research Association, San Francisco.

Calhoun, E. F. (1993) Action research: three approaches, *Educational Leadership*, 51(2), 62–5.

Calhoun, E. F. (1994) *How to Use Research in the Self Renewing School*. Alexandria, VA: The Association for Supervision and Curriculum Development.

Calhoun, E. F. (1996) The action network: action research on action research, in B. R. Joyce and E. Calhoun (eds.) *Learning Experiences in School Renewal*. Eugene, OR: The ERIC Clearinghouse on Educational Management.

Calhoun, E. F. (1997) *Literacy for All*. Saint Simons Island, GA: The Phoenix Alliance.

Calhoun, E. F. (1999) *The Picture-Word Inductive Model*. Alexandria, VA: The Association for Curriculum and Supervision Development.

Calhoun, E. F. and Allen, L. (1996) Results of schoolwide action research in the League of Professional Schools. Paper presented at the annual meeting of the American Educational Research Association, New Orleans.

Calhoun, E. F. and Glickman, C. D. (1993) Issues and dilemmas of action research in the League of Professional Schools. Paper presented at the annual meeting of the American Educational Research Association, Atlanta.

Carpenter, T. P., Fennema, E., Peterson P. L., Chiang, C., and Loef, M. (1988) Effects of cognitively-guided instruction on students' problem solving. Paper presented at the 1988 annual meeting of the American Educational Research Association.

Carpenter, T. P., Fennema, E., Peterson, P. L., Chiang, C., and Loef, M. (1989) Using knowledge of children's mathematics thinking in classroom teaching: an experimental study, *American Educational Research Journal*, 26: 499–532.

Carran, N. (1993) *The Teacher Satisfaction and Productivity Interview*. Ames, IA: Ames Community Schools.

Carroll, J. B. (1963) A model of school learning, *Teachers College Record*, 64: 722–33.

Carroll, J. B. (1977) A revisionist model of school learning, *Review of Educational Research*, 3: 155–67.

Carroll, J. B. (1989) The Carroll model: a 25-year retrospective and prospective view, *Educational Researcher*, 18(1): 26–31.

Ceram, C. W. (1951) *Gods, Graves, and Scholars: The Story of Archeology*. New York: Random House.

Chall, J. S. (1967/1983) *Learning to Read: The Great Debate*. New York: McGraw-Hill.

Chall, J. S. (1983) *Stages of Reading Development*. New York: McGraw-Hill.

Chall, J. S. (1990) Policy implications of literacy definitions, in R. L. Venezky, D. A. Wagner, and B. S. Ciliberti (eds.) *Toward Defining Literacy* (pp. 54–62). Newark, DE: International Reading Association.

Chamberlin, C. and Chamberlin, E. (1943) *Did They Succeed in College?* New York: Harper and Row.

Chesler, M. and Fox, R. (1966) *Role-playing Methods in the Classroom*. Chicago: Science Research Associates.

Clark, C. and Peterson, P. (1986) Teachers' thought processes, in M. Wittrock (ed.) *Handbook of Research on Teaching*. New York: Macmillan.

Clark, H. H. and Clark, E. V. (1977) *Psychology and Language: An Introduction to Psycholinguistics*. New York: Harcourt, Brace, Jovanovich.

Cleary, F. (1939) Why children read, *Wilson Library Bulletin*, 14: 119–26.

Clymer, T. (1963, 1996) The utility of phonic generalizations in the primary grades, *The Reading Teacher*, 50(3): 182–7.

Cochran-Smith, M. (1988) Mediating: an important role for the reading teacher, in C. Hedley and J. Hicks (eds.) *Reading and the Special Learner* (pp. 109–39). Norwood, NJ: Ablex.

Collins, A., Brown, J. S., and Newman, S. (1989) Cognitive apprenticeship: teaching students the craft of reading, writing, and mathematics, in L. B. Resnick (ed.) *Knowing, Learning, and Instruction: Essays in Honor of Robert Glaser*. Hillsdale, NJ: Erlbaum.

Collins, K. (1969) The importance of strong confrontation in an inquiry model of teaching, *School Science and Mathematics*, 69(7): 615–17.

Comer, J. (1988) Educating poor minority children, *Scientific American*, November: 42(8): 43–55.

Commission on Chapter I (1993) *Making Schools Work for Children of Poverty: A New Framework Prepared by the Commission on Chapter I*. Washington, DC: American Association for Higher Education.

Conant, J. B. (1961) *Slums and Suburbs*. New York: McGraw-Hill.

Cooley, W. (1993) The difficulty of the educational task: implications for comparing student achievement in states, school districts, and schools, *ERS Spectrum*, 11: 27–31.

Copeland, K., Winsor, P., and Osborn, J. (1994) Phonemic awareness: a consideration of research and practice, in F. Lehr and J. Osborn (eds.) *Reading, Language, and Literacy: Instruction for the Twenty-first Century* (pp. 25–44). Hillsdale, NJ: Erlbaum.

Corey, S. M. (1949) Curriculum development through action research, *Educational Leadership*, 7(3): 147–53.

Corey, S. M. (1953) *Action Research to Improve School Practices*. New York: Teachers College Press.

Cox, C. (1996) *Teaching Lnguage Arts*. Boston, MA: Allyn and Bacon.

Crandall, D., Eiseman, J., and Louis, K. (1986) Strategic planning issues that bear on the success of school improvement efforts, *Educational Administration Quarterly*, 22(2): 21–53.

Creemers, B. P. M. (1994) *The Effective Classroom*. London: Cassell.

Cuban, L. (1990) Reforming again, again, and again, *Educational Researcher*, 19(1): 3–13.

Cunningham, P. M. (1976) Investigating a synthesized theory of mediated word identification, *Reading Research Quarterly*, 11: 127–43.

Cunningham, P. M. (1979) Mediated word identification: a compare/contrast approach, in J. E. Button, T. C. Lovitt, and T. D. Rowland (eds.) *Communications Research in Learning Disabilities and Mental Retardation*. Baltimore, MD: University Park.

Cunningham, P. M. and Cunningham, J. W. (1987) Content area reading-writing lessons, *The Reading Teacher*, 40(3): 507–12.

Dalin, P., with Rolff, H.-G. and Kleekamp, B. (1993) *Changing the School Culture*. London: Cassell.

David, J. L. (1989) *Restructuring in Progress: Lessons from Pioneering Districts*. Washington, DC: National Governors' Association.

David, J. L. (1990) Restructuring: increased autonomy and changing roles. Invited address presented at the annual meeting of the American Educational Research Association, Boston.

David, J. L. (1991) What it takes to restructure education, *Educational Leadership*, 48(8): 11–15.

David, J. L. and Peterson, S. M. (1984) *Can Schools Improve Themselves? A Study of School-based Improvement Programs*. Palo Alto, CA: Bay Area Research Group.

Deal, T. E. (1993) The culture of the school, in M. Sashkin and H. Walberg (eds.) *Educational Leadership and School Culture* (pp. 226–73). San Pablo, Berkeley, CA: McCutchan.

Dewey, J. (1916) *Democracy in Education*. New York: Macmillan.

Dewey, J. (1937) *Experience and Education*. New York: Macmillan.

Dole, J. A., Duffy, G. G., Roehler, L. R., and Pearson, P. D. (1991) Moving from the old to the new: research on reading comprehension instruction, *Review of Educational Research*, 61(2): 239–64.

Dole, J. A., Brown, K. J., and Trathen, W. (1996) The effects of strategy instruction on the comprehension performance of at-risk students, *Reading Research Quarterly*, 31(1): 62–88.

Dreher, M. J. and Slater, W. H. (eds.) (1992) *Elementary School Literacy: Critical Issues*. Norwood, MA: Christopher-Gordon.

Drucker, P. F. (1985) *Innovation and Entrepreneurship: Practice and Principles*. New York: Harper and Row.

Drucker, P. F. (1989) *The New Realities: In Government and Politics, in Economics and Business, in Society and World View*. New York: Harper and Row.

Drucker, P. F. (1994) The age of social transformation, *Atlantic Monthly*, November: 53–80.

Duffelmeyer, Merkley, Fyfe, and Kruse (1994) Further validation and enhancement of the NAMES Test, *The Reading Teacher*, 48(2): 118–28.

Duffy, G. G. (ed.) (1990) *Reading in the Middle School* (2nd edn). Newark, DE: International Reading Association.

Duffy, G. G. and Roehler, L. R. (1989) Why strategy instruction is so difficult and what we need to do about it, in C. McCormick, G. Miller, and M. Pressley (eds.) *Cognitive Strategy Research: From Basic Research to Educational Applications*. New York: Springer-Verlag.

Duffy, G. G., Roehler, L. R., Sivan, E., Rackliffe, G., Book, C., Meloth, M., Vavrus, L., Wesselman, R., Putnam, J., and Bassiri, D. (1987) Effects of explaining the reasoning associated with using reading strategies, *Reading Research Quarterly*, 22, 347–68.

Duffy, G. G., Roehler, L. R., and Hermann, B. (1988) Modeling mental processes helps poor readers become strategic readers, *The Reading Teacher*, 41, 762–7.

Durkin, D. (1978–79) What classroom observations reveal about reading comprehension instruction, *Reading Research Quarterly*, 14(4): 481–533.

Durkin, D. (1986) Reading methodology textbooks: are they helping teachers teach comprehension? *The Reading Teacher*, 39(5): 410–17.

Durst, R. K. and Newell, G. E. (1989) The uses of function: James Brittons's category system and research on writing, *Review of Educational Research*, 59(4): 375–94.

Edelsky, C. (1990) Whose agenda is it anyway? *Educational Researcher*, 19(8): 7–10.

Ehri, L. C. (1994) Development of the ability to read words: update, in R. B. Ruddell, M. P. Ruddell, and H. Singer (eds.) *Theoretical Models and Processes of Reading* (4th edn). Newark, DE: International Reading Association.

Elefant, E. (1980) Deaf children in an inquiry training program, *The Volta Review*, 82: 271–9.

Elliott, J. (1991) *Action Research for Educational Change*. Buckingham: Open University Press.

Ellis, E. S. (1994) Integrating writing strategy instruction with content-area instruction: Part 1 – Orienting students to organizational devices, *Intervention in School and Clinic*, 29(3): 169–79.

Elmore, R. F. (1990) On changing the structure of public schools, in R. F. Elmore (ed.) *Restructuring Schools*. San Francisco: Jossey-Bass.

Elmore, R. F. (1996) Getting to scale with good educational practice, *Harvard Educational Review*, 66(1): 1–26.

El-Nemr, M. A. (1979) "Meta-analysis of the outcomes of teaching biology as inquiry." PhD thesis, Boulder, CO: University of Colorado.

Encyclopaedia Britannica (1993) Volume 13. Chicago: Encyclopaedia Britannica.

Englert, C. S. and Hiebert, E. H. (1984) Children's developing awareness of text structures in expository materials, *Journal of Educational Psychology*, 76: 65–74.

Englert, C. S. and Raphael, T. E. (1989) Developing successful writers through cognitive strategy instruction, in J. Brophy (ed.) *Advances in Research on Teaching: Volume I* (pp. 105–51). Greenwich, CN: JAI Press.

Englert, C. S., Raphael, T. E., Anderson, L. M., Gregg, S. L., and Anthony, H. M. (1989) Exposition: reading, writing and the metacognitive knowledge of learning disabled students, *Learning Disabilities Research*, 5(1): 5–24.

Englert, C. S., Raphael, T. E., Anderson, L. M., Anthony, H. M., and Stevens, D. D. (1991) Making strategies and self-talk visible: writing instruction in regular and special education classrooms, *American Educational Research Journal*, 28(2): 337–72.

Englert, C. S., Tarrant, K. L., Mariage, T. V., and Oxer, T. (1994) Lesson talk as the work of reading groups: the effectiveness of two interventions, *Journal of Learning Disabilities*, 27, 165–85.

Evans, M. and Hopkins, D. (1988) School climate and the psychological state of the individual teacher as factors affecting the use of educational ideas following an inservice course, *British Educational Research Journal*, 14(3): 211–30.

Fader, D. (1976) *The New Hooked on Books*. New York: Berkeley.

Fielding, L. C., Wilson, P. D., and Anderson, R. C. (1986) A new focus on free reading: the role of trade books in reading instruction, in T. E. Raphael (ed.) *The Contexts of School-based Literacy* (pp. 149–60). New York: Random House.

Fielding, L. G. and Pearson, P. D. (1994) Reading comprehension: what works, *Educational Leadership*, 51(5): 62–8.

Fitzgerald, J. (1995) English-as-a-second-language learners' cognitive reading processes: a review of research in the United States, *Review of Educational Research*, 65(2): 145–90.

Flaspeter, R. (1995) Sustained silent reading: implementation in the LEP class-room based on research results. Paper presented at the annual meeting of the Sunshine State Teachers of English to Speakers of Other Languages (TESOL). Jacksonville, FL. (ED 388107).

Flower, L. S. (1989) Cognition, context, and theory-building, *College Composition and Communication*, 40(3): 282–311.

Flower, L., Stein, V., Ackerman, J., Kantz, M., McCormick, K., and Peck, W. (1990) *Reading-to-write: Exploring a Cognitive and Social Process*. New York: Oxford University Press.

Foertsch, M. A. (1992) *Reading in and out of School*. Washington, DC: US Department of Education.

Fullan, M. G. (1982) *The Meaning of Educational Change*. New York: Teachers College Press.

Fullan, M. G. (1990) Staff development, innovation, and institutional development, in B. R. Joyce (ed.) *Changing School Culture Through Staff Development: 1990 ASCD Yearbook* (pp.43–65). Alexandria, VA: Association for Supervision and Curriculum Development.

Fullan, M. G. (1992) *Successful School Improvement*. Buckingham: Open University Press.

Fullan, M. G. (1993) *Change Forces*. London: The Falmer Press.

Fullan, M. G. and Miles, M. B. (1992) Getting reform right: what works and what doesn't, *Phi Delta Kappan*, 73(10): 744–52.

Fullan, M. and Park, P. (1981) *Curriculum Implementation: A Resource Booklet*. Toronto: Ontario Ministry of Education.

Fullan, M. and Pomfret, A. (1977) Research on curriculum and instruction implementation, *Review of Educational Research*, 47(2): 335–97.

Fullan, M. G. and Stiegelbauer, S. (1993) *The New Meaning of Educational Change*. New York: Teachers College Press.

Fullan, M., Miles, M., and Taylor, G. (1980) Organization development in schools: the state of the art, *Review of Educational Research*, 50(1): 121–84.

Gage, N. L. (1982) The future of educational research, *Educational Researcher*, 11(8): 11–12.

Gage, N. L. (1997) Competing visions of what educational researchers should do, *Educational Researcher*, 26(4): 4–12.

Gagne, R. (1965) *The Conditions of Learning*. New York: Holt, Rinehart, and Winston.

Gagne, R. M. (1975) *Essentials of Learning for Instruction*. New York: Holt, Rinehart, and Winston.

Gagne, R. M. and Briggs, L. J. (1979) *Principles of Instructional Design*. New York: Holt, Rinehart, and Winston.

Gallo, D. R. (1994) The writing processes of professional authors, *English Journal*, 83(5): 55–60.

Gandara, P. and Merino, B. (1993) Measuring outcomes of LEP programs: test scores, exit rates, and other mythological data, *Educational Research and Policy Analysis*, 15, 320–38.

Garcia, G. E., Stephens, D. L., Koenke, K. R., Harris, V. J., Pearson, P. D., Jimenez, R. T., and Janisch, C. (1995) *Reading Instruction and Educational Opportunity at the Middle School Level*. Urbana-Champaign, IL: University of Illinois, Center for the Study of Reading.

Garner, R. (1987) *Metacognition and Reading Comprehension*. Norwood, NJ: Ablex.

Garner, R., Belcher, V., Wingield, E., and Smith, T. (1985) Multiple measures of text summarization proficiency: what can fifth-grade students do? *Research in the Teaching of English*, 19, 140–53.

Garner, R., Gillingham, M. G., and White, C. S. (1989) Effects of "seductive details" on macroprocessing and microprocessing in adults and children, *Cognition and Instruction*, 6, 41–57.

Garnier, H. E., Stein, J. A., and Jacobs, J. K. (1997) The process of dropping out of high school: a 19-year perspective, *American Educational Research Journal*, 34(2): 395–419.

Gaskins, I. W., Downer, M., Anderson, R. C., Cunningham, P. M., Gaskins, R. W., and Schommer, M. (1988) A metacognitive approach to phonics: using what you know to decode what you don't know, *Remedial and Special Education*, 9: 36–41, 66.

Gaskins, I. W. and Elliot, T. T. (1991) *Implementing Cognitive Strategy Instruction Across the School: The Benchmark Manual for Teachers*. Media, PA: Brookline.

Gaver, M. (1963) *Effectiveness of Centralized Library Service in Elementary Schools*. New Brunswick, NJ: Rutgers University Press.

Gemignani, R. J. (1994) Juvenile correctional education: a time for change: update on research (US Department of Justice, Office of Juvenile Justice and Delinquency Prevention), *Juvenile Justice Bulletin* (ED 382861).

Gentile, C. (1992) *Exploring New Methods for Collecting Students' School-based Writing: NAEP's 1990 Portfolio Study*. Washington, DC: National Center for Educational Statistics, US Department of Education.

Glass, G. V. (1982) Meta-analysis: an approach to the synthesis of research results, *Journal of Research in Science Teaching*, 19(2): 93–112.

Glasser, W. (1969) *Schools Without Failure*. New York: Harper and Row.

Glickman, C. D. (1993) *Renewing America's Schools: A Guide for School-based Action*. San Francisco: Jossey-Bass.

Glickman, C. D. and Allen, L. (eds.) (1991) *Lessons from the Field: Renewing Schools Through Shared Governance and Action Research*. Athens, GA: Program for School Improvement, University of Georgia.

Goldenberg, C. and Gallimore, R. (1991) Changing teaching takes more than a one-shot workshop, *Educational Leadership*, 49(3): 69–72.

Good, T. L. and Brophy, J. E. (1987) *Looking in Classrooms* (4th edn). New York: HarperCollins.

Goodlad, J. I. (1984) *A Place Called School*. New York: McGraw-Hill.

Goodlad, J. and Klein, F. (1970) *Looking Behind the Classroom Door*. Worthington, OH: Charles A. Jones.

Gordon, W. J. J. (1961) *Synectics*. New York: Harper and Row.

Goswami, U. and Bryant, P. (1990) *Phonological Skills and Learning to Read*. Hove: Erlbaum.

Goswami, U. and Bryant, P. (1992) Rhyming, analogy, and children's reading, in P. B. Gough, L. C. Ehri, and R. Treiman (eds.) *Reading Acquisition* (pp. 107–43). Hillsdale, NJ: Erlbaum.

Graves, M. F. (1992) The elementary vocabulary curriculum: what should it be? in M. J. Dreher and W. H. Slater (eds.) *Elementary School Literacy: Critical Issues* (pp. 101–31). Norwood, MA: Christopher-Gordon.

Graves, M. F., Watts, S., and Graves, B. (1994) *Essentials of Classroom Teaching: Elementary Reading Methods*. Boston, MA: Allyn and Bacon.

Gray, J., Hopkins, D., Reynolds, D., Wilcox, B., Farrell, S., and Jesson, D. (1999) *Improving Schools: Performance and Potential*. Buckingham: Open University Press.

Greaney, V. (1980) Factors related to amount and type of leisure reading, *Reading Research Quarterly*, 15(3): 337–57.

Greaney, V. and Hagerty, P. E. (1987) Correlations of leisure-time reading, *Journal of Research in Reading*, 10, 3–20.

Grouws, D. and Ebmeier, H. (1983) *Active Mathematics Teaching*. New York: Longman.

Gunning, T. G. (1996) *Creating Reading Instruction for all Children* (2nd edn). Boston, MA: Allyn and Bacon.

Guthrie, J. T. and Pressley, M. (1992) Reading as cognition and the mediation of experience, in M. J. Dreher and W. H. Slater (eds.) *Elementary School Literacy: Critical Issues* (pp. 241–60). Norwood, MA: Christopher-Gordon.

Haggard, M. R. (1988) Developing critical thinking with the directed reading-thinking activity, *The Reading Teacher*, February: 526–33.

Hall, G. E. and Hord, S. M. (1987) *Change in Schools: Facilitating the Process*. New York: State University of New York.

Hall, G. and Loucks, S. (1977) A developmental model for determining whether the treatment is actually implemented, *American Educational Research Journal*, 14(3): 263–76.

Hall, G. and Loucks, S. (1978) Teacher concerns as a basis for facilitating and personalizing staff development, *Teachers College Record*, 80(1): 36–53.

Hallinger, P. and Murphy, J. (1985) Assessing the instructional management behavior of principals, *Elementary School Journal*, 86(2): 217–47.

Hargreaves, D. H. and Hopkins, D. (1991) *The Empowered School*. London: Cassell.

Harp, B. (1991) *Assessment and Evaluation in Whole Language Programs*. Norwood, MA: Christopher-Gordon.

Harris, K. and Pressley, M. (1991) The nature of cognitive strategy instruction: interactive strategy instruction, *Exceptional Children*, 57: 392–404.

Havelock, R. G., Guskin, A., Frohman, M., Havelock, M., Hill, M., and Huber, J. (1969) *Planning for Innovation through Dissemination and Utilization of Knowledge*. Ann Arbor, MI: Institute for Social Research.

Heathington, B. S. (1979) What to do about reading motivation in the middle school? *Journal of Reading*, 22(8): 709–13.

Heller, M. F. (1986) How do you know what you know? Metacognitive modeling in the content areas, *Journal of Reading*, 29(5): 415–22.

Heller, M. F. (1991) *Reading-writing Connections: From Theory to Practice*. New York: Longman.

Hendrickson, R. (1987) *The Henry Holt Encyclopedia of Word and Phrase Origins*. New York: Henry Holt.

Hensley, F., Calhoun, E. F., and Glickman, C. D. (1992) Results from site-based, action research schools: what has been accomplished? What are the next steps? Paper presented at the annual meeting of the American Educational Research Association, San Francisco.

Herman, R. and Stringfield, S. (1997) *Ten Promising Programs for Educating All Children*. Arlington, VA: Educational Research Service.

Hermann, B. A. (1990) Cognitive and metacognitive goals in reading and writing, in G. G. Duffy (ed.) *Reading in the Middle School* (2nd edn) (pp. 81–96). Newark, DE: International Reading Association.

Hertz-Lazarowitz, R. (1993) Using group investigation to enhance Arab–Jewish relationships, *Cooperative Learning*, 11(2): 13–14.

Heyns, B. (1978) *Summer Learning and the Effects of Schooling*. New York: Academic Press.

Hidi, S. and Anderson, V. (1986) Producing written summaries: task demands, cognitive questions, and implications for instruction, *Review of Educational Research*, 56(4): 473–93.

Hillocks, G. (1986) *Research on Written Composition: New Directions for Teaching*. Urbana, IL: ERIC Clearinghouse on Reading and Communication Skills.

Hillocks, G. (1987) Synthesis of research on teaching writing, *Educational Leadership*, 44(8): 71–82.

Hoetker, J. and Ahlbrand, W. (1969) The persistence of the recitation, *American Educational Research Journal*, 6: 145–67.

Hoffman, J. V., Roser, N. L., and Battle, J. (1993) Reading aloud in classrooms: from the modal to a "model," *Reading Teacher*, 46: 496–503.

Hollingsworth, S. and Sockett, H. (1994) *Teacher Research and Educational Reform*. Chicago: University of Chicago Press.

Holt, S. B. and O'Tuel, F. S. (1989) The effect of sustained silent reading and writing on achievement and attitudes of seventh and eighth grade students reading two years below grade level, *Reading Improvement*, 26: 290–97.

Hopkins, D. (1987) *Improving the Quality of Schooling*. Lewes: Falmer.

Hopkins, D., Ainscow, M., and West, M. (1994) *School Improvement in an Era of Change*. London: Cassell.

Hopkins, D., Ainscow, M., and West, M. (1996a) *Improving the Quality of Schooling for All*. London: David Fulton Publishers.

Hopkins, D., Ainscow, M., and West, M. (1996b) Unravelling the complexities of school improvement: a case study of the Improving the Quality of Education for All (IQEA) Project. Open University Course E838 reader, Organisational Effectiveness and Improvement in Education. Milton Keynes: Open University.

Hopkins, D., Ainscow, M., West, M., and Beresford, J. (1997) *Creating the Conditions for Classroom Improvement*. London: David Fulton Publishers.

Hopkins, D., Harris, A., Youngman, M., and Wordsworth, J. (1998) *Evaluation of the Initial Effects and Evaluation of Success for All in England*. Nottingham: Centre for Teacher and School Development, University of Nottingham.

Huberman, A. M. (1992) Successful school improvement: reflections and observations. Critical introduction to M. G. Fullan (1992) *Successful School Improvement*.. Buckingham: Open University Press.

Huberman, A. M. and Miles, M. B. (1984) *Innovation Up Close*. New York: Praeger.

Huberman, A. and Miles, M. (1986) Rethinking the quest for school improvement: some findings from the DESSI study, in A. Lieberman (ed.) *Rethinking School Improvement Research*. New York: Teachers College Press.

Hunt, D. E. (1983) The MOTAC studies, in B. R. Joyce, C. Brown, and L. Peck (eds.) *Flexibility and Teaching*. White Plains, NY: Longman.

Hunt, D. E. and Sullivan, E. V. (1974) *Between Psychology and Education*. Hinsdale, IL: Dryden.

Hunt, D. E., Joyce, B. R., and Del Popolo, J. (1964) An exploratory study of the modification of student teachers' behavior patterns. Unpublished paper, Syracuse University.

Hunt, D. E., Butler, L. F., Noy, J. E., and Rosser, M. E. (1978) *Assessing Conceptual Level by the Paragraph Completion Method*. Toronto: Ontario Institute for Studies in Education.

Ivany, G. (1969) The assessment of verbal inquiry in elementary school science, *Science Education*, 53(4): 287–93.

Janopoulos, M. (1986) The relationship of pleasure reading and second language writing proficiency, *TESOL Quarterly*, 20: 763–78.

Jenkins, J. R., Stein, M. L., and Wysocki, K. (1984) Learning vocabulary through reading, *American Educational Research Journal*, 21(4): 767–87.

Jennings, N. E. and Spillane, J. P. (1995) State reform and local capacity: encouraging ambitious instruction for all and local decision-making. Paper presented at the annual meeting of the American Educational Research Association, San Francisco.

Jetton, T. L. and Alexander, P. A. (1997) Instructional importance: what teachers value and what students learn, *Reading Research Quarterly*, 32(3): 290–308.

Jimenez, R. T. (1997) The strategic reading abilities and potential of five low-literacy Latina/o readers in middle school, *Reading Research Quarterly*, 32(3): 224–43.

Jimenez, R. T., Garcia, G. E., and Pearson, P. D. (1996) The reading strategies of Latina/o students who are successful English readers: opportunities and obstacles, *Reading Research Quarterly*, 31: 90–112.

Johnson, D. W. and Johnson, R. T. (1974) Instructional goal structure: cooperative, competitive, or individualistic, *Review of Educational Research*, 44: 213–40.

Johnson, D. W. and Johnson, R. T. (1975) *Learning Together and Alone*. Englewood Cliffs, NJ: Prentice Hall.

Johnson, D. W. and Johnson, R. T. (1979) Conflict in the classroom: controversy in learning, *Review of Educational Research*, 49(1): 51–70.

Johnson, D. W. and Johnson, R. T. (1981) Effects of cooperative and individualistic learning experiences on inter-ethnic interaction, *Journal of Educational Psychology*, 73(3): 444–9.

Johnson, D. W. and Johnson, R. T. (1990) *Cooperation and Competition: Theory and Research*. Edina, MN: Interaction Book Company.

Johnson, D. W. and Johnson, R. T. (1993) *Circles of Learning*. Edina, MN: Interaction Book Company.

Johnson, D. W. and Johnson, R. T. (1994) *Leading the Cooperative School*. Edina, MN: Interaction Book Company.

Johnson, D. W. and Johnson, R. T. (1996) Conflict resolution and peer mediated programs in elementary and secondary schools: a review of the research, *Review of Educational Research*, 66(4): 459–506.

Johnson, D. W., Maruyana, G., Johnson, R., Nelson, D., and Skon, L. (1981) Effects of cooperative, competitive, and individualistic goal structures on achievement: a meta-analysis, *Psychological Bulletin*, 89(1): 47–62.

Johnston, P. and Allington, R. (1991) Remediation, in R. Barr, M. L. Kamil, P. Mosenthal, and P. D. Pearson (eds.) *Handbook of Reading Research: Volume II* (pp. 984–1012). White Plains, NY: Longman.

Joyce, B. R. (ed.) (1969) *The Teacher Innovates*. New York: Teachers College Press.

Joyce, B. R. (ed.) (1990) *Changing School Culture Through Staff Development*. The 1990 ASCD Yearbook. Alexandria, VA: The Association for Supervision and Curriculum Development.

Joyce, B. R. (1991) Doors to school improvement, *Educational Leadership*, 48(8): 59–62.

Joyce, B. R. (1992) Cooperative learning and staff development: teaching the method with the method, *Cooperative Learning*, 12(2): 10–13.

Joyce, B. R. and Belitzky, A. (1997) *Creating a System*. Tallahassee, FL: The Florida State Department of Education.

Joyce, B. R. and Calhoun, E. F. (1995) School renewal: an inquiry not a formula, *Educational Leadership*, 52(7): 51–5.

Joyce, B. R. and Calhoun, E. F. (eds.) (1996) *Learning Experiences in School Renewal*. Eugene, OR: ERIC Clearinghouse for Educational Management.

Joyce, B. R. and Calhoun, E. F. (1997) *Creating Learning Experiences*. Alexandria, VA: The Association for Supervision and Curriculum Development.

Joyce, B. R. and. Calhoun, E. F. (1998) *Learning to Teach Inductively*. Needham, MA: Allyn Bacon.

Joyce, B. R. and Joyce, E. (1968) *Data Banks for Children*. New York: Teachers College, Columbia University.

Joyce, B. R. and Showers, B. (1980) Improving inservice training: the messages of research, *Educational Leadership*, 37(5): 379–85.

Joyce, B. R. and Showers, B. (1982) The coaching of teaching, *Educational Leadership*, 40(1): 4–16.

Joyce, B. R. and Showers, B. (1983) *Power in Staff Development through Research on Training*. Washington, DC: Association for Supervision and Curriculum Development.

Joyce, B. R. and Showers, B. (1995) *Student Achievement through Staff Development*. White Plains, NY: Longman.

Joyce, B. R. and Wolf, J. (1992) Operation Just Read and Write: toward a literate society. Paper presented at the annual meeting of the Association for Supervision and Curriculum Development, New Orleans.

Joyce, B. R. and Wolf, J. (1996) Readersville: building a culture of readers and writers, in B. R. Joyce and E. F. Calhoun (eds.) *Learning Experiences in School Renewal*. Eugene, OR: ERIC Clearinghouse for Educational Management.

Joyce, B. R., Brown, C., and Peck, L. (1981) *Flexibility in Teaching*. New York: Longman.

Joyce, B. R., Bush, R., and McKibbin, M. (1982) *The California Staff Development Study: The January 1982 Report*. Palo Alto, CA: Booksend Laboratories.

Joyce, B. R., Hersh, R., and McKibbin, M. (1983a) *The Structure of School Improvement*. New York: Longman.

Joyce, B. R., McKibbin, M., and Bush, R. (1983b) The seasons of professional life: the growth states of teachers. Paper presented at the annual meeting of the American Education Research Association, Montreal, Canada.

Joyce, B. R., Showers, B., and Bennett, B. (1987a) Synthesis of research on staff development: a framework for future study and a state-of-the-art analysis, *Educational Leadership*, 45(3): 77–87.

Joyce, B. R., Showers, B., and Rolheiser-Bennett, C. (1987b) Staff development and student learning: a synthesis of research on models of teaching, *Educational Leadership*, 45(2): 11–23.

Joyce, B. R., Murphy, C., Showers, B., and Murphy, J. (1989) School renewal as cultural change, *Educational Leadership*, 47(3): 70–8.

Joyce, B. R., Wolf, J., and Calhoun, E. F. (1993) *The Self-renewing School*. Alexandria, VA: Association for Supervision and Curriculum Development.

Joyce, B. R., Calhoun, E. F., Halliburton, C., Simser, J., Rust, D., and Carran, N. (1996) University town, in B. R. Joyce and E. F. Calhoun (eds.) *Learning Experiences in School Renewal*. Eugene, OR: ERIC Clearinghouse for Educational Management.

Joyce, B. R., Calhoun, E. F., and Hopkins, D. (1997a) *Models of Learning: Tools for Teaching*. Buckingham, UK and Philadelphia, PA: Open University Press.

Joyce, B. R., Calhoun, E. F., Puckey, M., and Hopkins, D. (1997b) Inquiring and collaborating at an exemplary school, *Educational Leadership*, 54(8): 63–8.

Joyce, B. R., Weil, M., and Calhoun, E. F. (1999) *Models of Teaching* (6th edn). Boston, MA: Allyn and Bacon.

Juel, C. (1988) Learning to read and write: a longitudinal study of fifty-four children from first through fourth grades, *Journal of Educational Psychology*, 80: 437–47.

Juel, C. (1992) Longitudinal research on learning to read and write with at-risk students, in M. J. Dreher and W. H. Slater (eds.) *Elementary School Literacy: Critical Issues* (pp. 73–99). Norwood, MA: Christopher-Gordon.

Kaufman, P., McMillen, M. M., and Bradby, D. (1992) *Dropout Rates in the United States: 1992*. Washington, DC: National Center for Educational Statistics, US Department of Education.

Kozol, J. (1992) *Savage Inequalities*. New York: HarperCollins.

Krashen, S. (1993) *The Power of Reading: Insights from the Research*. Englewood, CO: Libraries Unlimited.

Langer, J. A. (1986) *Children Reading and Writing: Structures and Strategies*. Norwood, NJ: Ablex.

Langer, J. A. and Allington, R. L. (1992) Curriculum research in writing and reading, in P. W. Jackson (ed.) *Handbook of Research on Curriculum* (pp. 687–725). New York: Macmillan.

Langer, J. A. and Applebee, A. N. (1986) *Writing and Learning in the Secondary School*. Urbana, IL: National Council of Teachers of English.

Langer, J. A. and Applebee, A. N. (1987) *How Writing Shapes Thinking: A Study of Teaching and Learning*. Urbana, IL: National Council of Teachers of English.

Langer, J. A., Bartolome, L., Vasquez, O., and Lucas, T. (1990) Meaning construction in school literacy tasks: a study of bilingual students, *American Educational Research Journal*, 27(3): 427–71.

Lawton, J. and Wanska, S. (1977) The effects of different types of advance organizers on classification learning, *The American Educational Research Journal*, 16(3): 223–39.

Lehr, F. and Osborn, J. (eds.) (1994) *Reading, Language, and Literacy: Instruction for the Twenty-first Century*. Hillsdale, NJ: Erlbaum.

Levin, J. R., McCormick, C. B., Miller, G. E., Berry, J. K., and Pressley, M. (1982) Mnemonic versus nonmnemonic vocabulary learning strategies for children, *American Educational Research Journal*, 19: 121–36.

Levin, M. and Levin, J. R. (1990) Scientific mnemonics, *American Educational Research Journal*, 27: 301–21.

Levine, D. U. (1991) Creating effective schools: findings and implications from research and practice, *Phi Delta Kappan*, January: 389–93.

Levine, D. U. and Lezotte, L. (1990) *Unusually Effective Schools: A Review and Analysis of Research and Practice*. Madison, WN: National Center for Effective Schools Research and Development, University of Wisconsin.

Levine, D. U. and Lezotte, L. W. (1995) Effective schools research, in *Handbook of Research on Multicultural Education* (pp. 525–47). New York: Macmillan (ED 382724).

Lewin, K. (1947) Group decisions and social change, in T. M. Newcomb and E. L. Hartley (eds.) *Readings in Social Psychology*. New York: Henry Holt.

Lewin, K. (1948) *Resolving Social Conflicts: Selected Papers on Group Dynamics*. New York: Harper and Row.

Little, J. W. (1982) Norms of collegiality and experimentation: workplace conditions of school success, *American Educational Research Journal*, 19(3): 325–40.

Little, J. W. (1990) The persistence of privacy: autonomy and initiative in teachers' professional relations, *Teachers College Record*, 91(4): 509–36.

Lloyd, C. V. and Anders, P. A. (1994) Research-based practices as the content of staff development, in V. Richardson (ed.) *Teacher Change and the Staff Development Process: A Case in Reading Instruction* (pp. 68–89). New York: Teachers College Press.

Lloyd, D. N. (1978) Prediction of school failure from third-grade data, *Educational and Psychological Measurement*, 38: 1193–200.

Lorayne, H. and Lucas, J. (1974) *The Memory Book*. Briercliff Manor, NY: Memory Press.

Lortie, D. (1975) *Schoolteacher*. Chicago: University of Chicago Press.

MacGinitie, W. H. (1991) Reading instruction: plus ça change . . . *Educational Leadership*, 50(7) (March issue): 55–8.

Madden, N. A., Slavin, R. E., Karweit, N. L., Dolan, L. J., and Wasik, B. A. (1993) Success For All: longitudinal effects of a restructuring program for inner-city elementary schools, *American Educational Research Journal*, 30(1): 123–48.

Maehr, R. and Buck, R. (1993) Transforming school culture, in M. Sashkin and H. Walberg (eds.) *Educational Leadership and School Culture*. San Pablo, Berkeley, CA: McCutchan.

Magner, M. M. (1991) "Academic progress of selected middle school students after release from remedial reading programs." PhD thesis, New York: Fordham University.

Malik, A. A. (1990) A psycholinguistic analysis of the reading behavior of EFL-proficient readers using culturally familiar and culturally nonfamiliar expository texts, *American Educational Research Journal*, 27(1): 205–23.

Mandeville, G. K. (1994) Class formation and the correlates of achievement in the elementary grades in South Carolina. Paper presented to the annual meeting of the American Educational Research Association, New Orleans.

Maslow, A. (1962) *Toward a Psychology of Being*. New York: Van Nostrand.

Massialas, B. and Cox, B. (1966) *Inquiry in Social Studies*. New York: McGraw-Hill.

McGill-Franzen, A. and Allington, R. L. (1991a) Every child's right: literacy, *Reading Teacher*, 45: 86–90.

McGill-Franzen, A. and Allington, R. L. (1991b) The gridlock of low achievement: perspectives on policy and practice, *Remedial and Special Education*, 12: 20–30.

McKenna, M. C., Kear, D. J., and Ellsworth, R. A. (1995) Children's attitudes toward reading: a national survey, *Reading Research Quarterly*, 30(4): 934–56.

McKeown, M. G. and Curtis, M. E. (eds.) *The Nature of Vocabulary Acquisition*. Hillsdale, NJ: Erlbaum.

McKibbin, M. and Joyce, B. R. (1980) Psychological states and staff development, *Theory into Practice*, 19(4): 248–55.

Menyuk, P. (1971) *The Acquisition and Development of Language*. Englewood Cliffs, NJ: Prentice Hall.

Meyer, B. J. F. (1979) Organizational patterns in prose and their use in reading, in M. L. Kamill and A. J. Moe (eds.) *Reading Research: Studies and Applications*. Clemson, SC: National Reading Conference.

Miles, M. B. (1992) 40 years of change in schools: some personal reflections. Paper presented at the annual meeting of the American Educational Research Association, San Francisco.

Mill, J. S. (1947) *On Liberty*. New York: Appleton-Century-Crofts.

Milligan, J. L. (1996) The seven most common mistakes made by remedial reading teachers, *Journal of Reading*, November 1996: 140–4.

Moore, D. and Davenport, S. (1988/1989) *The New Improved Sorting Machine*. Madison, WN: University of Wisconsin, National Center on Effective Secondary Schools.

Moore, D. R. and Davenport, S. (1989) *The New Improved Sorting Machine: Concerning School Choice*. Chicago: Designs for Change.

Moore, D. W., Moore, S. A., Cunningham, P. M., and Cunningham, J. W. (1994) *Developing Readers and Writers in the Content Areas* (2nd edn). White Plains, NY: Longman.

Moran, C., Tinajero, J. V., Stobbe, J., and Tinajero, I. (1993) Strategies for working with overage students, in J. V. Tinajero and A. F. Ada (eds.) *The Power of*

Two Languages: Literacy and Biliteracy for Spanish-speaking Students. New York: Macmillan/McGraw-Hill.

Morrow, L. M. (1983) Home and school correlates of early interest in literature, *Journal of Educational Research*, 76: 221–30.

Morrow, L. M. (1991) Promoting voluntary reading, in J. Flood, J. Jensen, D. Lapp, and J. Squire (eds.) *Handbook of Research on Teaching the English Language Arts* (pp. 681–90). New York: Macmillan.

Morrow, L. M. and Weinstein, C. (1982) Increasing children's use of literature through program and physical changes, *Elementary School Journal*, 83: 131–7.

Morrow, L. M. and Weinstein, C. (1986) Encouraging voluntary reading: the impact of a literature program on children's use of library centers, *Reading Research Quarterly*, 21: 330–46.

Mortimore, P., Sammons, P., Stoll, L., Lewis, D., and Ecob, R. (1988) *School Matters: The Junior Years*. London: Open Books.

Moss, B. (1995) Using children's nonfiction tradebooks as read-alouds, *Language Arts*, 72(2): 122–6.

Mullis, I. V. S., Dossey, J. A., Foertsch, M. A., Jones, L. R., and Gentile, C. A. (1991) *Trends in Academic Progress: Achievement of U.S. Students in Science, 1969–70 to 1990; Mathematics, 1973 to 1990; Reading, 1971 to 1990; Writing, 1984 to 1990*. Washington, DC: Prepared by Educational Testing Service under contract with the National Center for Education Statistics for the Office of Educational Research and Improvement, US Department of Education.

Mullis, I. V. S., Campbell, J. R., and Farstrup, A. E. (1993) *NAEP 1992 Reading Report Card for the Nation and the States*. Washington, DC: Prepared by Educational Testing Service under contract with the National Center for Education Statistics for the Office of Educational Research and Improvement, US Department of Education.

Muncey, D. E. (1994) Individual and schoolwide change in eight coalition schools: findings from a longitudinal ethnographic study. Paper presented at the annual meeting of the American Educational Research Association, New Orleans.

Muncey, D. E. and McQuillan, P. J. (1993) Preliminary findings from a five-year study of the Coalition of Essential Schools, *Phi Delta Kappan*, 74(6): 486–9.

Murphy, J. and Hallinger, P. (eds.) (1993) *Restructuring Schooling: Learning from Ongoing Efforts*. Newbury Park, CA: Corwin Press.

Murphy, J. and Louis, K. S. (1994) *Reshaping the Principalship Insights from Transformational Reform Efforts*. Thousand Oaks, CA: Corwin Press.

Myers, J. (1992) The social contexts of school and personal literacy, *Reading Research Quarterly*, 27: 297–333.

Myers, K. (ed.) (1995) *School Improvement in Practice: Schools Make a Difference Project*. London: Falmer Press.

Myers, M. (1985) *The Teacher-researcher: How to Study Writing in the Classroom*. Urbana, IL: The National Council of Teachers of English.

Nagy, W. E. and Anderson, P. A. (1984) How many words are there in printed English? *Reading Research Quarterly*, 19: 304–30.

Nagy, W. E. and Anderson, P. A. (1987) Breadth and depth in vocabulary knowledge: implications for acquisition and instruction, in M. G. McKeown and M. E. Curtis (eds.) *The Nature of Vocabulary Acquisition*. Hillsdale, NJ: Erlbaum.

Nagy, W. E., Anderson, R. C., and Herman, P. A. (1987) Learning word meanings from context during normal reading, *American Educational Research Journal*, 24: 237–70.

Nagy, W., Anderson, R. C., Schommer, M., Scott, J., and Stallman, A. (1989) Morphological families in the internal lexicon, *Reading Research Quarterly*, 24: 262–82.

Nagy, W. E., Winsor, P., Osborn, J., and O'Flahavan, J. (1994) Structural analysis: some guidelines for instruction, in F. Lehr and J. Osborn (eds.) *Reading, Language, and Literacy: Instruction for the Twenty-first Century* (pp. 45–58). Hillsdale, NJ: Erlbaum.

National Assessment of Educational Progress (NAEP) (1992) *The Reading Report Card for the Nation and the States*. Washington, DC: National Center for Educational Statistics, US Department of Education.

National Assessment of Educational Progress (NAEP) Home Page (1996) NAEP Reading Report Card: Findings from the National Assessment of Educational Progress, Executive Summary.

National Center on Education and the Economy (1990) *America's Choice: High Skills or Low Wages*. Rochester, NY: National Center on Education and the Economy.

National Center for Educational Statistics (1991) *National Educational Longitudinal Survey (NELS: 88)*. Washington, DC: Office of Educational Research and Improvement, US Department of Education.

National Center for Educational Statistics (1993) *Digest of Educational Statistics*. Washington, DC: Office of Educational Research and Improvement, US Department of Education.

National Center for Educational Statistics (1994) *Report in Brief: National Assessment of Educational Progress. NAEP 1992 Trends in Academic Progress*. Washington, DC: US Department of Education.

National Center for Educational Statistics (1995) *The Educational Progress of Women*. Washington, DC: US Department of Education, Office of Educational Research and Improvement.

National Education Commission on Time and Learning (1994) *Prisoners of Time*. Washington, DC: US Government Printing Office.

Neill, A. S. (1960) *Summerhill*. New York: Holt, Rinehart, and Winston.

Nelson, J. (1971) "Collegial supervision in multi-unit schools." PhD thesis, University of Oregon, Eugene.

Neuman, S. (1986) The home environment and fifth-grade students' leisure reading, *Elementary School Journal*, 86: 335–43.

Newell, G. E. and Durst, R. K. (eds.) (1993) *Exploring Texts*. Norwood, MA: Christopher-Gordon.

Noyce, R. M. and Christie, J. F. (1989) *Integrating Reading and Writing Instruction*. Boston, MA: Allyn and Bacon.

Oakes, J. (1986) *Keeping Track: How Schools Structure Inequality*. New Haven, CT: Yale University Press.

Oliver, D. and Shaver, J. P. (1966) *Teaching Public Issues in the High School*. Boston, MA: Houghton Mifflin.

O'Masta, G. A. and Wolf, J. M. (1991) Encouraging independent reading through the reading millionaires project, *The Reading Teacher*, 44(3): 656–62.

Palinscar, A. S. (1986) The role of dialogue in providing scaffolded instruction, *Educational Psychologist*, 2: 73–98.

Palinscar, A. S. and Brown, A. L. (1984) Reciprocal teaching of comprehension fostering and monitoring activities, *Cognition and Instruction*, 1(2): 117–75.

Palinscar, A. S., Brown, A. L., and Martin, S. M. (1987) Peer interaction in reading comprehension instruction, *Educational Psychologist*, 22, 231–53.

Palinscar, A. S., Winn, J., David, Y., Snyder, B., and Stevens, D. (1993) Approaches to strategic reading instruction reflecting different assumptions regarding teaching and learning, in L. J. Meltzer (ed.) *Strategy Assessment and Instruction for Students with Learning Disabilities: From Theory to Practice* (pp. 247–92). Austin, TX: Pro-ed.

Palmer, G. P. and Stewart, R. A. (1997) Nonfiction trade books in content area instruction: realities and potential, *Journal of Adolescent & Adult Literacy*, 40(8): 630–41.

Paris, S. G., Wasik, B. A., and Turner, J. C. (1991) The development of strategic readers, in R. Barr, M. L. Kamill, P. Mosenthal, and P. D. Pearson (eds.) *Handbook of Reading Research: Volume II* (pp. 609–40). New York: Longman.

Passow, A. H. (ed.) (1963) *Education in Depressed Areas*. New York: Teachers College.

Pearson, P. D. (1992) Reading, in M. C. Alkin (ed.) *Encyclopedia of Educational Research: Volume III* (pp. 1075–85). New York: Macmillan.

Pearson, P. D. (1993) Teaching and learning to read: a research perspective, *Language Arts*, 70, 501–11.

Pearson, P. D. and Camperell, K. (1994) Comprehension of text structures, in R. R. Ruddell, M. R. Ruddell, and H. Singer (eds.) *Theoretical Models and Processes of Reading* (4th edn) (pp. 448–68). Newark, DE: International Reading Association.

Pearson, P. D. and Dole, J. A. (1987) Explicit comprehension instruction: a review of research and a new conceptualization of instruction, *Elementary School Journal*, 88(2): 151–65.

Pearson, P. D. and Fielding, L. (1991) Comprehension instruction, in R. Barr, M. L. Kamill, P. Mosenthal, and P. D. Pearson (eds.) *Handbook of Reading Research: Volume II* (pp. 815–60). New York: Longman.

Peregoy, S. F. and Boyle, O. F. (1997) *Reading, Writing, and Learning in ESL*. White Plains, NY: Longman.

Peters, C. W. (1990) Content knowledge in reading: creating a new framework, in G. G. Duffy (ed.) *Reading in the Middle School* (pp. 63–80). Newark, DE: International Reading Association.

Peterson, P. L., Fennema, E., and Carpenter, T. (1988/1989) Using knowledge of how students think about mathematics, *Educational Leadership*, 46(4): 37–41.

Phillips, D. (1987) *Philosophy, Science, and Social Inquiry*. Oxford, UK: Pergamon.

Phillips, D. (1995) The good, the bad, and the ugly: the many faces of constructivism, *Educational Researcher*, 24(7): 5–12.

Pinnell, G. S. (1989) Helping at-risk children learn to read, *Elementary School Journal*, 90(2): 161–84.

Pinnell, G. S., Lyons, C. A., DeFord, D. E., Bryk, A. S., and Seltzer, M. (1994) Comparing instructional models for the literacy education of high-risk first graders, *Reading Research Quarterly*, 29: 8–38.

Pitts, S. (1986) Read aloud to adult learners? Of course! *Reading Psychology*, 7, 35–42.

Pollina, A. (1995) *Gender Balance: Lessons from Girls in Science and Mathematics*.

Potter, D. (1992) Higher standards for grade promotion and graduation: unintended effects of reform. Paper presented at the annual meeting of the American Educational Research Association, San Francisco.

Pressley, M. (1977) Children's use of the keyword method to learn simple Spanish vocabulary words, *Journal of Educational Psychology*, 69(5): 465–72.

Pressley, M. and Dennis-Rounds, J. (1980) Transfer of a mnemonic keyword strategy at two age levels, *Journal of Educational Psychology*, 72(4): 575–82.

Pressley, M., Levin, J., and McCormick, C. (1980) Young children's learning of foreign language vocabulary: a sentence-variation of the keyword method, *Contemporary Educational Psychology*, 5(1): 22–9.

Pressley, M., Levin, J. R., and Miller, G. (1981a) How does the keyword method affect vocabulary, comprehension, and usage? *Reading Research Quarterly*, 16: 213–26.

Pressley, M., Levin, J. R., and Miller, G. (1981b) The keyword method and children's learning of foreign vocabulary with abstract meanings, *Canadian Psychology*, 35(3): 283–7.

Pressley, M., Samuel, J., Hershey, M., Bishop, S., and Dickinson, D. (1981c) Use of a mnemonic technique to teach young children foreign-language vocabulary, *Contemporary Educational Psychology*, 6: 110–16.

Pressley, M., Levin, J. R., and Delaney, H. D. (1982) The mnemonic keyword method, *Review of Educational Research*, 52(1): 61–91.

Pressley, M., Levin, J. R., and Ghatala, E. (1984) Memory-strategy monitoring in adults and children, *Journal of Verbal Learning and Verbal Behavior*, 23(2): 270–88.

Pressley, M., Levin, J. R., and McDaniel, M. A. (1987) Remembering versus inferring what a word means: mnemonic and contextual approaches, in M. G. McKeown and M. E. Curtis (eds.) *The Nature of Vocabulary Acquisition* (pp. 107–27). Hillsdale, NJ: Erlbaum.

Pressley, M., Johnson, C. J., Symons, S., McGoldrick, J. A., and Kurita, J. A. (1989) Strategies that improve children's memory and comprehension of what is read, *Elementary School Journal*, 90: 3–32.

Pressley, M., Brown, R., El-Dinary, P. B., and Afflerbach, P. (1995a) The comprehension instruction that students need: instruction fostering constructively responsive reading, *Learning Disabilities Research and Practice*, 10(4): 215–24.

Pressley, M., Woloshyn, V. E., and Associates (1995b) *Cognitive Strategies Instruction that Really Improves Academic Performance* (2nd edn). Cambridge, MA: Brookline.

Prestine, N. A. (1992) Benchmarks of change: assessing essential school restructuring efforts. Paper presented at the annual meeting of the American Educational Research Association, San Francisco.

Quellmalz, E. S. and Burry, J. (1983) *Analytic Scales for Assessing Students' Expository and Narrative Writing Skills*. Los Angeles: Center for the Study of Evaluation, UCLA Graduate School of Education (CSE Resource Paper No. 5).

Raphael, T. E. and McMahon, S. I. (1994) Book club: an alternative framework for reading instruction, *Reading Teacher*, 48(2): 102–16.

Raphael, T. E., Englert, C. S., and Kirscher, B. W. (1986) *The Impact of Text Structure Instruction and Social Context on Students' Comprehension and Production of Expository Prose*. East Lansing: Michigan State University, Institute for Research on Teaching (Research Series No. 177).

Raphael, T. E., Englert, C. S., and Kirscher, B. W. (1989) Students' metacognitive knowledge about writing, *Research in the Teaching of English*, 23: 343–79.

Reynolds, D. (1985) *Studying School Effectiveness*. Lewes: Falmer Press.

Rhine, W. R. (ed.) (1981) *Making Schools More Effective: New Directions from Follow Through*. New York: Academic Press.

Richardson, V. (ed.) (1994) *Teacher Change and the Staff Development Process: A Case in Reading Instruction*. New York: Teachers College Press .

Richardson, V. and Hamilton, M. L. (1994) The practical-argument staff development process, in V. Richardson (ed.) *Teacher Change and the Staff Development Process*. New York: Columbia University, Teachers College Press.

Richardson, V., Anders, P., Tidwell, D., and Lloyd, C. (1991) The relationship between teachers' beliefs and practices in reading comprehension instruction, *American Educational Research Journal*, 28(3): 559–86.

Roebuck, F., Buhler, J., and Aspy, D. (1976) *A Comparison of High and Low Levels of Humane Teaching/Learning Conditions on the Subsequent Achievement of Students Identified as Having Learning Difficulties*. Final Report: Order No. PLD 6816–76 re. the National Institute of Mental Health. Denton, TX: Texas Woman's University Press.

Roehler, L. R. (1991) Enhancing the instructional complexities of reading instruction, Institute for Research on Teaching, Michigan State University: ERIC Clearinghouse on Reading and Communication Skills (ED 340005).

Roehler, L. R. and Duffy, G. G. (1991) Teachers' instructional actions, in R. Barr, M. L. Kamill, P. Mosenthal, and P. D. Pearson (eds.) *Handbook of Reading Research: Volume II* (pp. 861–83). New York: Longman.

Rogers, C. (1961) *On Becoming a Person*. Boston, MA: Houghton Mifflin.

Rogers, C. (1969) *Freedom to Learn*. Columbus, OH: Charles E. Merrill.

Rogers, C. (1971) *Client Centered Therapy*. Boston, MA: Houghton Mifflin.

Rogers, C. (1981) *A Way of Being*. Boston, MA: Houghton Mifflin.

Rogers, C. (1982) *Freedom to Learn for the Eighties*. Columbus: Charles E. Merrill.

Rolheiser-Bennett, C. (1986) "Four models of teaching: a meta-analysis of student outcomes." PhD thesis, University of Oregon, Eugene.

Rollow, S. G. and Bryk, A. S. (1993) Catalyzing professional community in a school reform left behind. Paper presented at the annual meeting of the American Educational Research Association, Atlanta.

Rosaen, C. (1990) Improving writing opportunities in elementary classrooms, *Elementary School Journal*, 90: 419–34.

Rosenholtz, S. J. (1989) *Teachers' Workplace: The Social Organization of Schools*. White Plains, NY: Longman.

Rosenshine, B. and Meister, C. (1994) Reciprocal teaching: a review of the research, *Review of Educational Research*, 64(4): 479–530.

Rubin, D. L. (1984) Social cognition and written communication, *Written Communication*, 1: 211–45.

Rubin, D. L. and Rafoth, B. A. (1988) *The Social Construction of Written Communication*. Norwood, NJ: Ablex.

Rutter, M., Maughan, B., Mortimore, P., Ouston, J., and Smith, A. (1979) *Fifteen Thousand Hours: Secondary Schools and Their Effects on Children*. Cambridge, MA: Harvard University Press.

Sadker, M. and Sadker, D. (1994) *Failing at Fairness: How America's Schools Cheat Girls*. New York: Scribner.

Sagan, C. (1995) *The Demon-Haunted World: Science as a Candle in the Dark*. New York: Random House.

Samuels, S. J. (1994) Word recognition, in R. B. Ruddell, M. R. Ruddell, and H. Singer (eds.) *Theoretical Models and Processes of Reading* (4th edn) (pp. 359–80). Newark, DE: International Reading Association.

Sarason, S. (1982) *The Culture of the School and the Problems of Change* (2nd edn). Boston, MA: Allyn and Bacon.

Sarason, S. (1990) *The Predictable Failure of School Reform: Can We Change the Course Before it's too Late?* San Francisco: Jossey-Bass.

Schaefer, R. J. (1997) *The School as a Center of Inquiry*. New York: Harper and Row.

Schlecty, P. (1997) *Better Schools: An Action Plan for Educational Reform*.

Schrenker, G. (1976) "The effects of an inquiry-development program on elementary schoolchildren's science learning." PhD thesis, New York University.

Schwab, J. (1965) *Biological Sciences Curriculum Study: Biology Teachers' Handbook.* New York: John Wiley and Sons.

Schwab, J. (1982) *Science, Curriculum, and Liberal Education: Selected Essays.* Chicago: University of Chicago Press.

Schwab, J. and Brandwein, P. (1962) *The Teaching of Science.* Cambridge, MA: Harvard University Press.

Seashore-Louis, K. and Miles, M. B. (1990) *Improving the Urban High School.* New York: Teachers College Press.

Senge, P. M. (1990) *The Fifth Discipline: The Art and Practice of the Learning Organization.* New York: Doubleday.

Sergiovanni, T. J. (1994) *Building Community in Schools.* San Francisco: Jossey-Bass.

Shaftel, F. and Shaftel, G. (1982) *Role Playing in the Curriculum.* Englewood Cliffs, NJ: Prentice-Hall.

Shanahan, T. (1988) The reading–writing relationship: seven instructional principles, *The Reading Teacher*, 41: 636–47.

Shanahan, T. (1990) Reading and writing together: what does it really mean? in T. Shanahan (ed.) *Reading and Writing Together: New Perspectives for the Classroom* (pp. 1–18). Norwood, MA: Christopher-Gordon.

Sharan, S. (1990) *Cooperative Learning: Theory and Research.* New York: Praeger.

Sharan, S. and Shachar, H. (1988) *Language and Learning in the Cooperative Classroom.* New York: Springer-Verlag.

Sharan, S. and Shaulov, A. (1990) Cooperative learning, motivation to learn, and academic achievement, in S. Sharan and Y. Sharan (eds.) *Cooperative Learning: Theory and Research* (pp. 173–202). New York: Praeger.

Shaver, J. P. (1995) Social studies, in G. Caweelti (ed.) *Handbook of Research on Improving Instruction.* Arlington, VA: Alliance for Curriculum Reform.

Shinn, M. R., Good, R. H., Knutson, N., Tilly, W. D., and Collings, V. L. (1992) Curriculum-based measurement of oral reading fluency: a confirmatory analysis of its relation to reading, *School Psychology Review*, 21(3): 459–79.

Showers, B. (1982) *Transfer of Training: The Contribution of Coaching.* Eugene, OR: Center for Educational Policy and Management.

Showers, B. (1984) *Peer Coaching: A Strategy for Facilitating Transfer of Training.* Eugene, OR: Center for Educational Policy and Management.

Showers, B. (1985) Teachers coaching teachers, *Educational Leadership*, 42(7): 43–9.

Showers, B. (1989) School improvement through staff development: levels of implementation and impact on student achievement. Paper presented at the International Conference on "School-based Innovations: Looking Forward to the 1990's", Hong Kong.

Showers, B., Joyce, B. R., and Bennett, B. (1987) Synthesis of research on staff development: a framework for future study and a state-of-the-art analysis, *Educational Leadership*, 45(3): 77–87.

Showers, B., Joyce, B. R., and Murphy, C. (1996) *The River City Program: Staff Development Becomes School Improvement*, in B. R. Joyce and E. F. Calhoun (eds.) *Learning Experiences in School Renewal.* Eugene, OR: ERIC Clearinghouse for Educational Management.

Showers, B., Joyce, B. R., Scanlon, M., and Schnaubelt, C. (1998) A second chance to learn to read, *Educational Leadership*, 55(6): 27–31.

Sigel, I. E. (1984) *Advances in Applied Developmental Psychology.* New York: Ablex.

Sirotnik, K. A. (1983) What you see is what you get: consistency, persistence, and mediocrity in classrooms, *Harvard Educational Review*, 53(1): 16–31.

Sirotnik, K. A. (1987) Evaluation in the ecology of schooling, in J. I. Goodlad (ed.) *The Ecology of School Renewal: The Eighty-sixth Yearbook of the National Society for the Study of Education*. Chicago: University of Chicago Press.

Sizer, T. R. (1985) *Horace's Compromise*. Boston, MA: Houghton-Mifflin.

Sizer, T. R. (1992) *Horace's School: Redesigning the American High School*. Boston, MA: Houghton Mifflin.

Skinner, B. F. (1953) *Science and Human Behavior*. New York: Macmillan.

Skinner, B. F. (1968) *The Technology of Teaching*. Englewood Cliffs, NJ: Prentice-Hall.

Skinner, B. F. (1971) *Beyond Freedom and Dignity*. New York: Knopf.

Slater, W. H. and Graves, M. F. (1989) Research on expository text: implications for teachers, in K. D. Muth (ed.) *Children's Comprehension of Text: Research into Practice* (pp. 140–66). Newark, DE: International Reading Association.

Slavin, R. E. (1983) *Cooperative Learning*. New York: Longman.

Slavin, R. E. (1997/1998) Can education reduce social inequity? *Educational Leadership*, 55(4): 6–10.

Slavin, R. E. and Madden, N. A. (1995) Success for all: creating schools and classrooms where all children can read, in J. Oakes and K. Quartz (eds.) *Creating New Educational Communities. The Ninety-fourth Yearbook of the National Society for the Study of Education* (pp. 70–86). Chicago: University of Chicago Press.

Slavin, R. E., Karweit, N. L., and Wasik, B. A. (1994a) *Preventing Early School Failure: Research on Effective Strategies*. Boston, MA: Allyn and Bacon.

Slavin, R. E., Madden, N. A., Dolan, L. J, Wasik, B. A., and Ross, S. M. (1994b) "Whenever and wherever we choose": the replication of "Success for All," *Phi Delta Kappan*, 75(8): 639–47.

Slavin, R. E., Madden, N. A., Dolan, L. J., and Wasik, B. A. (1996) *Every Child, Every School: Success for All*. Thousand Oaks, CA: Corwin.

Smith, F. (1992) Learning to read: the never-ending debate, *Phi Delta Kappan*, February: 432–41.

Smith, J. and Heshusius, L. (1986) Closing down the conversation: the end of the qualitative–quantitative debate among educational inquirers, *Educational Researcher*, 15(1): 4–12.

Smith, K. and Smith, M. (1966) *Cybernetic Principles of Learning and Educational Design*. New York: Holt, Rinehart, and Winston.

Smith, M. L. (1980) Effects of aesthetics education on basic skills learning. Boulder, CO: Laboratory of Educational Research, University of Colorado.

Smith, T. M. (1995) *The Educational Progress of Hispanic Students*. Washington, DC: National Center for Education Statistics, Office of Educational Research and Improvement, US Department of Education.

Smith, W. E. (1993) Teachers' perceptions of role change through shared decision making: a two year case study. Paper presented at the annual meeting of the American Educational Research Association, Atlanta.

Snow, C., Barnes, W., Chandler, J., Goodman, I., and Hemphill, H. (1991) *Unfulfilled Expectations: Home and School Influences on Literacy*. Cambridge, MA: Harvard University Press.

Snyder, T. D. and Hoffman, C. M. (1992) *Digest of Educational Statistics*. Washington, DC: US Department of Education.

Sparks, D. (1993) Insights on school improvement: an interview with Larry Lezotte, *Journal of Staff Development*, 14(3): 19–21.

Sparks, D. and Loucks-Horsley, S. (1992) *Five Models of Staff Development for Teachers*. Oxford, OH: The National Staff Development Council.

Spaulding, R. (1970) *E.I.P.* Durham, NC: Duke University Press.

Stahl, S. A. and Fairbanks, M. M. (1986) The effects of vocabulary instruction: a model-based meta-analysis, *Review of Educational Research*, 56: 72–110.

Stanovich, K. E. (1990) A call for an end to the paradigmatic wars in reading research, *Journal of Reading Behavior*, 22: 221–31.

Stauffer, R. G. (1969) *Directing Reading Maturity as a Cognitive Process*. New York: Harper and Row.

Stedman, L. C. (1995) The new mythology about the status of U.S. schools, *Educational Leadership*, 52(5): 80–4.

Stenhouse, L. (1975) *An Introduction to Curriculum Research and Development*. London: Heinemann.

Stenhouse, L. (1980) *Curriculum Research and Development in Action*. London: Heinemann.

Sternberg, R. J. (1987) Most vocabulary is learned from context, in M. G. McKeown and M. E. Curtis (eds.) *The Nature of Vocabulary Acquisition* (pp. 89–105). Hillsdale, NJ: Erlbaum.

Sternberg, R. J. and Powell, J. S. (1983) Comprehending verbal comprehension, *American Psychologist*, 38: 878–93.

Stevens, F. I. and Grymes, J. (1993) *Opportunity to Learn: Issues of Equity for Poor and Minority Students*. Washington, DC: National Center for Educational Statistics.

Stevens, R. J. (1988) The effects of strategy training on the identification of the main idea in expository passages, *Journal of Educational Psychology*, 80: 21–6.

Stevens, R. J., Slavin, R. E., and Farnish, A. M. (1991) The effects of cooperative learning and direct instruction in reading comprehension on main idea identification, *Journal of Educational Psychology*, 83(1): 8–16.

Stevenson, H. W. and Stigler, J. (1992) *The Learning Gap*. New York: Summit Books.

Stiegelbauer, S. and Anderson, S. (1992) Six years later: revisiting a restructured school in Northern Ontario. Paper presented at the annual meeting of the American Educational Research Association, San Francisco.

Stille, A. (1997) Perils of the sphinx, *The New Yorker*, February 10.

Stoll, L. and Fink, D. (1996) *Changing Our Schools: Linking School Effectiveness and School Improvement*. Buckingham: Open University Press.

Stotsky, S. (1983) Research on reading/writing relationships: a synthesis and suggested directions, *Language Arts*, 60(5): 627–42.

Strike, K. A. (1993) Professionalism, democracy, and discursive communities: normative reflections on restructuring, *American Educational Research Journal*, 30(2): 255–76.

Suchman, R. J. (1964) Studies in inquiry training, in R. Ripple and V. Bookcastle (eds.) *Piaget Reconsidered*. Ithaca, NY: Cornell University Press.

Suchman, R. J. (1981) *Idea Gook for Geological Inquiry*. Chicago: Trillium Press.

Taba, H. (1966) *Teaching Strategies and Cognitive Functioning in Elementary School Children* (Cooperative Research Project 2404). San Francisco: San Francisco State College.

Taylor, B. M. and Samuels, S. J. (1983) Children's use of text structure in the recall of expository material, *American Educational Research Journal*, 20(4): 517–28.

Taylor, B. M., Frye, B. J., and Maruyama, G. (1990) Time spent reading and reading growth, *American Educational Research Journal*, 27(2): 351–62.

Thelen, H. (1960) *Education and the Human Quest*. New York: Harper and Row.

Tiedt, I. M., Gibbs, R., Howard, M., Timpson, M., and Williams, M. Y. (1989) *Reading/Thinking/Writing*. Boston, MA: Allyn and Bacon.

Tierney, R. J. and Pearson, P. D. (1985) Toward a composing model of reading, in C. N. Hedley and A. N. Baratta (eds.) *Contexts of Reading* (pp. 63–78). Norwood, NJ: Ablex.

Tierney, R. J. and Shanahan, T. (1991) Research on the reading–writing relationship: interactions, transaction, and outcomes, in R. Barr, M. L. Kamill, P. Mosenthal, and P. D. Pearson (eds.) *Handbook of Reading Research: Volume II* (pp. 246–80). New York: Longman.

Tierney, R. J., Readence, J. E., and Dishner, E. K. (1980) *Reading Strategies and Practices: A Guide for Improving Instruction*. Boston, MA: Allyn and Bacon.

Tierney, R. J., Soter, A., O'Flahavan, J. F., and McGinley, W. (1989) The effects of reading and writing upon thinking critically, *Reading Research Quarterly*, 24: 134–73.

Tierney, R. J., Carter, M. A., and Desai, L. E. (1991) *Portfolio Assessment in the Reading-writing Classroom*. Norwood, MA: Christopher-Gordon.

Tobias, S. (1993) *Overcoming Math Anxiety*. New York: W. W. Norton.

Toffler, A. (1990) *Power Shifts*. New York: Bantam.

Treiman, R. (1992) The role of intrasyllabic units in learning to read, in P. Gough, L. C. Ehri, and R. Treiman (eds.) *Reading Acquisition* (pp. 65–106). Hillsdale, NJ: Erlbaum.

Tunnell, M. O. and Jacobs, J. S. (1989) Using "real" books: research findings on literature-based reading instruction, *The Reading Teacher*, March: 470–7.

United States Department of Education (1987) *What Works: Research about Teaching and Learning*. Washington, DC: United States Department of Education.

United States Department of Education (1993) *Fifteenth Annual Report to Congress on the Implementation of the Individual with Disabilities Education Act*. Washington, DC: United States Department of Education.

Wallace, J. and Wildy, H. (1993) Pioneering school change: lessons from a case study of school site restructuring. Paper presented at the annual meeting of the American Educational Research Association, Atlanta.

Wallace, R. C., Lemahieu, P. G., and Bickel, W. E. (1990) The Pittsburgh experience: achieving commitment to comprehensive staff development, in B. R. Joyce (ed.) *Changing School Culture Through Staff Development*. Alexandria, VA: Association for Supervision and Curriculum Development.

Waller, W. (1965) *The Sociology of Teaching*. New York: Wiley. (Originally published in 1932.)

Wang, M., Haertel, G., and Walberg, H. (1993) Toward a knowledge base for school learning, *Review of Educational Research*, 63(3): 249–94.

Weathersby, J. and Harkreader, S. (1998) *Staff Development and Student Achievement: Making the Connection in Georgia Schools*. Atlanta, GA: Council for School Performance.

Weaver, C. (ed.) (in press) *Reconsidering a Balanced Approach to Reading*. Urbana, IL: National Council of Teachers of English.

Weick, K. E. (1976) Educational organizations as loosely coupled systems, *Administrative Science Quarterly*, 21: 1–19.

Weil, M., Marshalek, B., Mittman, A., Murphy, J., Hallinger, P., and Pruyn, J. (1984) Effective and typical schools: how different are they? Paper presented at the annual meeting of the American Educational Research Association, New Orleans.

Weiner, B. (1994) Integrating social and personal theories of achievement striving, *Review of Educational Research*, 64(4): 557–73.

Weiss, C., Cambone, J., and Wyeth, A., reported in E. Miller (1995) Shared decision-making by itself doesn't make for better decisions, *The Harvard Education Letter*, 11(6): 1–4.

Weiss, I. R. (1978) *Nineteen Seventy-seven National Survey of Science, Social Science, and Mathematics Education*. National Science Foundation. Washington, DC: US Government Printing Office.

Wendelin, K. H. and Zinck, R. A. (1983) How students make book choices, *Reading Horizons*, 23: 84–8.

White, T., Power, M., and White, S. (1989a) Morphological analysis: implications for teaching and understanding vocabulary growth, *Reading Research Quarterly*, 24: 283–304.

White, T. G., Slater, W. H., and Graves, M. F. (1989b) Yes/no method of vocabulary assessment: valid for whom and useful for what? *Cognitive and Social Perspectives for Literacy Research and Instruction* (pp. 391–8). Chicago: National Reading Conference.

White, T. G., Sowell, J., and Yanagihara, A. (1989c) Teaching elementary students to use word-part clues, *Reading Teacher*, 42: 302–8.

White, T. G., Graves, M. F., and Slater, W. H. (1990) Growth of reading vocabulary in diverse elementary schools: decoding and word meaning, *Journal of Educational Psychology*, 82(2): 281–90.

White, W. A. T. (1986) "The effects of direct instruction in special education: a meta-analysis." PhD thesis, University of Oregon, Eugene.

Whitehead, A. (1929) *The Aims of Education*. New York: Macmillan.

William T. Grant Foundation, Commission on Work, Family, and Citizenship (1988) *The Forgotten Half: Non-college Youth in America*. Washington, DC: William T. Grant Foundation.

Williams, J. P. (1992) Reading instruction and learning disabled students, in M. J. Dreher and W. H. Slater (eds.) *Elementary School Literacy: Critical Issues* (pp. 157–81). Norwood, MA: Christopher-Gordon.

Winograd, P. N. (1984) Strategic difficulties in summarizing texts, *Reading Research Quarterly*, 19: 404–25.

Winograd, P. N. and Bridge, C. A. (1986) The comprehension of important information in written prose, in J. B. Baumann (ed.) *Teaching Main Idea Comprehension* (pp. 18–48). Newark, DE: International Reading Association.

Winograd, P. N. and Bridge, C. A. (1995) Teaching for literacy, in J. H. Block, S. T. Everson, and T. R. Guskey (eds.) *School Improvement Programs: A Handbook for Educational Leaders* (pp. 229–46). New York: Scholastic.

Winograd, P. and Greenlee, M. (1986) Students need a balanced reading program, *Educational Leadership*, 43(7): 16–21.

Wittrock, M. C. (1983) Writing and the teaching of reading, *Language Arts*, 60(5): 600–6.

Wittrock, M. C. and Alesandrini, K. (1990) Generation of summaries and analogies and analytic and holistic abilities, *American Educational Research Journal*, 27(3): 489–502.

Wolf, J. M. (1998) Just Read, *Educational Leadership*, 55(8): 61–3.

Wolpe, J. and Lazarus, A. (1966) *Behavior Therapy Techniques: A Guide to the Treatment of Neuroses*. Oxford: Pergamon Press.

Worthen, B. (1968) A study of discovery and expository presentation: implications for teaching, *Journal of Teacher Education*, 19: 223–42.

Worthy, J. and McKool, S. S. S. (1996) Students who say they hate to read: the importance of opportunity, choice, and access, in *Literacies for the 21st Century: Forty-fifth Yearbook of the National Reading Conference*. Chicago, IL: National Reading Conference.

Wysocki, K. and Jenkins, J. (1987) Deriving word meanings through morphological generalization, *Reading Research Quarterly*, 22: 66–81.

Index